The Bible Speaks Today
Series editors: Alec Motyer (OT)
John Stott (NT)
Derek Tidball (Bible Themes)

The Message of
the Word of God

The Bible Speaks Today: Bible Themes series

The Message of the Living God
His glory, his people, his world
Peter Lewis

The Message of the Resurrection
Christ is risen!
Paul Beasley-Murray

The Message of the Cross
Wisdom unsearchable, love indestructible
Derek Tidball

The Message of Salvation
By God's grace, for God's glory
Philip Graham Ryken

The Message of Creation
Encountering the Lord of the universe
David Wilkinson

The Message of Heaven and Hell
Grace and destiny
Bruce Milne

The Message of Mission
The glory of Christ in all time and space
Howard Peskett and Vinoth Ramachandra

The Message of Prayer
Approaching the throne of grace
Tim Chester

The Message of the Trinity
Life in God
Brian Edgar

The Message of Evil and Suffering
Light into darkness
Peter Hicks

The Message of the Holy Spirit
The Spirit of encounter
Keith Warrington

The Message of Holiness
Restoring God's masterpiece
Derek Tidball

The Message of Sonship
At home in God's household
Trevor Burke

The Message of the Word of God
The glory of God made known
Tim Meadowcroft

The Message of the Word of God

The glory of God made known

Tim Meadowcroft

Senior Lecturer in Biblical Studies
Laidlaw College, Henderson, New Zealand

Inter-Varsity Press

InterVarsity Press
P.O. Box 1400, Downers Grove, IL 60515-1426
Internet: www.ivpress.com
E-mail: email@ivpress.com

InterVarsity Press® is the book-publishing division of InterVarsity Christian Fellowship/USA®, a movement of students and faculty active on campus at hundreds of universities, colleges and schools of nursing in the United States of America, and a member movement of the International Fellowship of Evangelical Students. For information about local and regional activities, write Public Relations Dept., InterVarsity Christian Fellowship/USA, 6400 Schroeder Rd., P.O. Box 7895, Madison, WI 53707-7895, or visit the IVCF website at <www.intervarsity.org>.

Unless otherwise indicated, Scripture quotations are taken from the Holy Bible, Today's New International Version™ *Copyright* © *2001 by International Bible Society. All rights reserved.*

ISBN 978-0-8308-2414-4

Printed in the United States of America ∞

Library of Congress Cataloging-in-Publication Data

Meadowcroft, T. J.
  The message of the Word of God: the glory of God made known / Tim Meadowcroft.
      p. cm.—(The Bible speaks today)
  Includes bibliographical references.
  ISBN 978-0-8308-2414-4 (pbk.: alk. paper)
  1. Bible—Evidences, authority, etc. 2. Word of God (Christian theology)—Biblical teaching. I. Title.
  BS480.M395 2011
  220.1—dc23

                                                                      2011033469

P	17	16	15	14	13	12	11	10	9	8	7	6	5	4	3	2	1
Y	25	24	23	22	21	20	19	18	17	16	15	14	13	12	11		

Dedicated to my daughters:
Anna, Sarah, Katie, Elizabeth
With thanks

Contents

General preface   9
Author's preface   11
Abbreviations   13
Select bibliography   16

Introduction   23

Part 1. God speaks

1. The glory of God made known (Psalm 19)   33
2. God's word goes forth (Isaiah 55)   46
3. The wisdom of God's word (Proverbs 30:1–9)   61
4. The Lord God has spoken (Amos 3:1–8)   72
5. Through men and women moved by the Spirit (2 Peter 1:19–21)   84

Part 2. God speaks in the written word

6. The spoken word written (Exodus 19 – 20)   99
7. The covenant remembered (Deuteronomy 4:1–20)   112
8. The written word as witness (Luke 1:1–4)   126
9. The Scriptures and the resurrection of the Word (John 2:13–25)   137
10. The Scriptures interpreted and fulfilled by Jesus (Matthew 12:1–21)   146

Part 3. God speaks in Christ

11. The Word made flesh (John 1:1–14)   157
12. In these last days God has spoken (Hebrews 1:1–4)   165
13. Christ fulfils the Scriptures (Matthew 5:17–48)   175
14. God's word and righteousness (Romans 10:5–13)   187
15. Worthy to open the scroll (Revelation 5)   194

Part 4. God speaks today

16. Individual encounter with the word of God (Acts 8:26–39)   207
17. Scripture read in community (Nehemiah 8)   219
18. All Scripture is God-breathed and useful (2 Timothy 3:10–17)   233
19. The Spirit of love and truth (John 14:15–26)   244
20. Holding fast the traditions (2 Thessalonians 2:13–17)   256

Study Guide   267

BST | The Bible Speaks Today

GENERAL PREFACE

THE BIBLE SPEAKS TODAY describes three series of expositions, based on the books of the Old and New Testaments, and on Bible themes that run through the whole of Scripture. Each series is characterized by a threefold ideal:

- to expound the biblical text with accuracy
- to relate it to contemporary life, and
- to be readable.

These books are, therefore, not 'commentaries', for the commentary seeks rather to elucidate the text than to apply it, and tends to be a work rather of reference than of literature. Nor, on the other hand, do they contain the kinds of 'sermons' that attempt to be contemporary and readable without taking Scripture seriously enough. The contributors to *The Bible Speaks Today* series are all united in their convictions that God still speaks through what he has spoken, and that nothing is more necessary for the life, health and growth of Christians than that they should hear what the Spirit is saying to them through his ancient – yet ever modern – Word.

ALEC MOTYER
JOHN STOTT
DEREK TIDBALL
Series editors

Author's preface

As this volume goes to print I am deeply conscious of people and institutions to whom I owe much for the formation in me of a sense of the word of God. First, there is the great gift of having grown up in a Christian family. And as I wrote I also found my mind often going to four men who played significant roles in further shaping my own perception and experience of God's speaking. Paul Davidson, my boarding master for a number of years as I grew up in West Pakistan, helped to form in me the habit of regular personal Bible reading, and taught me that life is an adventure and risk is part of the life of faith. Bob Robinson, my pastor in student days, opened a door through which I glimpsed the possibilities of academic theology, and taught me much about the comprehensive rule of Christ the Word. Don Corban, my pastor, nurtured in me a call to pastoral ministry. And the late Francis Foulkes, my teacher, modelled for me an academic commitment placed at the service of the church.

It was a privilege to write a substantial portion of this book during three months at Bethlehem Bible College in the Palestinian Territories in 2009. The location influenced my reading in unanticipated ways, and conversations with Alex Awad, Munther Isaac, Yohanna Katanacho, Salim Munayer and other BBC staff were enriching and challenging. As well as provision from BBC, funding from the St John's Trust in Auckland helped to make the time there possible.

I am grateful for the generosity of Laidlaw College (formerly Bible College of New Zealand), my employer, for their encouragement and enabling of this project through the provision of time and money and a supportive environment. I especially mention Martin Sutherland in this respect and for his encouragement of the project. I also thank John Hitchen for reading an early draft, and other colleagues as well as students who have patiently listened to me talk about what I am writing. The Deane Memorial Library staff at Laidlaw College have been unfailingly helpful. Angelene Goodman was a superb research assistant in the final stages of the project. And I thank Sue Meadowcroft and Elizabeth Kose for their final proof reading.

I am honoured by the invitation from Derek Tidball for me to contribute to the Bible Themes series, and consider it an immense privilege to have been able to gather my thoughts in this manner. Both he and Philip Duce of Inter-Varsity Press have given crucial guidance in the preparation of this work, and I am grateful also for Alison Walley's copy-editing. The comments from an anonymous reader were also appreciated.

This book is dedicated to my daughters, Anna, Sarah, Katie and Elizabeth, who with their husbands and children bring joy and satisfaction in all sorts of ways, for which I remain deeply thankful. As ever, I owe more than I can express to my wife Sue, whose extraordinary strength continues to support and sustain me. For all these people and many unnamed I give thanks; they have made this volume better than it could otherwise have been. And finally, thanks be to God who continues to speak and act in Christ, in the text of Scripture and in the world around us.

Tim Meadowcroft
Auckland
April 2011

Abbreviations

AB	Anchor Bible
ABC	Asia Bible Commentary
ACCS	Ancient Christian Commentary on Scripture
AYB	Anchor Yale Bible
BC	Bible Commentary
BCOT	Baker Commentary on the Old Testament
BDAG	*A Greek-English Lexicon of the New Testament and Other Early Christian Literature*, 3rd edn, eds. Walter Bauer, Frederick W. Danker, William F. Arndt and F. Wilbur Gingrich (Chicago: University of Chicago Press, 2000)
BECNT	Baker Exegetical Commentary on the New Testament
BMW	The Bible in the Modern World
BNTC	Black's New Testament Commentaries
BST	The Bible Speaks Today
BSTBT	The Bible Speaks Today: Biblical Themes
BTCB	Brazos Theological Commentary on the Bible
CBQ	*Catholic Biblical Quarterly*
CD	*Damascus Document*
CIT	Current Issues in Theology
COQG	Christian Origins and the Question of God
CR:BS	*Currents in Research: Biblical Studies*
CSR	*Christian Scholars Review*
CTR	*Criswell Theological Review*
DBI	*Dictionary of Biblical Imagery*, eds. Leland Ryken, James C. Wilhoit and Tremper Longman III (Downers Grove/Leicester: IVP, 1998)
DDD	*Dictionary of Deities and Demons in the Bible*, 2nd edn, eds. K. van der Toorn, B. Becking and P. W. van der Horst (Leiden: Brill and Grand Rapids: Eerdmans, 1999)

13

DJG	*Dictionary of Jesus and the Gospels*, eds. Joel B. Green, Scot McKnight and I. H. Marshall (Downers Grove/ Leicester: IVP, 1992)
DPL	*Dictionary of Paul and His Letters*, eds. Gerald F. Hawthorne, Ralph P. Martin and Daniel G. Reid (Downers Grove/Leicester: IVP, 1993)
EDT	*Evangelical Dictionary of Theology*, ed. Walter A. Elwell (Grand Rapids: Baker Book House, 1984)
ERT	*Evangelical Review of Theology*
EvQ	*Evangelical Quarterly*
FBC	Focus on the Bible
ICC	International Critical Commentary
Int	*Interpretation*
ITC	International Theological Commentary
JBL	*Journal of Biblical Literature*
JETS	*Journal of the Evangelical Theological Society*
JPT	*Journal of Pentecostal Theology*
JSNT	*Journal for the Study of the New Testament*
JSNTSup	Journal for the Study of the New Testament, Supplement Series
JSOT	*Journal for the Study of the Old Testament*
JSOTSup	Journal for the Study of the Old Testament, Supplement Series
LBI	Library of Biblical Interpretation
LXX	Septuagint
NICNT	New International Commentary on the New Testament
NICOT	New International Commentary on the Old Testament
NIDB	*New Interpreter's Dictionary of the Bible*, 5 vols., ed. Katharine Doob Sakenfeld (Nashville: Abingdon Press, 2006-09)
NIDNTT	*New International Dictionary of New Testament Theology*, 4 vols., ed. Colin Brown (Grand Rapids: Regency Refence Library, 1975-85)
NIGTC	New International Greek Testament Commentary
NIV	New International Version
NIVAC	NIV Application Commentary
NovT	*Novum Testamentum*
NRSV	New Revised Standard Version
NTL	New Testament Library
NTS	*New Testament Studies*
OBT	Overtures to Biblical Theology
OTG	Old Testament Guides
OTL	Old Testament Library

PEQ	*Palestine Exploration Quarterly*
PNTC	Pillar New Testament Commentary
RB	*Revue Biblique*
RSV	Revised Standard Version
SBT	Studies in Biblical Theology
SHBC	Smyth & Helwys Bible Commentary
SJT	*Scottish Journal of Theology*
SNTSMS	Society for New Testament Studies Monograph Series
SP	Sacra Pagina
TNAC	The New American Commentary
TNIV	Today's New International Version
TNTC	Tyndale New Testament Commentaries
TOTC	Tyndale Old Testament Commentaries
TrinJ	*Trinity Journal*
TWOT	*Theological Wordbook of the Old Testament*, eds. R. Laird Harris, Gleason L. Archer, Jr and Bruce K. Waltke (Chicago: Moody Bible Institute, 1980)
TynB	*Tyndale Bulletin*
VT	*Vetus Testamentum*
WBC	Word Biblical Commentary
WTJ	*Westminster Theological Journal*
ZAW	*Zeitschrift für die Alttestamentliche Wissenschaft*

Select bibliography

Alexander, L., *The Preface to Luke's Gospel: Literary Convention and Social Context in Luke 1.1-4 and Acts 1.1*, SNTSMS 78 (Cambridge: Cambridge University Press, 1993).

Alter, R., *The Art of Biblical Narrative* (New York: Basic Books, 1981).

Andersen, F. I. and D. N. Freedman, *Amos: A New Translation with Introduction and Commentary*, AB 24A (New York: Doubleday, 1989).

Aune, D. E., *Prophecy in Early Christianity and the Ancient Mediterranean World* (Grand Rapids: Eerdmans, 1983).

——, *Revelation 1–5*, WBC 52A (Dallas: Word, 1997).

Bar-Efrat, S., *Narrative Art in the Bible* (Sheffield: Almond, 1989).

Barth, K., *The Doctrine of the Word of God, Church Dogmatics* I/2 tr. G. T. Thomson and H. Knight (Edinburgh: T&T Clark, 1936).

Bartholomew, C. G. and M. W. Goheen, *The Drama of Scripture: Finding our Place in the Biblical Story* (Grand Rapids: Baker, 2004).

Bartholomew, C. G., C. Greene and K. Möller (eds.), *After Pentecost: Language and Biblical Interpretation* (Grand Rapids: Zondervan, 2001).

Barton, J., *Reading the Old Testament, Method in Biblical Study* (London: Darton, Longman and Todd, 1984).

Barton, S., 'New Testament Interpretation as Performance', *SJT* 52 (1999), pp. 179–208.

Bauckham, R. J., *Jude, 2 Peter*, WBC 50 (Waco: Word, 1983).

Beale, G. K., *The Book of Revelation: A Commentary on the Greek Text*, NIGTC (Grand Rapids: Eerdmans, 1999).

——, *1–2 Thessalonians* (Downers Grove: IVP, 2003).

Beasley-Murray, G. R., *John*, WBC 36 (Dallas: Word, 1999).

Beckwith, R. T., *The Old Testament Canon of the New Testament Church and Its Background in Early Judaism* (London: SPCK, 1985).

Berlin, A., *Poetics and Interpretation of Biblical Narrative* (Winona Lake: Eisenbrauns, 1994).

Berquist, J. L., *Judaism in Persia's Shadow: A Social and Historical Approach* (Minneapolis: Fortress, 1995).

Best, E., *The First and Second Epistles to the Thessalonians* (London: Adam & Charles Black, 1972).

Biddle, M. E., *Deuteronomy*, SHBC (Macon: Smith & Helwys, 2003).

Birch, B. C., *Let Justice Roll Down: The Old Testament, Ethics, and Christian Life* (Louisville: Westminster John Knox, 1991).

Black, C. C., 'Exegesis as Prayer', *Princeton Seminary Bulletin* 23NS (2002), pp. 131–145.

Bock, D. L., *Luke Volume 1: 1:1–9:50*, BECNT (Grand Rapids: Baker, 1994).

——, *Acts*, BECNT (Grand Rapids: Baker, 2007).

Boring, M. E., *Revelation*, Interpretation (Louisville: John Knox, 1989).

Boyce, R. N., 'Isaiah 55:6-13', *Int* 44 (1990), pp. 56–60.

Brett, M. C., *Decolonising God: The Bible in the Tides of Empire*, BMW 16 (Sheffield: Sheffield Phoenix, 2008).

Brown, R., *The Message of Hebrews*, BST (Leicester: IVP, 1982).

——, *The Message of Deuteronomy*, BST (Leicester: IVP, 1993).

——, *The Message of Nehemiah: God's Servant in a Time of Change*, BST (Leicester: IVP, 1998).

Brown, R. E., *The Gospel According to John I–XII*, AB 29 (New York: Doubleday, 1966).

——, *The Gospel According to John XIII–XXI*, AB 29A (New York: Doubleday, 1970).

Bruce, F. F., *1 & 2 Thessalonians*, WBC 45 (Dallas: Word, 1982).

——, *The Book of the Acts,* rev. ed., NICNT (Grand Rapids: Eerdmans, 1988).

Brueggemann, W., 'Isaiah 55 and Deuteronomic Theology', *ZAW* 80 (1968), pp. 171–186.

——, *Hopeful Imagination: Prophetic Voices in Exile* (Philadelphia: Fortress, 1986).

——, *Isaiah 40–66*, WBC (Louisville: Westminster John Knox, 1998).

Burge, G. M., *John*, NIVAC (Grand Rapids: Zondervan, 2000).

Carson, D. A., *The Gospel According to John* (Leicester: IVP, 1991).

Carson, D. A. and J. D. Woodbridge (eds.), *Scripture and Truth* (Grand Rapids: Zondervan, 1983).

Charles, J. D., *Virtue Amidst Vice: The Catalog of Virtues in 2 Peter 1*, JSNTSup 150 (Sheffield: Sheffield Academic Press, 1997).

Coggins, R. J., *Haggai, Zechariah, Malachi*, OTG (Sheffield: JSOT, 1987).

Cohen, A., *The Psalms: Hebrew Text and English Translation with an Introduction and Commentary* (London: Soncino, 1945).

Cole, R. A., *Exodus: An Introduction and Commentary*, TOTC (London: IVP, 1973).

Collins, R. F., *I & II Timothy and Titus; A Commentary*, NTL (Louisville: Westminster John Knox, 2002).

Craigie, P. C., *Psalms 1–50*, WBC 19 (Waco: Word, 1983).

Davis, J., 'Acts 2 and the Old Testament: The Pentecost Event in Light of Sinai, Babel and the Table of Nations', *CTR* 7 (2009), pp. 29–48.

Douglas, M., *Purity and Danger: An Analysis of Concepts of Pollution and Taboo* (Middlesex: Penguin, 1966).

Dunn, J. D. G., *Romans 9–16*, WBC 38B (Dallas: Word, 1988).

Durham, J. I., *Exodus*, WBC 3 (Dallas: Word, 1978).

Ebeling, G., *Introduction to a Theological Theory of Language* (London: Collins, 1973).

Ellingworth, P., *The Epistle to the Hebrews*, NIGTC (Grand Rapids: Eerdmans, 1993).

Fensham, F. C., *The Books of Ezra and Nehemiah*, NICOT (Grand Rapids: Eerdmans, 1982).

Fitzmyer, J. A., *The Gospel According to Luke (I–IX)*, AB 28 (New York: Doubleday, 1981).

Fox, M. V., *Proverbs 10–31: A New Translation with Introduction and Commentary*, AYB 18B (New Haven: Yale University Press, 2009).

France, R. T., *Matthew*, TNTC (Leicester: IVP, 1985).

Franke, J. R., *Manifold Witness: The Plurality of Truth* (Nashville: Abingdon, 2009).

Franklyn, P., 'The Sayings of Agur in Proverbs 30: Piety or Scepticism?', *ZAW* 95 (1983), pp. 238–252.

Gardner, P., *2 Peter & Jude*, FBC (Fearn: Christian Focus, 1998).

Gloer, W. H., *1 & 2 Timothy–Titus*, SHBC (Macon: Smith & Helwys, 2010).

Goldingay, J. E., *Models for Scripture* (Grand Rapids: Eerdmans, 1994).

——, *Old Testament Theology Volume One: Israel's Gospel* (Downers Grove: IVP, 2003).

——, *The Message of Isaiah 40–55: A Literary-Theological Commentary* (London: T&T Clark International, 2005).

——, *Old Testament Theology, Volume Three: Israel's Life* (Downer's Grove: IVP, 2009).

Goodrick, E. W., 'Let's Put 2 Timothy 3:16 Back in the Bible', *JETS* 25 (1982), pp. 479–487.

Green, G. L., *The Letters to the Thessalonians*, PNTC (Leicester: Apollos, 2002).

Green, J. B., *The Gospel of Luke*, NICNT (Grand Rapids: Eerdmans, 1997).

Green, M., *The Second Epistle General of Peter and the General Epistle of Jude: An Introduction and Commentary*, TNTC (London: Tyndale, 1968).

——, *The Message of Matthew*, BST (Leicester: IVP, 2000).

Guthrie, G. H., *Hebrews*, NIVAC (Grand Rapids: Zondervan, 1998).

Habets, M., *The Anointed Son: A Trinitarian Spirit Christology* (Eugene: Pickwick, 2010).

Hagner, D. A., *Matthew 1–13*, WBC 33A (Dallas: Word, 1993).

Hicks, J. M., 'The Sabbath Controversy in Matthew: An Exegesis of Matthew 12:1–14', *Restoration Quarterly* 27 (1984), pp. 79–91.

Holmgren, F. C., *Israel Alive Again: A Commentary on the Books of Ezra and Nehemiah*, ITC (Grand Rapids: Eerdmans, 1987).

Hui, A., 'The Spirit of Prophecy and Pauline Pneumatology', *TynB* 50 (1999), pp. 93–115.

Jensen, P., *The Revelation of God* (Leicester: IVP, 2002).

Johnson, L. T., *The Acts of the Apostles*, SP 5 (Collegeville: Liturgical Press, 1992).

——, *Hebrews: A Commentary*, NTL (Louisville: Westminster John Knox, 2006).

Keener, C. S., *A Commentary on the Gospel of Matthew* (Grand Rapids: Eerdmans, 1999).

Kelly, J. N. D., *The Epistles of Peter and of Jude*, BNTC (London: Adam & Charles Black, 1969).

Knight, G. A. F., *Servant Theology: A Commentary on the Book of Isaiah 40–55*, ITC (Grand Rapids: Eerdmans, 1984).

Knight, G. W., *The Pastoral Epistles*, NIGTC (Grand Rapids: Eerdmans, 1992).

Kraemer, D. C., 'On the Relationship of the Books of Ezra and Nehemiah', *JSOT* 59 (1993), pp. 73–92.

Kraus, H.-J., *Psalms 1–59: A Commentary*, tr. H. C. Oswald (Minneapolis: Augsburg, 1988).

Kruse, C., *John*, TNTC (Leicester: IVP, 2003).

Lane, W. L., *Hebrews 1–8*, WBC 47A (Dallas: Word, 1991).

Longman, T., *Proverbs*, BCOT (Grand Rapids: Baker Academic, 2006).

MacQuarrie, J., *Principles of Christian Theology* (London: SCM, 1966).

McGowan, A. T. B., *The Divine Spiration of Scripture: Challenging Evangelical Perspectives* (Nottingham: Apollos, 2007).

McKane, W., *Proverbs: A New Approach*, OTL (London: SCM, 1970).

McKnight, E. V. and C. Church, *Hebrews-James*, SHBC (Macon: Smith & Helwys, 2004).

Marshall, I. H., *Luke: Historian and Theologian* (Exeter: Paternoster, 1970).

———, *The Acts of the Apostles: An Introduction and Commentary*, TNTC (Leicester: IVP, 1980).

———, *The Pastoral Epistles*, ICC (Edinburgh: T&T Clark, 1999).

Mays, J. L., *Psalms*, Interpretation (Louisville: John Knox, 1994).

Mey, J. L., *Pragmatics: An Introduction* (Oxford: Blackwell, 2001).

Milne, B., *The Message of John: Here is Your King*, BST (Leicester: IVP, 1993).

Mitchell, A. C., *Hebrews*, SP 13 (Collegeville: Liturgical Press, 2007).

Moo, D. J., *The Epistle to the Romans*, NICNT (Grand Rapids: Eerdmans, 1996).

———, *Romans*, NIVAC (Grand Rapids: Zondervan, 2000).

Moloney, F. J., *The Gospel of John*, SP 4 (Collegeville: Liturgical Press, 1994).

Morris, L., *The Gospel According to Matthew* (Leicester: IVP, 1992).

Motyer, A., *The Day of the Lion: The Message of Amos*, BST (London: IVP, 1974).

———, *The Prophecy of Isaiah* (Leicester: IVP, 1993).

Murphy, R. E., *Proverbs*, WBC 22 (Nashville: Thomas Nelson, 1998).

Neyrey, J. H., *2 Peter, Jude: A New Translation with Introduction and Commentary*, AB 37C (New York: Doubleday, 1993).

Nolland, J., *Luke 1–9:20*, WBC 35A (Dallas: Word, 1989).

Osborne, G. R., *Revelation*, BECNT (Grand Rapids: Baker Academic, 2002).

Oswalt, J. N., *The Book of Isaiah Chapters 40–66*, NICOT (Grand Rapids: Eerdmans, 1998).

Packer, J. I., *Beyond the Battle for the Bible* (Westchester: Cornerstone, 1980).

Pattemore, S. W., *The People of God in the Apocalypse: Discourse, Structure, and Exegesis*, SNTSMS 128 (Cambridge: Cambridge University Press, 2003).

Paul, S. M., *Amos: A Commentary on the Book of Amos*, Hermeneia (Minneapolis: Fortress, 1991).

Pilkington, A., 'Introduction: Relevance Theory and Literary Style', *Language and Literature* 5 (1996), pp. 157–162.

du Plessis, I. I., 'Once More: The Purpose of Luke's Prologue (Lk 1 1–4)', *NovT* 16 (1974), pp. 259–271.

Polanyi, M., *Personal Knowledge, Towards a Post-Critical Philosophy* (Chicago: University of Chicago Press, 1958).

Polkinghorne, J., *Belief in God in an Age of Science* (New Haven: Yale University Press, 1998).

Porter, S. L. and C. D. Stanley (eds.), *As It Is Written: Studying Paul's Use of Scripture* (Atlanta: SBL, 2008).

Provan, I., V. P. Long and T. Longman, *A Biblical History of Israel* (Louisville: Westminster John Knox, 2003).

Rae, M., *History and Hermeneutics* (London: T&T Clark, 2005).

Ridderbos, H., *The Gospel According to John: A Theological Commentary*, tr. J. Vriend (Grand Rapids: Eerdmans, 1997).

Richard, E. J., *First and Second Thessalonians*, SP 11 (Collegeville: Liturgical Press, 1995).

Saarinen, R., *The Pastoral Epistles with Philemon & Jude*, BTCB (Grand Rapids: Brazos, 2008).

Sargent, B., 'The Dead Letter? Psalm 119 and the Spirituality of the Bible in the Local Church', *EvQ* 81 (2009), pp. 99–115.

Schlatter, A., *Romans: The Righteousness of God*, tr. S. S. Schatzmann (Peabody: Hendrickson, 1995).

Schreiner, T. R., *1, 2 Peter, Jude*, TNAC 37 (Nashville: Broadman & Holman, 2003).

Schweizer, E., *Matthew*, tr. D. E. Green (London: SPCK, 1976).

Senior, D. P. and D. J. Harrington, *1 Peter, Jude and 2 Peter*, SP 15 (Collegeville: Michael Glazier, 2003).

Smith, G., *Amos: A Commentary*, LBI (Grand Rapids: Regency, 1989).

Smith, J. K. A., 'The Closing of the Book: Pentecostals, Evangelicals and the Sacred Writings', *JPT* 11 (1997), pp. 233–250.

Stott, J. R. W., *Understanding the Bible* (Sydney: ANZEA, 1972).

———, *The Message of Acts: To the Ends of the Earth*, BST (Leicester: IVP, 1990).

———, *The Message of Romans: God's Good News for the World*, BST (Leicester: IVP, 1994).

Sweet, J. P. M., *Revelation* (Philadelphia: Westminster, 1979).

Thielicke, H., *The Evangelical Faith: Volume Three, Theology of the Spirit*, tr. and ed. G. W. Bromiley (Grand Rapids: Eerdmans, 1982).

Thiselton, A. C., *New Horizons in Hermeneutics* (Grand Rapids: Zondervan, 1992).

Tidball, D., *The Message of Holiness: Restoring God's Masterpiece*, BSTBT (Leicester and Downers Grove: IVP, 2010).

Towner, P. H., *The Letters to Timothy and Titus*, NICNT (Grand Rapids: Eerdmans, 2006).

Trebilco, P. and S. Rae, *1 Timothy*, ABC (Singapore: Asia Theological Association, 2006).

Turner, D. L., *Matthew*, BECNT (Grand Rapids: Baker Academic, 2008).

Vanhoozer, K. J., *Is There a Meaning in this Text? The Bible, the Reader and the Morality of Literary Knowledge* (Leicester: Apollos, 1998).

———, *The Drama of Doctrine: A Canonical-Linguistic Approach to Christian Theology* (Louisville: Westminster John Knox, 2005).

———, '"One Rule to Rule Them All?" Theological Method in an Era of World Christianity', in C. Ott and H. A. Netland (eds.), *Globalizing Theology: Belief and Practice in an Era of World Christianity* (Grand Rapids: Baker Academic, 2006), pp. 85–126.

Volf, M., *After Our Likeness: The Church as the Image of the Trinity* (Grand Rapids: Eerdmans, 1998).

Wagner, J. R., 'From the Heavens to the Heart: The Dynamics of Psalm 19 as Prayer', *CBQ* 61 (1999), pp. 245–261.

Waltke, B. K., *The Book of Proverbs Chapters 15–31*, NICOT (Grand Rapids: Eerdmans, 2005).

Webster, J., *Holy Scripture: A Dogmatic Sketch*, CIT (Cambridge: University Press, 2003).

Welker, M., *God the Spirit*, tr. J. F. Hoffmeyer (Minneapolis: Fortress, 1994).

Westcott, B. F., *The Gospel According to St John* (London: James Clark & Co, 1958 [1880]).

Wilkins, M. J., *Matthew*, NIVAC (Grand Rapids: Zondervan, 2004).

Williamson, H. G. M., *Ezra, Nehemiah*, WBC 16 (Waco: Word, 1985).

———, *Variations on a Theme: King, Messiah and Servant in the Book of Isaiah* (Carlisle: Paternoster, 1998).

Witherington, B., 'The Preface of Luke-Acts and Historiography', *NTS* 31 (1985), pp. 576–581.

———, *1 and 2 Thessalonians: A Socio-Rhetorical Commentary* (Grand Rapids: Eerdmans, 2006).

———, *Matthew*, SHBC (Macon: Smyth & Helwys, 2006).

Wolterstorff, N., *Art in Action: Toward a Christian Aesthetic* (Carlisle: Solway, 1980).

———, *Divine Discourse: Philosophical Reflections on the Claim that God Speaks* (Cambridge: Cambridge University Press, 1995).

Wright, C. J. H., *The Mission of God: Unlocking the Bible's Grand Narrative* (Leicester and Downers Grove: IVP, 2006).

Introduction

The volumes in this series – The Bible Speaks Today: Bible Themes – each explore a key theme or doctrine of the Christian faith as that theme or doctrine emerges in the Bible. The assumption is that the words of Scripture carry a particular primacy in the matter of Christian belief, however we might define that primacy, and so it is worth dedicating time and effort to reminding ourselves of what the Bible actually says about the themes and doctrines held dear by Christians through the centuries. As originally conceived this volume in the series was to have been on 'The Message of the Bible'. It does not take a great deal of imagination to see that a volume on what the Bible says about the Bible is problematic. Since the Bible is a defined set of texts that gradually emerged over time, the texts that make up the Bible could have had no concept of a Bible *per se* during their formation. The theme of the Bible could only have emerged after the event of the Bible. This was the key interpretive hurdle facing me as I began to write. When I described the project to a respected senior biblical studies scholar, he remarked: 'Oh, I'd never have the *chutzpah* to do that.' At that point I wondered what I had got myself into by agreeing to write this volume in the Bible Themes series.

1. The word of God

However, two important and reassuring things gradually emerged. The first was that it would be helpful to examine the somewhat more general theme of Scripture, which is the concept of the word of God in the form of written text, rather than the theme of the particular text itself, namely, the Bible. In doing so it became clear that the Bible has a lively sense of God speaking in a unique way within and through the text of Scripture, and there is much that can be said on this theme. This includes the proposal that when the New

Testament talks about the Scriptures or the written word of God it potentially is speaking of the collection of texts that includes what we now call the New Testament, even though the exact borders of that collection would only finally emerge under the guidance of the Holy Spirit through the historical process. That is why I refer more often to 'Scripture' or 'the Scriptures' than to 'the Bible'. By 'Scriptures' I mean the Christian Scriptures that have been accepted by the church as canonical and called the Bible, but I also mean the idea of the Bible. I do not define what is 'canonical' but write with the Protestant canon in mind. I hope, though, that those from other Christian traditions than my own, who set the boundaries of the canon in slightly different places, may also usefully read of the Scriptures in this volume.

More importantly, and secondly, a study of the Bible on the subject of the Bible quickly reveals that the Bible is only one aspect, albeit an indispensable aspect, of an even wider and more important concept, the word of God. While the Bible is in every sense the word of God, the Bible is also at the same time a vehicle of the word of God. Therefore any coherent comment on what the Bible says about the Bible, the Christian Scriptures, must address the wider notion that God speaks. And so it gradually emerged that this volume should be on *The Message of the Word of God*. The distinction between the Bible and the word of God, to which I return below, is a topic to which the texts themselves often return.

2. The outline and approach

Accordingly, the message of the word of God is considered around four key propositions, each of which is expressed in a five-chapter division. The first is the extraordinary notion that God speaks. This introduces us to the breadth of God's speaking, both in the text of Scripture and by means of the world that God has made. Following on from this, the second proposition is that God speaks in the written words of Scripture in a particular way. This is because the Scriptures are unique in nature. The third proposition is that God speaks in Christ. The word of God is finally and fully revealed and heard in the person of Jesus. At least three things follow from this: that the word of God in Scripture is a witness to the revelation of God in Jesus; that Jesus provides a model for interpretation of the Scriptures; and that the Scriptures are best understood and interpreted in the light of Christ. The fourth proposition is that God speaks today. The first three ideas are not merely historical statements of what has been or what may be known by means of the texts; they also indicate how it is that the voice of God continues in the present day to be heard in the light of Christ and through the reading of Scripture.

The Bible itself is not a systematic treatment of doctrines and themes, but rather a narrative with a number of sub-plots along the way. Accordingly, in any sustained attempt to explore what the Bible says about something, which this volume attempts to be, it is best to follow the storied approach of the Bible itself. As a result, this volume does not purport to be a systematic treatment of a doctrine of Scripture, for the Bible itself is not that. There is a place for more systematic theological treatments of that doctrine, although it is interesting and a little unsettling to note that an approach such as is taken by the Bible Themes series does raise a somewhat different set of concerns than do more explicitly theological treatments. If the reader finds things missing from this volume or more lightly treated than might have been expected, it may be because they are not concerns of the texts themselves.[1] At the same time, it has not been possible to say everything or examine every text that is relevant to the 'word of God'. Nevertheless, I hope that the major features of the landscape of God's speaking are herein introduced to the reader. And hopefully also a narrative of sorts emerges in the ordering of the texts under examination that reflects something of the biblical story itself. Each chapter is a discrete treatment of a passage, but each is written in the light of the others to the end that a coherent, if not systematic, treatment of the 'The Message of the Word of God' emerges.

Incidentally, the text that I will primarily be referring to is Today's New International Version (TNIV), with an eye on the Hebrew, Aramaic and Greek manuscripts that it translates.

3. The speech-act of God

Notwithstanding the biblical narrative approach taken to the theme in question, there are a number of points that emerge consistently. Before outlining the most important of these, however, I note the one paradigm that I have found to be consistently useful in identifying an important thrust in the biblical notion of the word of God. It comes from the field of pragmatic linguistics and is known as speech-act theory. This approach to understanding the act of communication distinguishes between the words spoken, the intention behind their speaking and the effect on the hearer of their having

---

[1] It may also be that they are simply missing. But I hope not.

been uttered. In doing so, it draws attention to the action intended by speaking, whether that be to threaten or declare or pronounce or inform or entertain or any one of a number of other potential intents of speaking. It then considers the effect or outcome of the act of communication. The concepts developed in this theory are helping readers of Scripture to appreciate afresh that when God speaks he acts, and that God acts by speaking.[2] This understanding is set up in the creation account where God creates the world and human society by means of his word. It continues as God becomes part of his creation in the incarnation, in the form of one referred to as 'the Word' or *logos*.[3] It regularly expresses itself as the importance of language in knowing God. Although I (mostly) avoid the technical language of linguistics, the idea of the active and effective word of God, or the inseparability of speech and action, undergirds this volume.

The central place of Jesus in hearing the voice of God, alongside the helpfulness of linguistic insights, means that I will sometimes speak of 'the word of God' and sometimes of 'the Word of God'. The former expression refers to the notion that God speaks. The latter refers to the speaking of God in the incarnate Christ. The variation between upper and lower case 'w' in 'word' is intended to maintain the distinction between the two. Occasionally, of course, especially in the latter half of this book, the two become indistinguishable.

4. The reader and Scripture

One outcome of this emphasis on the active intent and outcome of language is that both sides of an utterance or text must be taken account of: the speaker or writer and the hearer or reader. This means that an appreciation of the fact that God speaks must focus both on the word of God and on the response of the reader or hearer to the word of God.[4] With respect to the text of Scripture itself, which is such an important element in God's speaking, attention must be paid both to the nature and message of Scripture and to its reading and interpretation. Any account of the word of

---

[2] For a wide-ranging exploration of the usefulness of speech-act theory in the interpretation of Scripture see C. G. Bartholomew, C. Greene and K. Möller (eds.), *After Pentecost: Language and Biblical Interpretation*, Scripture and Hermeneutics 2 (Grand Rapids: Zondervan, 2001).

[3] John 1.

[4] In that respect, another branch of linguistics, Relevance Theory, will be referred to at one point.

God that ignores one or other of these sides of the speech-act is incomplete.

In that respect, epistemology is an important handmaid to the study of Scripture. This broadly entails the question of how we know what we know. As I will note from time to time, a modernist approach to knowledge embraces the notion of doubt and of a sharp distinction between that which is known and the knower, whose task is to investigate everything as a non-involved observer. Such an approach has dogged the practice of biblical studies in the West over the last two centuries, and in doing so driven a wedge between knowledge and application and between history and faith. Like modernity itself, the contemporary postmodern context is a mixed phenomenon. But one of its blessings is a greater openness to a more subjective approach to knowledge: one that accepts that knowledge and belief have to do with one another; one that seeks to understand the Bible on its own terms as God's story. In that environment the faith of the reader and the transformative impact on the reader of his or her reading is an inescapable part of the appreciation of Scripture.

A corollary of this is that the Bible is not primarily an object of investigation from which emerges a set of impersonal propositions about its nature. It is a phenomenon to be entered into and engaged with. That is certainly how the Bible itself understands the word of God. As a result, a study such as this does not result so much in a set of doctrinal proposals as in an appreciation of the impact on the reader of the amazing fact that God has spoken and continues to speak.

5. The glory of God

While it is difficult to generalize, there are three aspects or effects of this speaking that emerge time and again in this study. The first is that God's speaking has to do with the glory of God. God's glory is revealed in the fact that he speaks and his words may be discerned. Whatever else we might say about what God is like, or of his splendour and majesty and power and comprehensive nature, the primary reality is that God speaks. Scripture drives us back again and again to that fundamental reality. And what an ongoing miracle that is. Beyond the splendour of nature, beyond the fear of Sinai, beyond even the bruising judgment of God, is the extraordinary truth that God enters into relationship with humanity. Any study about the word of God, which is the primary vehicle of that relationship, is a study of the glory of God.

6. The people of God

The second and third effects of God's speaking take a pragmatic turn. The second is the observation that time and again God speaks in the service of bringing a people into being. In the Old Testament, this is often around the formation of a covenant people and the conduct of their life together. In the New Testament, the development of a people of God who together follow Jesus is a regularly recurring theme in the context of God's speaking. Related to that is a third effect of God's speaking, which is that this people who are called into being by the word of God are a people who themselves become the word of God, and in so doing declare the word of God to others. This too we will see as we work through our various passages.

7. Psalm 119

Psalm 119 does not get a chapter of its own in this volume, but it does deserve reflection in the light of these various themes.[5] As is well known, this psalm is an exhaustive reflection on God's word. In fact eight different Hebrew terms are used to refer to the word of God although with some variation in translation. They are roughly: law, word, promise, rulings, statutes, commandments, testimonies, precepts.[6] The issue of whether or not these terms refer to written texts or to the psalmist's own experience of God's speaking is debated, although there is a consensus that the poet responsible for this psalm has in mind the impact of written texts that bring the word of God. That being the case, it is also likely that he or she has in mind more than simply the *torah* (usually translated as 'law') in the sense of the five books of the Pentateuch. He or she possibly is writing late enough to encompass other texts that were attaining authoritative status.[7] The eight different Hebrew words used of the texts can be differentiated from each other, but they broadly refer to the experience of meeting God in the text of Scripture, and I am not here differentiating them.

In light of my comments in sections 4 to 6 above, it is intriguing to see how much an analysis of the concerns of Psalm 119 responds to the impact of the word of God discerned in the body of this volume.

---

[5] Much of what follows is drawn from B. Sargent, 'The Dead Letter? Psalm 119 and the Spirituality of the Bible in the Local Church', *EvQ* 81 (2009), pp. 99–115.

[6] Sargent, 'The Dead Letter?', p. 104, charts them and their possible translations.

[7] See ibid., pp 105–106, on the case for this.

The first thing to comment on is the evident love for and commitment to the text of Scripture on the part of the writer. Any number of verses could be picked to demonstrate this. The psalmist 'loves' the word,[8] he or she 'delights' in it,[9] and is 'consumed with longing' for it.[10] The psalmist basks in the reception of God's speaking as he or she 'meditates' on what is heard.[11] All of this comes together in a cluster around Psalm 119:47–48: 'for I delight in your commands because I love them. I reach out for your commands, which I love, that I may meditate on your decrees.' To have access to anything that calls forth this type of whole-hearted response is something to treasure. No wonder the psalm is also peppered with references to the value of the text; it is 'more [valuable] than pure gold' and 'sweeter than honey'.[12] The entire response to the word of God takes place in the context of a passionate and all-absorbing commitment. An appreciation of Scripture cannot be undertaken without a response to it. It is in the very nature of God's word to be heard in context and to be responded to accordingly. That is why interpretation and response, and even the guardianship of the word, are part of what we think about in this volume.

It is also why the effect of the word of God emerges. For the texts that the psalmist encounters confront their reader and call forth a response. They are to be 'fully obeyed',[13] kept[14] and followed.[15] This arises from the love for God's word already noted.[16] As a result the psalmist experiences a number of things: salvation, freedom, understanding, hope, comfort, identity, and the list goes on.[17] All of these point to the active effects of the word of God encountered in the text of Scripture by a reader whose heart is open to hear God speak. While a response is somewhat muted in this particular psalm it is strongly implied by the final stanza, in which the poet's 'lips overflow with praise' and he or she finds a 'tongue' to 'sing of [God's] word'.[18] Psalm 119 tends to reflect the individual, but much of what the poet experienced of God's active word provides the raw materials from which to form a people of God. And so, Psalm 119 prefigures for us a sense of God's speech-act as it emerges in

[8] Ps. 119:48.
[9] Ps. 119:16.
[10] Ps. 119:20.
[11] Ps. 119:48.
[12] Ps. 119:127, 103.
[13] Ps. 119:4.
[14] Ps. 119:69.
[15] Ps. 119:166.
[16] See the link in Ps. 119:167.
[17] See for example Ps. 119:41, 45, 73, 74, 82, 111.
[18] Ps. 119:171–172.

Scripture along with a dynamic expectation of God's impact on the hearer.

8. Doctrinal comment

If this all seems rather too pragmatic and not doctrinal enough, my response is that that is the position to which the text of Scripture has led me. Having said that, though, there are several aspects of a doctrine of Scripture that do emerge and are important. The first is that this conversation between God and the readers or hearers of the word is to be conducted constantly under the guidance of the Holy Spirit. This is true of the text itself, of those who played a role in producing the text, and in its readers and interpreters.[19]

I have used the word 'conversation' to indicate that the word of God is inherently effective and requiring of a response. That does not mean, though, that the conversation partners – humanity and God – are co-equal. The text of Scripture is quite explicitly God's story. He is the initiator. His respondents are free to respond in a range of ways but not all of those ways will be appropriate in the sense of realizing God's intent in speaking. It is in respect of God as initiator that we may speak of the authority of Scripture.

Accordingly, a proper distinction needs to be made between Scripture as the word of God and Scripture as a vehicle of the word of God. This paradox will emerge over and over in the chapters ahead. The Bible is the word of God; to waver on this point reduces it to the plaything of its readers. But the Bible is also not the sum total of the word of God, in that it must be read and interpreted and appropriated into life under the quickening of the Holy Spirit and in the light of Christ if the voice of God is to be heard. To ignore this is potentially to reduce the reading of the Bible to an act of idolatry. It is the face of God made known to us in Christ that we seek.

In a unique way the Bible enables us to see his face. To that end, we can say that the Bible is thoroughly true and complete, fit for its purpose and unique amongst texts. And so let us hear more of what it says about the word of God.

---

[19] For theological comment on this see J. R. Franke, *Manifold Witness: The Plurality of Truth* (Nashville: Abingdon, 2009), pp. 74–77.

Part 1
God speaks

Psalm 19
1. The glory of God made known

Most summers my family and I camp at a glorious spot on the east coast of Northland in New Zealand. We are on a narrow isthmus with a classic pohutukawa-fringed ocean beach on one side and a tidal estuary and harbour on the other. From our place on the isthmus we can walk about half an hour up and over a headland to a rocky tidal lagoon. This headland faces east over the Pacific Ocean. One morning I decided to walk out to the highest point of the headland and watch the sun rise over the ocean. As I stood waiting for the sun I heard and saw something that will stay with me forever.

Clouds began to develop on the horizon at a rate just fast enough to obscure the sun's emergence. After some minutes of waiting in vain for a glimpse of the sun through or above the clouds, I shifted my gaze southwards to the sky above the hills on the other side of the harbour. To my astonishment the isolated puffs of clouds to the south were tinged with the most magnificent colours, and changing their hues even as I watched. The sun, although hidden by cloud, was casting its beauty anyway. After some time observing this, while keeping an eye on the gathering clouds in the east, I turned further round to the west, now with my back to the sun's struggle. Looking out across the hills ranging inland, I began to see tendrils of fine mist dancing towards me, hugging the contours of the hills as they were blown along. The mist drew closer and expanded, gradually enveloping the sheep facing me in the paddock. And then, with a blast of cool air somehow out of tune with the promise of that summer morning, it engulfed me also. Suddenly it was cold. I turned back to the east, and of course by now there was no sign of even the ocean horizon, let alone the sun.

As I turned back again to the western hills I noticed just in front of me a small completely circular rainbow formed on the fine mist. Then I saw that in the centre of that rainbow was a shadow. I moved several steps sideways and as I did so the rainbow moved. And so did the shadow. I moved again with the same result. Wherever I moved, the shadow remained in the centre of the rainbow. And I was that shadow. Gradually the mist dissipated and the rainbow with it, and as I looked again to the east I saw that the sun was now above the clouds and well on its journey across the skies for another day.

I sensed that God was speaking to me in the silence of his creation. And then I began to think about all of this in the light of God's other book, the Scriptures. I was left overwhelmed with a sense of the power of the risen Son over the gathering clouds of evil, and moved by the beauty of God's unexpected work in the world even when we are not able to glimpse the full glory of the Son. At such moments the cool blast of sin threatens to obscure him even more. Yet it is at those very moments that the rainbow promise of God comes to surround us with the assurance that God remembers 'the everlasting covenant between God and all living creatures of every kind on the earth'.[1] On that January morning, facing a somewhat challenging year in several respects, I knew beyond a shadow of a doubt that I rested in the centre of God's perfectly formed love, a love shown in Jesus that no evil can ultimately obscure. How did I know? Because the heavens of God declared it and because the law of the Lord in Scripture interpreted it for me. Had I been thinking of Immanuel Kant at that moment I might have recalled his surprising declaration: 'There are two things that fill my soul with holy reverence and ever-growing wonder – the spectacle of the starry sky that virtually annihilates us as physical beings, and the moral law which raises us to infinite dignity as intelligent agents.'[2] In any case, further reflection on that moment on a Northland headland has led me to Psalm 19 with its affirmation of the speech of God.

1. The message of the structure

There is a progression of thought in Psalm 19 that can be described in various ways, but however it is done, most agree that there is a distinct shift in direction between verses 6 and 7. Until verse 6 the focus is on creation as the voice of God and as the outcome of God's glory. From verse 7 the written word of God, the *law*, becomes the centre of interest. So marked is the disjunction that many commentators have supposed that here are two distinct psalms which have

[1] Gen. 9:16.
[2] Quoted by A. Cohen, *The Psalms: Hebrew Text and English Translation with an Introduction and Commentary* (London: Soncino, 1945), p. 53.

somehow ended up being bundled together. That was the prevailing opinion as the form-critical approaches to biblical criticism reached their zenith through the early and middle part of the twentieth century. An increasing appreciation of the artistry and intent of the final form of the text has more recently led others to assume coherence and some kind of intent in the juxtaposition of these two types of material. The intent may be in the mind of a single human author or it may be an outcome of the way the psalms have been collected.[3] Either way, the question is now posed: although there is a marked shift in thought between the first and second part of the psalm, what might this shift actually mean?

When that question is considered we find considerable coherence in the material. There is a clear progression of thought discernible: the created world in some way 'speaks' of God (1–4a); the glory of God spoken of in creation is typified by the progress of the *sun* personified as a *bridegroom* (4b–6); the things of which the glory of creation speaks are more explicitly uttered in the written word of God (7–11); this in turn leads to prayer in the form of a sober reflection on the listener's own words to and of God (12–14).

But the coherence lies in more than a poetic progression of thought, important though that may be. The coherence is also theological in that it makes an important statement about the nature of God's speaking. This speaking is heard both by observation and appreciation of God's creation and by reading and considering the words of God in the *law*. There is much to say about how this actually works, how we relate these two forms of revelation to one another, what respective weighting we might give to them, or how this might inform the way we exercise discipleship within the world. And we will come to those things during the course of this study of the message of the word of God.

For the moment, though, it is worth pausing to absorb this one profound truth: that God speaks and God's words may be seen, heard and understood. And this speaking occurs not just in the reading of God's *law* or *ordinances* or *precepts* or *commands* or *statutes*, all words used to describe the Hebrew idea of *torah* but which may also be applied to what Christians now understand to be the Scriptures; it may also be discerned in the activity of the world around us. The verb in verse 2 translated as *pour forth* is a poetic term most common in Proverbs and Psalms and it almost always applies to human speech, sometimes as a negative quality.[4]

---

[3] J. L. Mays, *Psalms*, Interpretation (Louisville: John Knox, 1994), p. 97.

[4] For example, the evil uttered by the wicked in Prov. 15:28, and the words of praise to God in Ps. 119:171.

Similarly the sweetness of God's written words (10) and the impatient energy of the life-giving sun (5–6) are not distinguished from each other in their importance as vehicles of the voice of God. Both call forth *words* and *meditation* (14) from those who encounter them.

2. The paradox of God's speech

But the coherence I have referred to has its roots in a paradox. On one side of the paradox we find *The heavens declare* and *the skies proclaim* (1); indeed so prolific are their declarations that they *pour forth speech* (2), a phrase that might more literally be translated 'day after day bubbles forth speech'. And the scope of all this speech is *into all the earth . . . to the ends of the world* (4). The voice of creation is deafening and inescapable, and as constant as a reliable spring. Yet nestled into these assertions comes verse 3: *They have no speech* and *no sound is heard from them*. Numerous attempts have been made by interpreters to tackle this paradox. The tidiest, and therefore the one about which we should be the most cautious, is perhaps that reflected in the NIV translation: 'There is no speech or language *where* their voice is not heard.' By introducing 'where' into the start of the second half of the couplet a link is introduced that is not present in the Hebrew. This results in the rather simplistic notion that creation speaks but sometimes we are deaf and do not hear it.[5]

This solution misses the point in that it assumes a distinction between the type of speech carried on by the heavens and that available in human words. The Hebrew, however, implies that the voice of creation is of the same order as that which can be recognized in a human voice. The verb *declare* has the sense of recounting or rehearsing and usually refers to human communication. The heavens rehearse God's glory just as Abraham's servant tells Isaac all about his search for Isaac's bride,[6] or the fathers in the faith recount what God has done.[7] A similar point could be made of the verb translated *proclaim*. The words in verse 3 translated as *speech*, *words* and *sound* are also not distinct from the words used to describe human discourse. In that respect, the revelation of God in nature is not different in kind from the revelation of God in the

---

[5] H.-J. Kraus, *Psalms 1-59: A Commentary*, tr. H. C. Oswald (Minneapolis: Augsburg, 1988), p. 271: 'the discourse of the heavens is not carried on in words.'
[6] Gen. 24:66.
[7] Ps. 44:1.

written word. What can be said of one can be said of the other. And both, as we have noted, lead on to prayer.

Care is needed in what we do with this. It is not the case that the story of creation is all that is required to know God. Were that so, the second half of the psalm would not be necessary. Nor is it the case that the poetic forms chosen are merely metaphorical while the 'real' voice is the comprehensible voice of the written form. If that were so, the first part of the psalm would be unnecessary. Instead, somehow we must find a way to live in the paradox that God speaks as truly in the world that he has made and in which he has placed humanity as in the various instruments of revelation. And that somehow the trees and mountains and animals in their own way, a way with which humanity can never fully engage, exist in praise of God.[8]

Because of that, the glory of God can barely be expressed within the limitations of language. Were that not so, we would quickly lose a sense of the transcendence and otherness of God. A vivid example of this comes from the experience of Elijah at Mount Horeb. In hiding, depressed and alone after his epic battle on Mount Carmel with the prophets of Baal, and fearful of Queen Jezebel, Elijah stood out on the mountainside looking for the voice of God. He witnessed a powerful wind, an earthquake and a fire, but could hear the Lord in none of those phenomena. Finally, in a way that defies the despair of Simon and Garfunkel's 'The Sound of Silence' (1964), came 'the sound of finely ground silence'.[9] And somehow in that silent communication Elijah was made ready to hear the voice of God.[10]

Whatever else might be said about this, in one sense the clamour and the silence together of the voice of God (3–4) simply reflect the human struggle to hear God. The notion that the works of God may be seen and heard and spoken about is an extraordinary one; it is not something that humanity ever fully comes to grip with. Notwithstanding the doctrine of Christian assurance, we live much of our lives with a sense that God remains just out of reach, that we see 'only a reflection',[11] that the voice of God is often silent or distressingly subject to our own distortions. At the same time we are creatures in whom God has set eternity,[12] who have a capacity

---

[8] M. S. Northcott, *The Environment and Christian Ethics* (Cambridge: University Press, 1996), p. 181, argues that 'in the Hebrew perspective humanity and the cosmos have moral significance, and both are required to make a moral response to the creator, a response to God which reflects his glory and offers the return of gratitude, praise and worship. . .'.

[9] My translation, 1 Kgs 19:12. See NRSV, 'a sound of sheer silence'.

[10] 1 Kgs 19:11–12.

[11] 1 Cor. 13:12.

[12] Eccl. 3:11.

to glimpse beyond the mundane facts of our existence, who may, however inadequately, know and speak of God. This is the paradox within which the life of faith is lived: that we sense an aspect of our existence that remains beyond the reach of human language and which we call the word of God, while at the same time this word of God comes in the frail garb of human language. This is nowhere more strongly felt than at those moments when God is encountered in the activity of the wider creation.

3. The word of God in creation

There are well-established links formed by creation language between Genesis 1 – 3 and Isaiah 40 – 55.[13] In making his point the psalmist reflects the craftsman language of those two great sections of Scripture. The second half of verse 1 can be translated literally: 'the works of his hands are revealing the pressed firmament'. The word I have translated as 'pressed firmament' is the same as that used in Genesis 1:6–7 of the 'vault' between the heavens and the earth ('firmament' in RSV). The picture is of God beating out the firmament as a craftsman beats patterns into and forms vessels out of precious metals. This picture is also recalled in Isaiah 42:5 where the Lord 'spread out' the earth.[14] Although the correspondence is not always as exact, Isaiah 40 – 55 reflects the early chapters of Genesis at various other points. See for example Isaiah 40:12, a picture of God weighing out and marking off the created order, or Isaiah 40:22, in which he 'stretches out the heavens like a canopy, and spreads them out like a tent to live in'. Just as God, like a worker in precious metals, beat out creation like pressed metal by his spoken word, so now creation itself speaks out the glories of the God who spoke it into being.

By linking the psalm into the tradition reflected in Isaiah 40 – 55, the nature of *glory* is further clarified. In the parallelism of verse 1, the *glory of God* corresponds to the *work of his hands*.[15] The glory of God may be seen in the creation which God has made and which speaks of him. At the same time Isaiah 40:5 looks at 'glory' from a slightly different yet related angle. In the context of the prophet's vision of the people's return through the desert from exile, he

---

[13] See S. Lee, *Creation and Redemption in Isaiah 40–55*, Jin Dao Dissertation Series 2 (Hong Kong: Alliance Bible Seminary, 1995), p. 2.

[14] The Hebrew noun in Gen. 1:6–7, *rāqîaʿ*, is from the same word family as the verb in Isa. 42:5, *rāqaʿ*.

[15] NRSV echoes older translations with 'handiwork'.

declares, 'the glory of the LORD will be revealed, and all people will see it together. For the mouth of the LORD has spoken'. The Hebrew connecting word translated as 'for' (*kî*) at the start of the final phrase is capable of a different interpretation. It may also be translated as 'that'; hence, 'that the mouth of the Lord has spoken'. In what does the glory of the Lord reside, in that case? In the fact that the Lord speaks, and then acts to save his people. This is in line with the creation account in Genesis 1. There the handiwork of God in creation comes into being by the word of God. It is hardly a surprise, then, that both word and created order are spoken by and speak of the Lord, and that therein lies God's glory.

4. Creation as God's handiwork

At the same time, it is also no surprise that the creation emphasis of Isaiah 40 – 55 is accompanied by a concern about idolatry.[16] Once the creatures lose sight of the one to whom the glory of God in creation points, the one who also speaks and acts in their history, then there is idolatry.[17] And in the ancient world of this psalm the object most likely to be ascribed the glory due to God was the sun. The Babylonian hymns to the sun god *Shamesh* and various Egyptian hymns to different sun-gods illustrate this.[18] And this is an understandable reaction from those who have no sense of a Creator who is both within and apart from his creation. Of all parts of creation, the sun is apparently most worthy of praise. All life depends on its rays; it reflects a joy in living typified by the joy known to a man who has consummated his relationship with the woman of his dreams (5); it conveys a sense of power and possibility felt in physical achievement (5); and it is utterly reliable, tracing its course day after predictable day (6). Yet in the world of the psalmist the sun is subject to the creator craftsman, who by *[pitching] a tent* (4b) for it proves to be its master.[19] The arena of the sun is not a magnificent palace for its worship but its daily circuit is one part of the handiwork of God.

---

[16] See the withering sarcasm directed by the prophet in the parodies of those who worship idols made from created materials in Isa. 40:18–20; 44:9–20; 46:1–11. See also Ps. 115.

[17] That is one reason Isa. 40 – 55 never deals with creation apart from history, the work of the Creator apart from his explicit dealings with his creatures. See B. W. Anderson, *Creation Versus Chaos: The Reinterpretation of Mythical Symbolism in the Bible* (New York: Association Press, 1967), pp. 119–123.

[18] Kraus, *Psalms 1–59*, pp. 272.

[19] J. R. Wagner, 'From the Heavens to the Heart: The Dynamics of Psalm 19 as Prayer', *CBQ* 61 (1999), p. 252.

The joy, the power, the possibility, the reliability, the life-giving essence of the sun all derive ultimately from the one who created it. The sun is the chief signpost to that being.

And *nothing is deprived of its warmth* (6). It is generally agreed that this phrase is intended positively.[20] There is no place that does not benefit from the life-giving rays of the sun. But perhaps we might also consider that it speaks of the all-pervasive presence of the One who created the sun, and foreshadows the possibility of judgment. And therein lies a conundrum. These first six verses of Psalm 19 proclaim the clarity of God's voice in creation. Yet the extended metaphor of the sun as *bridegroom* has put the reader in mind of those who somehow do not hear the voice clearly and worship the sun instead of the glory of God. Which takes us back to the paradox of the simultaneous noise and silence of creation in declaring God's glory.

Those who examine the created world most closely, the scientific community, illustrate this at work. There are those for whom the voice of creation speaks clearly of the voice of God. Scientist and Anglican clergyman John Polkinghorne, for example, comments that 'we are not misled by the world'. For him 'the whole effect of scientific experience is to engender belief that we attain a tightening grasp of an actual reality'. And further, 'God is not a deceiving demon'.[21] It is his experience as a mathematician that 'the rational beauty of the cosmos indeed reflects the Mind that holds it in being'.[22] On the other hand there are those whom the glory of God's handiwork does not draw to prayer. Indeed the religious impulse that this handiwork invokes in some is for Richard Dawkins a mere 'by-product' of the gullibility that can spin off from obedience to the voice of experience for the sake of preservation of a species.[23] The main thing in Dawkin's vision is 'the something else' that humanity would be better off using to fill the gap '[cluttered] up' by God. [24] In terms of the creation tradition of Isaiah 40 – 55, we might name this 'something else' as an idol, the mere 'image' of its maker. In terms of Psalm 19, Dawkins appreciates the *sun* but not the one who has *pitched [its] tent*. For some the silence of verse 3

[20] For example Mays, *Psalms*, p. 97.

[21] L. F. Harris, 'Divine Action: An Interview with John Polkinghorne', *Cross Currents* 48.1 (1998); <http://www.crosscurrents.org/polkinghorne.htm> (accessed 19 February 2008).

[22] J. Polkinghorne, *Belief in God in an Age of Science* (New Haven: Yale University Press, 1998), p. 4.

[23] R. Dawkins, *The God Delusion* (London: Bantam, 2006), pp. 172–179, argues that religion is a 'by-product'.

[24] Dawkins, *God Delusion*, p. 347.

simply remains silence; for others the very silence is part of the voice of God. This too is part of the paradox.

5. The turn to wisdom in the law

The response by the psalmist is a turn to wisdom at the start of verse 7.[25] C. S. Lewis considers that the psalmist at this point 'felt, effortlessly and without reflecting on it, so close a connection, indeed ... such an identity between his first theme and his second that he passed from the one to the other without realizing that he had made any transition'.[26] The link is the searching heat of the sun, from which nothing may be hidden (6). Just as this typifies the revelation of God in nature, so it puts the poet in mind of that other great agent of revelation, the *law of the Lord* (7).[27] Just as the sun spreads its heat to the benefit of all creatures, so the wholesome reviving effect of this *law* is to make *wise* (7), a condition as necessary as being warmed and nourished by the rays of the sun. Indeed the impact of the sun is reflected in the hymn to the *law of the Lord* that follows in verse 7–9. It fills the *heart* with *joy* (8), it is such as to *[give] light to the eyes* (8), and there is an enduring quality about *the fear of the Lord* (9) as there is about the ever-reliable sun. At the same time, in the Psalmist's declarations beats a regular rhythm of contentment that there is something right and good and well directed about this *law*. It is *perfect* or unblemished (7), it is *trustworthy* or reliable (7), it is *right* or straight (8) and also *radiant* or clear (8), and it is *sure* (9), perhaps in the sense that a plumb line is true. Just as the sun unerringly runs the course that has been set for it (5), so does the law given by the one who sets the course of the sun. In short, the word of the Lord produces a well-lived life, one that is pleasurable and good and appropriately focused on the one who is the source of blessing.

The word translated as *law* (7) is *torah*. As understood by the psalmist it is a term not narrowly focused on the law as a series of prescriptions (and here the limitations of English translation do not serve us well) nor necessarily on the first five books of the Bible, the Pentateuch. Rather it is best taken as the instruction of Yahweh

---

[25] We will have more to say on wisdom in ch. 3.

[26] C. S. Lewis, *Reflections on the Psalms* (London: Fontana, 1961), p. 56.

[27] Historically, this link has been expressed with the metaphor of the two books written by God, the book of nature and the book of Scripture. P. M. J. Hess, 'Nature and the Word of God in Inter-Religious Dialogue', p. 2; <http://www.metanexus.net/conference2004/pdf/Hess.pdf> (accessed 16 April 2008).

that 'comes to human beings and marks off the way for them'.[28] As Hans-Joachim Kraus puts it, 'human beings confront the [*torah*] as a working power. In it they have perceived the living address of God (Psalm 119), by it they have been revived (Ps. 19:7) and delighted (Ps. 19:8).'[29] This experience of the instruction of the Lord in the lives of people is always the aim of biblical wisdom literature, no matter how complicated the route to that state of affairs may sometimes be. And so the turn taken by the psalmist towards the spoken words of God with humanity is couched in wisdom terms. This culminates in the classic wisdom picture contained in verses 10–11 of the value (*more precious than gold*), pleasure (*sweeter than honey*) and benefit (*great reward*) of the word of God to his people.

This sense of rightness or order is reflected in the almost perfectly symmetrical form of the poetry in verses 7–9. There is a series of six statements, each with the same length of line and stress pattern and grammatical structure. The grammatical balance is well represented by the TNIV translation, but no English translation can quite convey the rhythmic beat of these lines in the Hebrew. Cumulatively they emphasize several key points about the speaking of God. First, that these words are words of Yahweh; in every line they are *of the* LORD. The one who calls his people into covenant speaks them. Secondly, as we have seen already, at each point there is something good about this speaking. The words somehow reflect the beauty of the world made by the one who speaks. How could it be otherwise? The words of God are such as to induce trust, joy, endurance, purity. Indeed, as we heed the advice of Paul to dwell on 'whatever is true, whatever is noble, whatever is right, whatever is pure, whatever is lovely, whatever is admirable . . . anything [that] is excellent or praiseworthy',[30] we find that naturally we are drawn towards the place where such things are most fully in evidence, at the point of the glory of God. And Psalm 19 shows them in the eloquent handiwork of God as well as in his revealed speech preserved in the Scriptures. Who knows if Paul was setting out to draw a parallel with Psalm 19 in his choice of words? Certainly, at two points his list coincides with two elements in the ancient Greek translation. Paul's fellow disciples are asked to dwell on what is 'true' just as the ordinances of God are *sure* (9), and also on what is 'pure' just as the fear of the Lord is *pure*.[31]

---

[28] Kraus, *Psalms 1–59*, p. 273.

[29] Ibid.

[30] Phil. 4:8.

[31] The word for *pure* is present in both Gk Ps. 19:9 and Phil. 4:8; the word represented by *sure* in TNIV. Ps. 19:9 is the same word translated as 'true' in Phil. 4:8.

The third element in each of the first four lines describes the effect on the hearer of the words of the Lord: they revive, they bring wisdom, they give joy and they enlighten. This is a pointer towards the effect of the fact that God speaks. The word of God as heard in the *law* is effective; it makes a difference.

6. The fear of the Lord

A close reading of the sixfold expression of the *law* contained in verses 7–9 (*law*, *statutes*, *precepts*, *commands*, *fear* and *ordinances*) invites the challenge: spot the odd one out. At first glance the term *fear* seems out of place. The poetics of these lines suggest that *fear* should be approximately synonymous with all the other terms, yet it pinpoints what seems to be a response to the words of the Lord rather than those words themselves.[32] A helpful starting point is Peter Craigie's comment that the six 'aspects' of the *torah*, as he calls them, may be thought of as 'all-embracing'.[33] Therefore the fear of the Lord is an inherent part of God's self-revelation. In the same way that law, ordinance, statute, precept and all the other synonyms developed in Psalm 119 are vehicles of God's speech with human-kind, so the fear of God may function as a means by which God speaks with his people.

'Fear' as used in the Old Testament Scriptures contains the idea of emotional response, respect, reverence, worship, and ultimately an appreciation that the worshipper is in the presence of a being who is worthy of that worship.[34] All of these things are essential to the human apprehension of God speaking. 'The fear of the LORD is the beginning of wisdom'[35] because such fear is inherent in the *law* by which God makes himself heard by humanity. And that is also why an appreciation of the word of God occurs most fully within the context of the creature worshipping the creator.

To explore the point a little further, most of the terms deployed for the *torah* convey something that in the minds of most

---

[32] One explanation is that the text is disturbed at this point and the word that may be translated as 'promise' has been corrupted in the process of textual trans-mission. However, there is no manuscript evidence for this being the case, and it seems preferable to wrestle with the text in the form in which we have received it. This decision applies the text-critical principle of *lectio difficilior*, accepting the more difficult reading. Given the tendency of copyists to simplify and iron out dif-ficulties in their copying, that a difficult reading has survived that process makes it more likely to have been original.

[33] P. C. Craigie, *Psalms 1–50*, WBC 19 (Waco: Word, 1983), p. 181.

[34] *TWOT* 1, pp. 907–908.

[35] Prov. 9:10.

English-speaking readers is external, static, in some sense even pre-scriptive. In contrast, fear is internal, dynamic and primarily affective. Fear is something that is experienced subjectively as a result of encountering something that is external. In short it is a term that is fundamentally relational in a way that the other terms for *torah*, on the face of it, are not. In Hebrew poetry, the device of parallelism is seldom as simple as the poet saying exactly the same thing twice using slightly different language each time. The different parts of the parallel structure more often clarify and deepen the meaning of each element in the structure. That the term *fear* is in poetic parallel with *law, statute, command, precept* and *ordinance* invites us to dig a little, to entertain the possibility that the poetic structure tells the reader something both about fear and about these other terms. First, the parallelism suggests that the idea of 'the law' should not be reduced to a set of legal instructions that are merely to be complied with; they are instruments of God's grace that draw those who encounter them into relationship. Looking at things from the other side, the context in which the term *fear of the Lord* is set suggests that this fear is not merely emotional and subjective; it beckons into a relationship that is articulate and comprehensible and not merely something that is experienced at an emotional level (although it is that too).

This appreciation of the human encounter with the God who speaks articulately with humanity is somewhat at odds with the concept of knowing (technically, epistemology) that has dominated Western thought in the modern period. Modernist epistemology has embraced the distinction between knowing and belief, and has declared that belief is subjective while knowledge is objective in that it is that which may be known by the application of doubt and the scientific method. Such an approach has dominated the study of theology and Scripture, in the academy and in parts of the church, for many generations.[36] But increasingly the mood of our own age is permitting a recognition that this approach does not quite work. A leader in this field has been the philosopher and scientist, Michael Polanyi, with his ground-breaking presentation of what he calls 'personal knowledge'. In a compelling analysis he demonstrates that ultimately the subject and object cannot be kept apart in the process of discovery. Rather, Polanyi demonstrates, true knowledge is personal in that it is knowledge that does not respect the distinction

---

[36] For an extended discussion of this, see N. Wolterstorff, 'Scholarship Grounded in Religion', in A. Sterk (ed.) *Religion, Scholarship, and Higher Education, Perspectives, Models, and Future Prospects* (Notre Dame: University of Notre Dame, 2002), pp. 3–15.

between the subject and the object. In short it is knowledge that is grounded in belief, in the commitment on the part of the knower to that which is known.[37] The enthronement of doubt by Descartes as the only respectable intellectual stance to take towards any search for truth is seen to be no longer sufficient. Although Polanyi does not say this, a theological analysis of his ideas is in tune with the concept of the incarnation, of true knowing being founded in the fact that God enters into relationship with his world as Jesus. The incarnation of God as 'the word' or *logos* is the final demonstration that God speaks.[38] Part 3 of this study examines in more detail the fact that God speaks in Christ.

7. The turn to prayer

If the fear of the Lord is an intrinsic part of the revelation of God in the *law*, then one might expect that the encounter with that aspect of the word of God constitutes, among other things, a call to prayer. And that is precisely the turn made at verse 12. The psalmist, overwhelmed by the voice of God both in creation and then in the *law*, finds his own tongue in prayer. While the law of the Lord is sweet and pure, it is also as searching as the sun, penetrating to the *hidden faults* (12) of those who encounter this God who speaks. A sense of one's sin is one result of the encounter. But with this comes the confidence that forgiveness and the assurance of innocence are possible.

The encounter with the voice of God also draws the hearer into a dialogue. As God speaks, so God's creatures are invited to speak.[39] In creation this expresses itself in the declaration of the glory of God. Amongst the human community, for those who have ears to hear, it leads to repentance and the desire to speak in a way that is *pleasing in [God's] sight* (14). As this prayer is answered, humanity, guided by the words of Scripture, takes up its voice with the rest of the created order in declaring the handiwork of God, and in the process becomes that very handiwork that in its turn bears witness to the voice of God.

---

[37] See M. Polanyi, *Personal Knowledge, Towards a Post-Critical Philosophy* (Chicago: University of Chicago Press, 1958), pp. 269–298, in ch. 9 on 'The Critique of Doubt'.

[38] John 1:1–14.

[39] Wagner, 'From the Heavens to the Heart', p. 261.

Isaiah 55
2. God's word goes forth

Attendance at worship was falling. The young people in particular were conspicuous by their absence. When the elders gathered,
they grumbled about accommodation, looked back on better
days, and wondered whether God was yet working (or even
present) in their midst. Each day brought reports of someone
from the flock who was 'selling out', turning toward the values
of an increasingly alien world, chasing after other gods – a better
spot in the market, the trust and respect of those in power, a
secure and stable life for them and their family. Other congregations were growing and growing rapidly, but the gods they worshipped did not seem to be the God of the ancestors, the Lord
who had always brought them victory in the past. Where was this
God, they wondered, now?[1]

Richard Boyce's imaginative depiction of the gathered life of Jewish
exiles under the Babylonian empire could so easily describe church
life in the West at the beginning of the twenty-first century. The
church seems to have less and less to say to our world, or even to its
own adherents. Religious enthusiasm, when it is expressed, is often
clumsy and somehow out of touch with the questions of the age. The
promotion of the marketer as the new high priest in society results
in an obsession with appearance over substance at almost every level
of public life, from fashion to politics, and even to matters of faith.
The materialistic apathy that surrounds the faithful is profoundly
debilitating in its effects. And the breakdown of a moral consensus
in society leaves believers uncertain how to respond with both grace
and truth. In a post-Christendom world, Christians find themselves
increasingly on the fringe.

[1] R. N. Boyce, 'Isaiah 55:6–13', *Int* 44 (1990), p. 56.

From time to time something of the moral poverty in which we live breaks like a wave over us, causing us to pay attention briefly. As I write this, New Zealand has just heard evidence at a trial of several young men and women responsible for the appalling mistreatment and death of a three-year-old child. The picture that emerged of endemic violence and abuse is simply impossible to ignore at such moments. In a different and more pervasive way, the financial crisis that broke over the global economy in the second half of 2008 has occasioned public discussion about the infectious and corrosive nature of greed, and the inability of humans to pull back from harmful behaviour until it is too late. At such moments, society as a whole senses that a moral response is called for. But even then it is often hard for Christians to break the mould of indifference and self-interest which we share with those around us.

From what we know of life in the Babylonian exile, the Hebrew people were free – indeed, commanded by God – to make a living in Babylon, to go about their daily lives more or less undisturbed, to form their own religious communities and even to 'seek the peace and prosperity of the city'.[2] Yet still they ached for something more as they tried to make sense of life in an exilic context and to come to terms with being surrounded by a Babylonian cosmology that ascribed all power to the forces represented by the heavenly bodies.[3] In short, they struggled in the terms laid out above by Boyce. Into that context, the words of Isaiah spoke of new hope and possibility, a possibility formed around a renewed covenant brought into being by the ever-reliable word of God. The very word or speech of God acts to bring new possibility into being.

As Walter Brueggemann has illustrated, the exiles' sense of being on the margins of an alien world is not very different from our own as we struggle to maintain a fingerhold in a Western society that has largely rejected a Christian account of the great questions of life.[4] Like those Hebrew exiles, we too are worn down by constant contact with a world that has a different set of values and hopes from our own. We too are often tempted to give in to those things and to doubt that we ourselves have anything real to offer the world around us. Like the exiles, we are in regular need of being re-invigorated by Christian hope and possibility. For us, too, the effectiveness of the word of God in establishing a relationship between God and humanity and in bringing the impossible to pass

[2] Jer. 29:4–7.
[3] Ps. 137.
[4] W. Brueggemann, *Hopeful Imagination: Prophetic Voices in Exile* (Philadelphia: Fortress, 1986), p. 6.

is essential. And so Isaiah's account of God at work through the power of his word in Isaiah 55 speaks as powerfully to the Christian church today as it did to the exiles all those generations ago.[5]

In the words of Isaiah 55 we are reminded of the affirmation of Part 1 of this study, that God speaks and God's voice may be heard. We discover also that this voice is an effective one; when God speaks things happen. In that God's word is sent forth with a task to do, *speech* and *act*, two words I have already used in this section, come together. It is no accident then that a branch of pragmatic linguists known as Speech-Act Theory has come to prominence in the study of biblical interpretation, as interpreters search for greater understanding of the process whereby God's word impacts the lives of those who encounter it.[6]

Briefly, speech-act focuses on the category of *locution*.[7] Locution refers to the actual words spoken or written in a piece of communication. But words themselves in a vacuum seldom communicate much at all. For communication to occur, the intended effect of the words spoken must be appreciated: to persuade, to threaten, to promise, to comfort, to inform and so forth. What effect does the speech mean to have? The intended effect of a piece of communication has been labelled *illocution* by the linguists. The same words can have quite different intentions according to the context in which and the intent with which they are uttered. For example the words 'you are now husband and wife' are meant to entertain and perhaps inform if they are uttered in a movie in which two of the characters get married. If I am standing at the front of a church next to a woman and the person speaking those words is licensed to marry people and is directing them to me and the woman, the illocution (or intention) is profoundly different. Speech is inherently something that makes things happen or brings about states of being, sometimes more powerfully and obviously than at other times.

---

[5] The dating of this section of Isaiah (40 – 55) is contested broadly between those who argue for an eighth-century date, well before the Babylonian exile, and those who see these chapters as originating in the exile experience. While I assume the later date, even if an early date is accepted for the entire Isaiah scroll, ch. 40 – 55 are still best read as applicable to the exile experience. On dating, compare A. Motyer, *The Prophecy of Isaiah* (Leicester: IVP, 1993), pp. 25–30, with J. E. Goldingay, *The Message of Isaiah 40–55: A Literary-Theological Commentary* (London: T&T Clark International, 2005), pp. 3–5.

[6] See for example the contributions from K. J. Vanhoozer, D. R. Stiver, N. Wolterstorff and A. C. Thiselton in C. Bartholomew, C. Greene and K. Möller (eds.), *After Pentecost: Language and Biblical Interpretation*, Scripture and Hermeneutics 2 (Grand Rapids: Zondervan, 2001).

[7] For an introduction to these things, see J. L. Mey, *Pragmatics: An Introduction* (Oxford: Blackwell, 2001), pp. 92–133.

But in thinking about speech as an act the intention of the speaker or writer (the illocution) is not all that has to be taken into account. There is also the outcome of the act of speech, which is known in the trade as the *perlocution*, the effect of the speech.[8] The effect of my hearing the words quoted above in a movie is that I am entertained, while the effect of hearing them for myself at the front of a church is that I am now a married man. There is rather a big difference! Sometimes of course the intention of an utterance or a piece of writing may have a different effect than that intended. A threat, for example, may not achieve the desired outcome. As a parent of teenagers I often used to find that it did not! Why that might be so is also part of the study that is opened up by a speech-act approach to language. All of this is relevant to and helpful in considering the question of the effectiveness of the word of the God who speaks. The technicalities of pragmatic linguistics will not further detain us in this volume, but some of its insights will continue to inform an unfolding appreciation of the message and action of God's word.

1. Structural matters

While the focus of this chapter is the word of God as described in verses 10–11, it is important to understand that word in the wider context both of Isaiah 55 and the second half of the book of Isaiah as a whole. Some of the prophetic books are shaped into a clear narrative,[9] but for the most part they are in the nature of collected written anthologies of the prophets' spoken messages over the time of their ministries. The result is that the books display a thematic unity around the message of the prophet, but it is not always obvious what the logical relationships might be between different sections. I am convinced by the argument that Isaiah 55 is best read as a coherent literary unit.[10] I am also convinced by the logical flow of the chapter as described by Walter Brueggemann:[11] verses 1–5 describe the invitation into a renewed covenant that God offers to his people on the basis of the ancient covenant with the house of David; verses 6–9 then switch to the imperative mood as God appeals to the people

---

[8] Unfortunately linguists love to make up words like illocution and perlocution, but I will not burden the reader further with them. Intention and effect are close equivalents.

[9] Jonah and Haggai for example.

[10] M. C. A. Korpel, 'Metaphors in Isaiah LV', *VT* 46 (1996), p. 48. *Contra* those who read vv. 1–5 and 6–13 as units distinct from each other.

[11] W. Brueggemann, 'Isaiah 55 and Deuteronomic Theology', *ZAW* 80 (1968), pp. 173–174.

to accept the invitation, assuring them of forgiveness as he does so; verses 10–11 concern the word of Yahweh, which both looks back to the earlier promises and also brings to fulfilment the renewed promises of God; the concluding verses 12–13 are then a vivid picture of the transformation that comes through accepting Yahweh's invitation and obeying his commands. As Brueggeman puts it in summary: 'the transformation occurs because life is now given (v. 1–5). Israel turns to life (v. 6–9) and Yahweh guarantees it (v. 10–11).'[12]

Some have also linked the message of Isaiah 55 with what immediately precedes it, namely the reference to the 'heritage of the servants of the Lord'.[13] If the thirsty and penniless people of God think they are bankrupt, then think again. They have an inheritance, which the prophet now reveals as a renewed covenant brought into being by the word of God. Indeed, the link goes back further because the comfort promised in Isaiah 40 is on the basis of the fact that 'the mouth of the Lord has spoken'.[14] This promised comfort culminates in the reflection of Isaiah 55 on the effective word of Yahweh in formulating a new covenant with God's people.[15] In fact, the words of chapter 55 reach further back than just chapter 40. They can also be read as the culmination of the response of God to the situation set up by the puzzling material of Isaiah 6:9–13. There the word of the Lord through the prophet promises to close eyes and ears to the things of God: 'Make the heart of this people calloused; make their ears dull and close their eyes.'[16] Not unreasonably, Isaiah asks how long this must go on, to which God replies that it must be until the time when 'the holy seed will be the stump in the land'.[17] Whatever exactly this much contested phrase means, there is a link through to chapter 55 in which the word of the Lord *yields seed for the sower* (10). The word of God in judgment set out in Isaiah 6:9–13 now reveals its counterpoint in hope and comfort through the institution of the new covenant and the transformation that will flow from that covenant, all as a result of the word of God. Possibly Jesus picked up on this same dynamic in his parable of the

---

[12] Brueggemann, 'Isaiah 55', p. 194. Although I would want to say that Yahweh does more than guarantee it; he brings it about by the act of his speech.

[13] Isa. 54:17b. See Goldingay, *The Message of Isaiah 40–55*, p. 543.

[14] Isa. 40:5.

[15] One of the assumptions of a speech-act approach to language is that language implies relationship. K. J. Vanhoozer, 'From Speech Acts to Scripture Acts: The Covenant of Discourse and the Discourse of Covenant', in Bartholomew, Greene and Möller (eds.), *After Pentecost*, pp. 1–49, demonstrates that it is therefore no surprise that the act of God's word is closely connected to the formation of covenant.

[16] Isa. 6:10.

[17] Isa. 6:13.

sower,[18] where the seed of the word of God brings obduracy and judgment along with eventual assurance of the divine purposes.[19]

With that in mind we turn to the nature of God's word as it emerges in verses 10–11, before considering more of its effects in light of the surrounding material in Isaiah 55.

2. As the rain and the snow . . .

There is a clear poetic structure within verses 10–11. The start of each verse is around the grammatical structure, *as* . . . (10), *so* . . . (11). The process described in verse 11 thus mirrors that of verse 10. At the same time, each verse pivots on an important Hebrew particle *'im*. The term is represented by the TNIV in verse 10 by *without* in the phrase *without watering the earth*, with the translators opting in verse 11 for *but* in the phrase *but will accomplish*. It is not an easy expression to capture exactly in English. The NRSV prefers 'until'; 'unless' is also a possibility. The TNIV and NRSV between them indicate the general conditional feel of the term. In any case, in each instance an agent is sent out, and is not permitted to return 'unless/without/until' certain effects have occurred as a result of the agent's action. The structure of each of these two verses so closely reflects the other that the reader cannot help but read one in the light of the other. The *as* . . . *so* scaffolding of the two verses also makes clear that the more abstract verse 11 is to be understood in the light of the picture taken from nature in verse 10. As with any reading of metaphor, the metaphor of rain and snow illumines that to which it is being likened, the *word* of God, and the text assumes some familiarity on the part of the reader with the metaphor itself.

So we turn to verse 10, a picture of precipitation which in its various forms causes the earth to sprout forth its vegetation for the benefit of humanity. The vegetables grow, the trees absorb the carbon dioxide, and the beauty of the world around is enhanced because the rains and the snows come in their seasons. In Auckland, where I am writing this, it is easy to take this miracle for granted, blessed as we are with plenty of rain and a green lush environment most of the year. Sometimes, as I watch the lawn grow, I wish it were a bit less lush! But in many parts of the world, including in the Judean hills familiar to the earliest hearers of Isaiah's words, rain and snow are scarce and valuable commodities. They are

---

[18] Mark 4:3–20.
[19] C. E. Evans, 'On the Isaianic Background of the Sower Parable', *CBQ* 47 (1985), p. 467.

eagerly awaited and carefully managed when they arrive. In such an environment agricultural and horticultural management centres around making the most of every drop of water that arrives. None is taken for granted and when the rains fail a grim time is in store.

But when *the rain and the snow* do their work the effect is there for all to see. First of all, it *[waters] the earth*. The verb used has the sense of giving something a good soaking, of abundance and plenty. The earth itself, not merely its foliage, receives the benefits of rains from the Lord's hands. The result is that it *buds*, a word that in Hebrew explicitly concerns reproduction. And it also *flourishes*, a term of extravagance and abundance. Together *bud and flourish* speak of the miraculous self-sustaining fertility and fruitfulness of nature made possible through the watering of the earth.

The final two lines of verse 10 then point out the usefulness of all this fertility. The benefit is to those who depend on the fruitfulness of the earth for their well-being, and two kinds of dependence are highlighted. First, the well-watered earth provides the means for its own sustainability; there is *seed for the sower*. Secondly, it provides sustenance for those who depend on it. These two aspects reflect the two verbs, *bud and flourish*, both of which are in the causative form. The rains and snow cause the ground to reproduce, as a result of which its reproductive capacity is sustained in the form of seeds. At the same time, they cause the ground to produce extravagantly, thus providing *bread for the eater*. It may not be pushing the metaphor too hard to note that, while the watering of the earth is something over which humanity has little control, the resulting fruitfulness comes about partly through human participation in the process.[20] Whether or not that particular point was intended by the prophet, it is part of the creation tradition shared by the early chapters of Genesis and these chapters of Isaiah. Therefore that the *sower* should appear in verse 10 echoes the commissioning of Adam and Eve to tend the garden and enable it to bear fruit.[21]

3. . . . So is God's word

The word that goes out from God's mouth, the prophet says, may be understood in the same way. There are several key aspects of God's word that are treated in verse 11: it is effective; it does not return empty; it is sent forth with a purpose; and that purpose has to

---

[20] There is a rich vein of reflection here on how God and humanity work together in the care of creation, but that is for another time.
[21] Gen. 2:15.

do with the will of God. This all sounds very abstract, but it achieves an immediacy and everyday relevance when considered in light of the metaphor that has just preceded it.

Let us first think of one aspect of both the metaphor and what it illustrates that is not mentioned in the preceding section, namely, that it does not return without/unless/until it achieves that for which it is sent. It has been pointed out that the prophet is unlikely to have had a scientific understanding of the precipitation cycle in speaking of the rain and snow returning to heaven once it has watered the earth.[22] But he was drawing on an established sense of the *word* of God as agent sent forth on a particular commission and then returning with that commission accomplished. By the time that these words were written there was an understanding of wisdom as the agent of God in the world,[23] and the beginnings of an identification of the word of God, the *torah*, with this wisdom work of God in the world.[24] Thus, when the prophet speaks of God's word *[achieving] the purpose* or *[accomplishing]* something, a sense of the word's activity on behalf of God is not far away. Something of this sense is also captured by Jeremiah's vision of the almond blossom showing him that God is 'watching to see that [God's] word is fulfilled'.[25] In the same way, in the mind of the poet at this point, the rain once it has ceased may be thought of as having returned whence it came, the evidence of its effect remaining in the form of a fertile earth.

For a twenty-first-century reader, with a knowledge of the water cycle, the opposite effect is at work. The idea of water moving on in the cycle once it has done its work helps to illuminate for us a sense of the word of God as effective agent, that does its work, leaves its impact and then moves on. And in both the metaphor and the actual reference the process is inevitable. The apostle Paul captured something of this in his concept of the power of the gospel in bringing about the will of God.[26]

I am not a particularly good gardener, and there are a range of reasons why plants under my care do not flourish.[27] But even for me

[22] B. Couroyer, 'Note sur II Sam., et Is., LV, 10–11', *RB* 88 (1981), p. 512.
[23] Prov. 8:22–36.
[24] E. J. Epp, 'Wisdom, Torah, Word: The Johannine Prologue and the Purpose of the Fourth Gospel', in G. F. Hawthorne (ed.), *Current Issues in Biblical and Patristic Interpretation* (Grand Rapids: Eerdmans, 1975), p. 135: 'the two terms [Wisdom and Torah] were often interchangeable and . . . the writer or hearer of a Wisdom hymn could just as well be thinking of Torah.'
[25] Jer. 1:12.
[26] See for example Rom. 1:16 and 1 Cor. 1:17–25. For further see R. L. Plummer, 'A Theological Basis for the Church's Mission in Paul', *WTJ* 64 (2002), pp. 256–260.
[27] To illustrate the problem, I recently staked up what appeared to be a self-sown tomato plant, only for my wife to point out that it was in fact a potato.

they are much more likely to do well when they are watered; that is the way things work. So it is when the word of God is brought to bear on a situation; there cannot but be an effect. But the phrasing adds an extra twist to that. Not only is there something inevitable about the process; there is also something persistent. The rains and snow do not return whence they came *until* their task is completed, or *without* completing their task. Likewise, the word of God does not merely glance into a situation to see if it can help; it persists until the desired effect is achieved. Every spring, when the rains come, the barren Judean wilderness blossoms briefly. It is impossible not to notice the effect. When God's word has been at work it is similarly evident, in ways to which we turn below and which in this context primarily reflect God's formation of covenant relationship with his people.

The role of God in this process is further illumined by a subtle difference between the nature metaphor and the *word* itself. The language of verse 10 does not indicate any particular cause for the rain and snow, other than its source in *heaven*.[28] The agents are the beneficiaries of the rain and snow, namely, the sower and the eater, whose task it is to appropriate the earth's abundance. Unlike in verse 10, the agent of God's word in verse 11 is the speaker: Yahweh, from whose mouth the word *goes out*. At the same time, the beneficiary of God's word is also Yahweh in the sense both that the word is sent forth with a particular purpose in the divine mind and that the effect of the word is a cause of delight. The TNIV phrase, *what I desire*, begins to capture the sense of divine delight which is inherent in the term. By implication, just as the sower and eater benefit from the rains, so the Lord benefits from the word of God.

This is somewhat counter-intuitive in that we might have thought that humankind in some way would benefit. It is a remarkable emphasis that God benefits from his own word. However, the metaphor also allows for the possibility that humankind is the beneficiary. The sower and the eater of verse 10 are likely to be identified in the mind of readers and hearers as people like themselves, therefore the effectiveness of the word of God that *does not return to [God] empty* (11) is assumed also to be of benefit to men and women who encounter it. Somehow the two things hold together in a way that reinforces the understanding of God as a character within his own

---

[28] Of course to the Hebrew mind, the source of all forces of nature is inescapably Yahweh, but that is not the point being made here. Indeed, arguably by the time of this writing in the exilic period, *heaven* had come to be used as a shorthand for the God of heaven. See J. J. Collins, *Daniel*, Hermeneia (Minneapolis: Fortress, 1993), pp. 229–230.

story which infuses the Old Testament Scriptures. The equation of Yahweh (11) with the sower and eater (10) is a subtle reminder that human beings are co-workers with God. God's purposes in verse 11 in some way relate to the response of the sower and eater of verse 10 in bringing into effect the purposes of God. God both enters into our experience with his word and also endows us with something of himself through his word.

As we have seen, the effect brings delight to Yahweh. Something of the content of this delight emerges through the nature metaphor of verse 10 with its picture of extravagant fertility and joy in the delights of God's good creation. The pleasure that the human experience of these things brings is akin to that felt by God at the effect of his word. At the same time, those on whom the word acts are similarly affected with pleasure both at its extravagant fruitfulness and at its self-sustaining possibility. When God truly works in a situation, he does so in a way that enables the work to be sustained through the participation of God's co-workers.[29]

4. God's word in the call to covenant

So far we have identified that God's word is effective. But what effect is in mind? Given that we are reading Isaiah 55 as a complete unit, these two verses on the word that goes out from God's mouth (10–11) respond to the key emphases that have been identified in the chapter as a whole. By working through each of those emphases we may appreciate more fully the nature of the impact of God's word. Rain and snow are inherently interesting natural phenomena that may quite legitimately be described and experienced, but the poet in this context is less interested in doing that and more concerned with what happens as a result of the rain and snow. In the same way, the word of God may also be described and experienced for its own sake, and indeed the enterprise of doing so is almost endlessly interesting. But the prophet here is more concerned with the impact of the word of God on that which it encounters. Similarly, in this section we remain focused on the fact that God speaks and that God's word goes forth and is effective.[30]

And so to verses 1–5, which we have summarized as God's invitation into a renewed covenant. In the previous chapter on Psalm 19

---

[29] To name one potential application of this insight, in the language of Christian development work, God's word builds 'capacity' rather than dependence amongst those to whom it comes.

[30] Parts 2, 3 and 4 of this volume look more at how this actually works.

we saw God's word active in creation and also in Scripture. In Isaiah 55 the metaphors chosen echo a link with creation but also sharpen the focus onto the covenant-making word of God. There are several aspects to this. First of all, it is a word that is spoken by direct address into the situation in which the people find themselves. The opening word in the Hebrew is an attention grabbing *hôy!* (1, translated as *Come*). Pay attention! you who are thirsty and hungry and without the means to acquire food and drink. The covenant-making word of God is for such as you, because the result is the unimaginably *richest of fare* (2). This message can be taken in both a spiritual and a 'secular' sense. On the one hand, it recalls the metaphor of famine for those who are under the judgment of God desperately looking for a word from God.[31] On the other, it foreshadows the later physical experience of those who returned from exile struggling to make ends meet like people whose wages are going into a purse with holes.[32] For them, the failings in their covenant relationship were being expressed physically. These words should not be spiritualized in a way that excludes a physical application of them. God speaks both for the poor and for the poor in spirit.[33] It has also been observed that the covenant-making experience of the exodus itself brings together both of those elements. It was a time of physical deliverance from oppression along with provision of food and water, but at the same time the broader canvas of the establishment of the people of God was always in view.[34] God's word comes to people in their particular struggles and uncertainties. Much later, those who gathered around Jesus would hear him echo this invitation as he called people to the 'rivers of living water'.[35]

And God speaks not only to alleviate the suffering and respond to the longings of individuals; he speaks also to bring a people into being. In the remarkable verse 3, the Lord through the prophet remembers the everlasting covenant made with King David,[36] and effectively incorporates into that promise 'all who would believe from all the nations'.[37] To view the dynamic from a slightly different angle: 'The covenant relationship David once enjoyed with God is

---

[31] Amos 8:11–13.

[32] Hag. 1:6.

[33] Compare Matt. 5:3 and Luke 6:20.

[34] G. A. F. Knight, *Servant Theology: A Commentary on the Book of Isaiah 40–55*, ITC (Grand Rapids: Eerdmans, 1984), p. 190.

[35] John 7:38. M. A. Daise, '"If Anyone Thirsts, Let That One Come to Me and Drink": The Literary Texture of John 7:37b-38a', *JBL* 122 (2003), pp. 687–699.

[36] 2 Samuel 7.

[37] W. C. Kaiser, 'The Unfailing Kindnesses Promised to David: Isaiah 55:3', *JSOT* 45 (1989), p. 97.

now to be enjoyed by the nation as a whole.'[38] God's effective word, like the snow and rain on a thirsty earth, enables the formation of a people of God; God's word comes to build communities of the faithful.

To what end are these communities formed? To the end that their calling will be fulfilled as a people who draw other nations also into the covenant. The people are *endowed . . . with splendour* (5) so that the influence of the Lord God, the Holy One of Israel might be evident. The involvement of the people of the covenant in the mission of God, which is hinted at regularly in Isaiah 40 – 55, is strongly and explicitly in evidence at this point. The activity of the word of God speaks into being a people who then further the work of God in forming a people of faith. God's word comes to build communities of the faithful, so that those communities in their turn become agents in God's covenant-making intention.[39] This reflects the dynamic we noted in the metaphor of verse 10, that the rain and snow water the earth not only to provide bread for the hungry, but also to enable the sower to propagate and extend the fruitfulness of the earth. In the same way, the people spoken into being are also intended in some sense to be self-sustaining. This point needs to be made with care. It is always the case that the church remains dependent on the word of God for any effective work, but it is also the case that a viable and faithful church has its own effect in widening the circle in which the word of God exercises its influence.

5. God's word in the appeal for a response

Verses 6–9 have been characterized as an appeal to God's people to respond to God's words. In terms of our study of the effect of God's word, it demonstrates the effectiveness of God's speech-act in drawing people into his covenant. In verse 6, much loved of evangelists, the English implies that God is only *near* and able to *be found* at particular moments, and that it is important to respond at those moments before the word recedes. This translation of the Hebrew preposition as *while* does highlight the need for a response to God's word, and in that respect is in tune with what emerges in verses 7–8; a sense of urgency is appropriate to this theme. However, another more literal translation of verse 6 reads as follows: 'Seek the Lord

---

[38] H. G. M. Williamson, *Variations on a Theme: King, Messiah and Servant in the Book of Isaiah* (Carlisle: Paternoster, 1998), pp. 118–119.

[39] C. J. H. Wright, *The Mission of God: Unlocking the Bible's Grand Narrative* (Leicester and Downers Grove: IVP, 2006), p. 352.

in his being found; call on him in his being near.' That translation has a less urgent ring about it, but it does draw out another likely intent of this verse, namely, that God's presence is not in doubt.[40] He is near and he is available to be found. Therefore, harking back to the opening of this chapter, those who are thirsty and hungry and penniless can confidently come. This is assurance rather than threat. The word of God, which does not return without doing its work, is always at hand for those who seek and come.[41]

At the same time, there is a paradox inherent in the framing of this section. If God's immanence is expressed in verse 6, it is also the case that the difference between the *ways* and *thoughts* of Yahweh (8) and of the hearers of this message is as vast in scale as the difference between the *heavens* and the *earth* (9). The Hebrew term translated as *thoughts* has the sense of 'device' or 'plan'. It has to do with all the factors at work that result in the formation of a person's intent, for good and ill. Then *ways* relates to the action or way of life that arises from the intention formed by the will. There are all sorts of limitations to the human heart and mind, from the impulse to evil to the scars created by life's hurts to external forces at work on us to the simple fact of our boundedness in time and space. As a result the paths we take in life reflect these limitations. God's will, however, is not bound by any of those limitations and as a result the actions undertaken by God are truly reliable and appropriate and good. Although God is always near, as verse 6 suggests, God is also always vastly different (9).

The miracle of the incarnation is that this God enters into the world of humanity and enables the gap to be bridged. One effect of this is that through the activity of God's word it becomes possible for humankind to begin to see the world through God's eyes, and so to begin to form ways of life that more adequately reflect the truth and goodness of God.[42] That is what verse 7 is about: the beginning of the alignment of the human will with that of God, with a consequent alignment of the way of life with that of God. The particular means by which this occurs in verse 7 is repentance and forgiveness.

And this forgiveness is effected by God's word. The link emerges in the poetic shaping of verses 8–11. Each of these verses begins with the Hebrew particle *kî*, variously translated by TNIV as *for* or *as*. There is a wide array of usage for this little word, but almost all of

---

[40] Goldingay, *The Message of Isaiah 40–55*, p. 551.
[41] Deut. 30:14 indicates that this is not only a New Testament concept.
[42] J. N. Oswalt, *The Book of Isaiah Chapters 40–66*, NICOT (Grand Rapids: Eerdmans, 1998), p. 444.

them relate to cause and effect in some form or other.[43] Hence verse 8 reflects that the need for humanity to amend their ways and be pardoned arises from the difference between humanity's ways and God's ways. The scale of this difference is further reinforced by the comparison with heaven and earth in verse 9. And then the *kî* at the start of verse 10 links the effective word of God with the call to turn to Yahweh and to be pardoned. By implication, the outcome is that the ways and thoughts of those who turn will more closely resemble those of Yahweh who pardons. And this comes about through the word of God.

Thus it is in God's speaking that the covenant people of God learn the thoughts or intentions of God, and so are enabled to live out the ways of God in situations in which they find themselves.

6. God's word in transformation

To conclude his reflection, the prophet reverts to the world of nature. This time, however, he goes far beyond the metaphor of the watering of the earth (10). That was an everyday matter, albeit important and miraculous in its own way. Now the prophet does two further things with nature. First he evokes a sense of the whole of creation dancing for joy before its creator. The beauty and extravagance and differentiation of nature point us to God readily enough. But as humans we cannot ever enter into the experience of other parts of creation responding to God, although we can imagine that it might be so. Verse 13a, however, seems to take us into the realm of the truly unimaginable. In such a place the thornbush becomes one of the plants of the cypress family,[44] and instead of briars a flowering myrtle grows. Transformation has truly taken place but in ways beyond our wildest dreams. Because God speaks.

But perhaps this vision of a transformed nature is not as beyond human ken as might be thought at first glance. The verb translated as *will grow* (13) is an extremely common word, which is often translated as 'to go up'. It is not unusual to find it being used, as here, of the cycles of plant and animal life, but it is a verb also occasionally used evocatively of the people of God. In yet another link back to chapter 40, the herald of Zion is enjoined to 'go up on a high mountain',[45] while the servant of chapter 53 'grew up . . . like

---

[43] B. K. Waltke and M. O'Connor, *An Introduction to Biblical Hebrew Syntax* (Winona Lake: Eisenbrauns, 1990), pp. 636–673.
[44] Translated as *juniper* in TNIV and 'cypress' in NRSV.
[45] Isa. 40:9.

a root out of dry ground'.[46] Tellingly, amongst the so-called Songs of Ascent 'the tribes go up' to Jerusalem.[47] And so the people who *go out in joy* (12), thus echoing the movement of the exodus, now go up as God's people to new possibility.[48] In this way the choice of vocabulary contains a giant hint that the transformation of nature is not only a sign of the cosmic influence of the word of God; it is also a pointer to the radical change in the people of God and their circumstances brought about by the effective word of God.[49] *You* (12), the people of God, will do more than watch the mountains and hills dancing for joy. Such will be your own transformation that you too will know a *joy* and *peace* that will lead to singing and dancing and clapping as at the time of *torah* celebration in the synagogue each year.[50] For the active word of God will have transformed as truly as if a thornbush has turned into a juniper or briars into the myrtle. Once again, as a metaphor from nature illustrated the agency of God's word (10), so now another metaphor from nature indicates the degree of transformation that God has in mind for the exiled people. In this way their imaginations are formed by God so that they can see beyond the limits of their exiled circumstances, as ours also may be as we struggle to stand true in the secularized West. Their and our 'heritage'[51] has become one of joy and possibility.

And as God's people are transformed by the word of God the effects stand as an *everlasting sign* (13) for what God has done, something that will endure to his memory and as a lasting tribute in a way that a statue or a building in memory of some person or event never can. God's word goes forth that God might be remembered and worshipped. Through the transforming effects of God's word on his people hope is rekindled and the cycle of praise of the creator continues.

---

[46] Isa. 53:2.

[47] Ps. 122:4. Still today Jewish people are said to 'make *aliah* [a going up]' when they migrate to Israel.

[48] W. Brueggemann, *Isaiah 40–66*, WBC (Louisville: Westminster John Knox, 1998), p. 162.

[49] See Goldingay, *The Message of Isaiah 40–55*, p. 557, on links drawn by early Jewish commentary between 'the blossoming of the land' and 'the community's spiritual transformation'.

[50] The annual festival at the end of *Sukkoth* in which the congregation sings and dances in celebration of the *torah* scrolls and of the end of the annual cycle of *torah* readings.

[51] Isa. 54:17.

Proverbs 30:1–9
3. The wisdom of God's word

Most people, as beings made in the image of God, desire to live well: to pass on something to the next generation; to have a sense that they are part of something bigger than themselves; to know that they have made a contribution; to do the right thing (however 'the right thing' might be understood); to be able at the end of it all to shape their lives into a narrative that makes sense. All of this seems possible to the extent that people are able to make good life choices and to exercise a measure of control over their environment. And from time to time we feel as if we are achieving it. Most human beings also occasionally despair at the elusiveness of this well-lived life: at a sense of meaninglessness; at alienation from others; at a propensity to do the wrong thing; at incoherence and chaos; and at the sheer smallness of human endeavour against the backdrop of an expanding cosmos. At such moments we echo the refrain of the book of Ecclesiastes, 'Everything is meaningless'.[1]

Mostly we live our lives moving between these two extremes; indeed we could not function if we did not do so. We would become subject either to an overweening pride or to a crippling despair, and both are disastrous. All of this is further confused by an endemic tendency within us to rationalize our own selfish motives and actions and justify them as good and useful. Yet even that is further evidence of this inbuilt sense that it is a good thing to live well, a sense that in most people is never fully crushed by sinful nature.

A significant proportion of the Old Testament addresses itself to this human conundrum. It offers advice about making good choices and taking charge; it wrestles with the fact that things can go wrong for even the best-lived life; and it addresses the sinful tendencies of human nature that make it hard both to live a well-lived life and to

[1] Eccl. 1:2.

deal well with tragedy and disaster. All of this constitutes the biblical quest for wisdom. We find it in the mundane advice of Proverbs, in the uncomprehending submission of Job to God in the face of tragedy, in the struggle on the part of Ecclesiastes to make sense of the contradictions of the human experience.[2] And ultimately we are led to the one overarching reality that 'the fear of the LORD is the beginning of wisdom, and knowledge of the Holy One is understanding'.[3] We also find that a central component in the formation of wisdom within human beings is the *word of God* (5). It is no accident that part of God's answer to Solomon's prayer for wisdom was that he should heed God's 'decrees and commands'.[4] This link between the word of God and wisdom is encapsulated in the final section of the book of Proverbs, especially 30:1–9 and the central affirmation of that section: *Every word of God is flawless; he is a shield to those who take refuge in him* (5).

1. The unity of the passage

To best appreciate the import of that statement, however, two interpretive decisions must be made. The first relates to chapter 30 as a whole. In that context, I assume that verses 1–9 should be taken as a distinct unit.[5] Assuming that, there then arises a further question, the answer to which has an immediate impact on our understanding of the thrust of this passage. It concerns whether or not there is a change of speaker after verse 4. How we answer that question determines whether we read these sentiments as 'piety or scepticism'.[6] If the first four verses are those of a weary sceptic, then the words of verses 5 and 6 are spoken by another and are set against the weariness and agnosticism of the speaker in verses 1–4. If, however, these verses are a unity, then they become an expression of 'piety'. In them the speaker confronts the limitations of his sin-bound humanity and world-weariness in the face of the world and its creator. As he does so he finds a response in

---

[2] Such material is of course not confined to these books alone. Note for example the wisdom psalms, parts of the prophets and even in the history, most notably in the story of Solomon (1 Kgs 3 – 4).

[3] Prov. 9:10.

[4] 1 Kgs 3:14.

[5] This is a finely balanced argument with those who see vv. 1–14 as the opening section, but see B. K. Waltke, *The Book of Proverbs Chapters 15–31*, NICOT (Grand Rapids: Eerdmans, 2005), p. 464, who calls these verses the 'author's autobiography'.

[6] P. Franklyn, 'The Sayings of Agur in Proverbs 30: Piety or Scepticism?', *ZAW* 95 (1983), pp. 238–252.

the word of God which itself leads on to prayer (7–9). This latter position is supported by what has been called the 'beautiful structural symmetry' of verses 1–9.[7] After all, the position expressed in verses 2–4 is precisely that at which Job arrives in Job 38 – 42.[8] And Psalm 73 contains a similarly frank confession accompanied by a strong affirmation of faith. In this exposition, I am presuming that unity.

2. Agur

That being the case, the sentiments of verses 1–9 are spoken by *Agur son of Jakeh* (1). Almost nothing is known of Agur but much has been speculated. Whatever else we might say about him, it is probable that Agur is not an Israelite. The Israelite intellectual tradition regularly interacts with the wisdom conventions of its neighbours, and this is one further instance of this phenomenon.[9] A decision to read verses 1–9 as by the same speaker means, remarkably, that a non-Israelite affirms the importance of the words of God (5–6). But there is more. Although the translation of verse 1 is contested, it is clear that Agur is the speaker and that what he speaks is *an inspired utterance* (1). The term so translated (*nĕ'um*) is most commonly used with respect to an oracle or prophetic saying attributed to Yahweh.[10] Very occasionally it refers to another important or prophetic figure.[11] Its usage with Agur is highly unusual and hence significant. He is not merely affirming the importance of the words of God; Scripture at this point is apparently allowing him to be responsible for delivering them. Taken together with the fact that the prayer in verses 7–9 addresses Yahweh, we might say with William McKane that Agur here becomes 'fully integrated into the fold of Yahwism'.[12]

Previously we have noted the importance of God's speaking for the formation of the covenant. The link of God's word with wisdom leads us now to think more expansively about the possibilities for this covenant. It is something that is potentially applicable to all the peoples that God has made. In that respect, it is remarkable that the otherwise unknown figures of *Agur son of Jakeh*, and Lemuel,

[7] Ibid., p. 251.
[8] Job 42:3 for example.
[9] See 1 Kgs 4:29–34.
[10] From a random sampling of the 376 occurrences in the Old Testament see Isa. 1:24; Jer. 1:8; Amos 9:12; Hag. 1:9.
[11] Balaam for example, Num. 24:15–16.
[12] W. McKane, *Proverbs: A New Approach*, OTL (London: SCM, 1970), p. 647.

son of his mother,[13] close the collection of wisdom sayings that are inaugurated by 'Solomon son of David'.[14] Solomon, as 'king of Israel' and 'son of David', was a child of the covenant, yet his is not the last word; that is given to Agur and Lemuel. Their presence in this Israelite collection hints that the words and acts of God have a public relevance that is larger than the interests of those who gather into communities of faith. This is inherent in the vision of Psalm 19 with which this study of the word of God began. And it will be further unpacked in our consideration of Nehemiah 8.[15]

This does more than reinforce an expanded notion of who was in the family of Yahweh. In light of our consideration of God's word going forth in Isaiah 55, it breathes a confidence that this word brings wisdom to every corner of the created order. This ought to engender a similar confidence within those who read and discern the word of God that it may be applied to every conceivable sphere of life. It has to do with politics and economics, with family life, with academic pursuits, with scientific exploration, with the arts and literature – and the list could go on. When Christians separate the wisdom of everyday life from the wisdom that is more traditionally associated with church life and personal spirituality, they make a distinction that is defied by the biblical picture of wisdom at work.[16] In linking the words and actions of God to wisdom, then, we are saying that God speaks into the whole of life.

This holistic understanding of wisdom, and hence of the applicability of the fact that God speaks, may be illustrated from the wisdom terminology in Daniel 1. Daniel and his friends were recruited to learn the intellectual tradition of their Babylonian masters,[17] but this tradition is expressed in terms that would have been familiar to the Jewish captives. At the end of their training, the young men have received wisdom from God,[18] and, conversely, the terminology used there would have been familiar to their Babylonian captors. Daniel could 'understand visions and dreams of all kinds' and he had the skills to become an accomplished imperial administrator. Both types of knowledge are wisdom, both arise from the fear of God, and both have to do with the fact that God speaks into the world that he has

---

[13] Prov. 31:1.

[14] Prov. 1:1.

[15] See ch. 17.

[16] For more on this dynamic in the New Testament, see J. M. Hitchen, 'Confirming the Christian Scholar and Theological Educator's Identity through New Testament Metaphor', *ERT* 35 (2011), pp. 276–287.

[17] Dan. 1:4.

[18] Dan. 1:17.

made.[19] And the participation of Agur in this word reminds us of the same thing, that God's word has as much to do with Monday as with Sunday, as much to do with the running of a foreign kingdom as with the conduct of the covenant between God and his people.

3. The problem

As indicated above, the translation of verse 1a is highly contested.[20] The issues need not detain us, for whatever translation is finally settled on the world-weariness of the speaker is evident. Thus the question concerns the source of this world-weariness; is it an outcome of the regular endurance of the slings and arrows of life, or is it perhaps more from an acute sense of the distance between the speaker and the wisdom for life that he needs? Certainly this latter option emerges in verse 2, as Agur is overwhelmed by his closeness to the brutes.[21] With that comes a sense of separation from the *knowledge of the Holy One* (3). In expressing himself in this way, Agur captures the dilemma of the human condition. The experience of human identity, as against that of the animals, is a wonderful thing but at times our limitations overwhelm us. At the same time, as beings created in the image of God and hence with 'eternity in the human heart',[22] we glimpse something bigger and better, yet just out of reach.[23] This we identify with the divine, as Agur has done in verses 3–4.

At the same time he is acutely conscious of the boundaries formed by his humanity, existing as he does between the brutes and God. He expresses this through a series of questions in verse 4. The second and third questions recall from Proverbs 8 the sense of God the creator as the master craftsman.[24] As such he *[gathers] up the wind* and *[wraps] up the waters in a cloak* (4). The first question reflects the unattainability of the nature of this divine creator: *who has gone up to heaven and come down?*

The final puzzling question has occasioned much debate: *What*

---

[19] T. J. Meadowcroft and N. Irwin, *The Book of Daniel*, ABC (Singapore; Asia Theological Association, 2004), pp. 34–35.

[20] As illustration, compare T. Longman, *Proverbs*, BCOT (Grand Rapids: Baker Academic, 2006), p. 515, with TNIV.

[21] R. E. Murphy, *Proverbs*, WBC 22 (Nashville: Thomas Nelson, 1998), p. 225, captures this nicely with his translation: 'I am not God, that I should prevail.'

[22] Eccl. 3:11.

[23] For an exploration of the place of humanity in encounter with both our animal nature and the divine see N. Hoggard Creegan, 'Being an Animal and Being Made in the Image of God', *Colloquium* 39 (2007), pp. 185–203.

[24] Prov. 8:27–29.

is his name, and what is the name of his son? (4). There are a range of suggestions as to what this might mean.[25] In the context of this reflection by the *son of Jakeh* drawing to a conclusion proverbs collected in the name of the son of David, I take it to be a yearning to participate in God as a son would participate in the life of a family into which he had been born. Yet the question is left hanging, and the yearning is for the moment left unanswered. The resulting gap has been aptly called 'the tension between the sovereignty of God and the vagaries of human existence'.[26] To find a way of living in this tension is the course of wisdom.

This may be expressed with a different metaphor which will come to the fore in our study of Exodus 19[27] and is foreshadowed here: the boundary between the limitations of humanity and the holiness of God. Ways must be found to cross this boundary, or in terms expressed by Agur, *[to go] up to heaven and come down* (4).

4. The word of God

By the time we get to verse 7 Agur has presumably found a way across this boundary because he addresses God directly. What has happened to enable him to do so is the discovery of the *word of God*, and that it is *flawless* (5) and is not to be added to. When Agur discerns the *word of God* his modifying *every* suggests that he has in mind not so much a set of writings as the more fluid notion that God speaks. His choice of the noun *'amrat* (translated as *word*) in verse 5a, which is related to the verb 'to speak', reinforces this sense of the word as spoken by God, as does the plural reference in verse 6 to *his words*. At the same time, this material probably dates from a time when the notion of authoritative Scriptures is beginning to take shape.[28] The path of wisdom is then at least partially understood as dedication to the task of knowing and applying these Scriptures.[29] This would not have replaced, however, a dynamic sense of the word of God as *torah*, as that which is sent forth from God to do God's work in the world.[30] So we are dealing with the fundamental

[25] For a summary of the possibilities, see M. V. Fox, *Proverbs 10–31: A New Translation with Introduction and Commentary*, AYB 18B (New Haven: Yale University Press, 2009), pp. 856–857.

[26] R. W. Byargeon, 'Echoes of Wisdom in the Lord's Prayer (Matt 6:9–13)', *JETS* 41 (1998), p. 362.

[27] See ch. 6.

[28] Longman, *Proverbs*, p. 25.

[29] McKane, *Proverbs*, p. 648.

[30] See ch. 2 on Isa. 55:11.

notion that God speaks in a way that may be grasped and appropriated by humanity, but this does not exclude a reflection on the written word also. Indeed both senses are implicit in what follows. The idea of *every word* implies a general sense that God speaks; the concept of *his words* as a corpus which may not be *add[ed] to* suggests a defined, and perhaps by now textualized, body of material that is recognized as having that status.

The first thing to note about the nature of God's speaking is that it is *flawless* (5). This word contains the idea of something being tried and tested by fire and thus cleansed of impurity. This says two important things about the word of God: first, that it has been tried and tested. It is not the product of human flippancy or some fly-by-night idea; it stands up to scrutiny because it has been through the fires. At the same time, secondly, the smelting image implies that it has been purged of any impurity. The word of God is not partly the word of God or somehow infected by elements that are not the word of God. It is *flawless* in that those parts have been eliminated from the mix (if in fact they were ever present). This is important to grasp because the undeniable humanity of the means by which the word of God usually comes to its hearers, and is discerned as such, may easily be confused with the word itself.

Before expanding on the significance of this I note the second characteristic of the words of God, that they may not be *add[ed] to* (6). This implies that there is a body of material that is sufficient for the purpose. When there is doubt about this sufficiency there is the temptation to add or subtract in some way from the word. The writer is clear that to do so is tantamount to lying (6). While the language may appear strong, it is making the point that any dilution of the word of God amounts to a compromise of truth.

As we have seen, the subject of this discussion, the word of God as understood by the compiler of the book of Proverbs, is wider than simply a set of texts. In fact, it is probably not primarily about a set of texts. But we have also seen that a written corpus of material is also likely to be part of what is in mind. Chapters 6 and 7 of this volume explore more fully the importance of and dynamic by which the two are related.

5. Infallibility and sufficiency

Theologically, the views being expounded here have profound consequences. The two qualities stated – that the word is *flawless* and that it may not be added to – together amount to what are sometimes called the infallibility and sufficiency of Scripture. The use of the term 'infallible' with respect to Scripture expresses the manner in which the Bible is God-given in its entirety, and therefore in no way at odds with the character of God, while at the same time showing signs of its humanity in such features as diversity of perspective and some looseness in the matter of accuracy of detail. At a deep level, the diversity does not detract from the fact that the Bible is God speaking and speaking within that diversity. The fact that Scripture does not always concern itself with detailed accuracy to twenty-first-century standards of precision similarly does not detract from the trustworthiness of Scripture as God speaking through the human authors and the processes of compilation, preservation and interpretation.[31] As Wayne Grudem puts it, Scripture is 'infallible' in that 'it is as trustworthy and reliable as the God who speaks in it (Ps. 119:160; 2 Tim. 3:16)'.[32] As the writer of Proverbs would put it, it is as *flawless* as something that has had all impurities smelted out of it.

If this sounds to be something of a contradiction in terms it is important to remember the tension that we have already noted within these verses, namely, that the word of God is likely to refer both to the Scriptures and to the broader notion that God speaks. To express it another way, the Bible is the word of God but the word of God is not confined to the Bible. This phenomenon has already emerged in our exposition of Psalm 19, and will continue to be something with which we wrestle in this volume. This means that the textual witness to the voice and actions of God, the Bible, and the reading and appropriations of the text display the fingerprints of humanity. But the voice of God that emerges by means of the text and humanity's encounter with the text is the word of God in all its purity as if refined by fire. How this may be so is found in a robust confidence in the Spirit of God breathing through the whole process.[33]

It is interesting that John Stott in his iconic volume *Understanding the Bible* (1972) handled the question of the infallibility of Scripture by avoiding the double negative inherent in the word, preferring instead to work with the positive categories of inspiration, authority

---

[31] See the exploration of these matters by J. E. Goldingay, *Models for Scripture* (Grand Rapids: Eerdmans, 1994), pp. 333–341.

[32] W. A. Grudem, 'Scripture's Self-Attestation and the Problem of Formulating a Doctrine of Scripture', in D. A. Carson and J. D. Woodbridge (eds.), *Scripture and Truth* (Grand Rapids: Zondervan, 1983), p. 58.

[33] J. Webster, *Holy Scripture: A Dogmatic Sketch*, CIT (Cambridge: University Press, 2003), pp. 29–30. See also the detailed exposition of this in ch. 5.

and revelation.[34] Many years later, in addressing the debates around infallibility, Stott pleaded explicitly for a positive description of the nature of Scripture by citing the 1989 affirmation by the National Association of Evangelicals regarding Scripture: 'We affirm the complete truthfulness and the full and final authority of the Old and New Testament Scriptures as the Word of God written. The appropriate response to it is humble assent and obedience.' Therefore, the statement continues, the Bible as God's word is 'completely true and trustworthy'.[35]

As we have already seen, if the word and words of God are *flawless* it stands to reason that they should also be regarded as complete. This is implicit in the observation that anybody who presumes to *add to his words* is a *liar* (6). This points towards another important formulation of Scripture: its sufficiency. I take this to be saying two things about the fact that God speaks and hence by implication about the text that encapsulates this: first, with respect to content, that the wisdom of God's speaking is complete; secondly, with respect to the collection of Scripture, that there is nothing further to be added.

The two ideas are closely related but not quite the same thing. They need to be distinguished in order to make quite clear exactly what is meant by the sufficiency of Scripture. Because the word of God is a wider concept than the text of Scripture, it does not mean that the text we call the Bible is the only book that needs to be read or its contents the sum total of all that needs to be known. This point will be made a number of times in this volume. That the heavens declare the glory of God[36] means that there is a whole world of knowledge beyond the text that is in some sense the words of God, in that the cosmos and knowing about that cosmos bear the imprint of its creator in a way that may be discerned and articulated.[37] In that respect there is nothing to be added to the words of

---

[34] J. R. W. Stott, *Understanding the Bible* (Sydney: ANZEA, 1972), pp. 181–204.

[35] Cited by J. R. W. Stott, *Evangelical Truth: A Personal Plea for Unity* (Leicester: IVP, 1999). I am not treating the word 'inerrant' but note here Stott's stronger objections to that term, including his comment on its inadequacies as a 'double negative' (pp. 73–74). For some it is identical to 'infallible' (see for example J. I. Packer, *Beyond the Battle for the Bible* [Westchester: Cornerstone, 1980], p. 51). For others, 'inerrant' says more than 'infallible' (see for example Grudem, 'Scripture's Self-Attestation', pp. 57–58). This highlights the problematic nature of the term as historical developments have gradually driven a wedge between the near synonyms. For more on the distinction between 'infallible' and 'inerrant', see P. Jensen, *The Revelation of God* (Leicester: IVP, 2002), pp. 197–203.

[36] Ps. 19:1.

[37] See P. Duce, *Reading the Mind of God: Interpretation in Science and Theology* (Leicester: Apollos, 1998), pp. 11–26, on 'reading the book of creation'.

God, although, from a human perspective, there is always more to be discovered and experienced.

On the other hand, the function of Scripture within the broader concept of the word of God is complete. This is expressed in various ways. One is the Reformation formulation that Scripture contains all that is needful for salvation and for the life of faith.[38] This should not be, and was never intended to be, taken to mean that the wider wisdom of the word of God is somehow less necessary to the life of faith. In fact, as I argue at various points in this volume, Scripture provides the framework within which humanity may relate to the vast array of human knowledge and find therein the wisdom of God. In technical terms, we might say that Scripture has an epistemological function which is sufficient,[39] in that Scripture is taken to be the complete and definitive witness to the acts of God in Christ, the one in whom 'all things hold together'.[40] Therefore all knowledge may be, indeed must be, understood and appropriated in the light shed by Jesus. In that respect any denial of the completeness and adequacy of Scripture, whatever form it might take, amounts to a lie.[41] Thus we are reminded by Agur.

6. Encountering the word in life

Having recognized the poverty of his own brutish lack of wisdom and the enervating effects of that state (1–4) and having also recognized the voice of God the creator (5–6), Agur puts the two together in prayer (7–9). The link is made by carrying forward the notion of lying (6 and 8). His making the link is also foreshadowed in his perception of God in verses 5–6, the nature of whose words we have explored above, as a *shield to those who take refuge in him* (5). Somehow Agur recognizes that an encounter with the words

---

[38] Various formulations could be cited to illustrate this. Since, by accident of history and eventually conviction, I am an Anglican, I note Article 6 from The Thirty-Nine Articles: 'Holy Scripture containeth all things necessary to salvation: so that whatsoever is not read there-in, nor may be proved thereby, is not to be required of any man, that it should be believed as an Article of the Faith, or be thought requisite or necessary to salvation.'

[39] B. K. Waltke, 'Agur's Apologia for Verbal, Plenary Inspiration: An Exegesis of Proverbs 30:1–6', in G. G. Scorgie, M. L. Strauss and S. M. Voth (eds.), *The Challenge of Bible Translation: Communicating God's Word to the World* (Grand Rapids: Zondervan, 2003), p. 313.

[40] Col. 1:17.

[41] Closely related to this is the concept of the uniqueness of Scripture as opposed to other texts. In that respect, see ch. 18 on 2 Tim. 3:10–17.

of God is a place of safety which contrasts with the weariness and insecurity of not knowing.

But once it comes to his prayer he also recognizes that this place of safety and the wisdom that comes with it can easily be lost. It can be lost by one or other of two further forms of falsehood: one is the self-sufficiency that can come with wealth; the second is the denial of the other that can come with poverty. The problem with wealth is that it can so easily deny the necessity of God at all. This leads back to the un-wisdom with which Agur began his piece. The problem with poverty is that it can deny the rights of others made in the image of God and in so doing implicitly dishonour the God who created them. Agur has come to the point of recognizing the path of wisdom by means of his encounter with the words of God and has glimpsed the importance of a lifestyle that will keep him in contact with those words. This is not to suggest that poverty or wealth inevitably become a denial of God; it is to recognize how easily either can alienate the person from God and how dependent we are on God to avoid that.

It is interesting to note that the concern with lies focuses on both the tendency to alter the word of God contained in Scripture and the tendency to live unwisely, either by ignoring God or by taking matters into our own hands and so dishonouring him. The implicit link between the two forms of falsehood is strong and suggestive. It indicates that stewardship of the word of God and living wisely and well belong together. The path to wisdom lies along the reception of the word of God, both as it comes to us in life and as it is witnessed to in the Scriptures. The fear of the Lord, at least partly expressed in respect for the sufficiency and trustworthiness of his Scriptures, enables a life well lived, a life of the sort for which Agur longed.

Amos 3:1–8
4. The Lord God has spoken

All of us know people who speak of God and their personal experience of conversing with God in wondrously clear and definite terms. God's requirements of them seem to arrive as clearly as a set of instructions in the letter box or the self-destructing tape for the Mission Impossible team. There are some personalities that are wired as mystics, and there is no suggestion that their experience is other than genuine. But there are others who struggle to know God's day-to-day requirements of them. Such people can feel inferior to their more mystical brothers and sisters. There can be many reasons for this sense of inferiority, but I suspect that a common one is an unspoken assumption that the word of God is something that is only fully available to a chosen few who have special insight into these things. The popularity of celebrity Christian speakers around the world suggests that there are many who, despite knowing with their heads that God has no favourites, imagine that there are some people who are closer to the counsel of God than they are. And they are closer, it is further assumed, because the divine counsel is essentially a mystery that mostly remains hidden. This way of thinking is a modern-day equivalent of the Gnostic heresy that the early church struggled with over the first two or three centuries of its existence. Arguably, much of the New Testament is dedicated to countering it. In essence, Gnosticism says that God is known through induction into the heavenly mysteries that only the chosen may know. Faith is a matter of uncovering secrets – if you can.

The wisdom poem by Amos that we are about to explore continues a theme that is a wonderful counter to those who think of the word of God in those terms. In our exploration so far of the great theme that God speaks and may be heard, it has been striking to notice the everyday nature of this meeting between God and his creatures. While in one sense the human-divine encounter is never less than a miracle, in another sense it is not a mystery accessible only to the chosen few. In Psalm 19 we saw that God speaks in the marvels of nature and in the written words of the *torah*. Later Isaiah 55 understands the word of God in terms of commercial transactions and the work of the sower and the reaper. Then Agur explores the word of God in light of the limitations of his own human nature and his desire to be delivered both from sins induced by having too much and from those that arise as particular temptations for the extremely poor.[1] In each instance the word of God transcends the context in which it is experienced as well as the metaphors by which it is understood; it is something whose scope and nature we will never fully appreciate in this life. Nevertheless, it is also a word for the everyday and for those people, the vast majority of us, who occupy the mundane realities of life. That God's word is so regularly spoken of in those terms is a warning to anybody who would rarify and mystify the word of God. Indeed, as this poem is about to show us, nothing could be more natural than that God speaks and his voice may be heard.

1. A wisdom poem

Amos 3:3–8 has long been recognized as a well-constructed poem that reflects the wisdom tradition. It is typical of wisdom literature in its focus on the mundane things of life and creation: setting up appointments; wars and threats of disaster; catching birds; the predatory rhythms of nature; the frisson of fear that sometimes catches us unawares. It is in these things that the activity of God within creation and among God's creatures is found.

It is also typical of wisdom literature in its rhetorical structure, based as it is around a series of questions. Verses 3–6 consist of seven questions which are tightly patterned in a way that is impossible to capture exactly in English translation.[2] In different ways all of the questions convey some kind of logical connection from the worlds of society and nature: if such and such is the case, could so and so happen? The answer in each case is an expected 'no, of course not'. The first five questions (3–5) instance human and animal behaviour; the structure of the first four of them repeats a pattern while the

---

[1] Prov. 30:1–9.
[2] For details of the patterning in these verses see S. M. Paul, *Amos: A Commentary on the Book of Amos*, Hermeneia (Minneapolis: Fortress, 1991), pp. 109–114.

final one (6) is structured differently, foreshadowing a change in direction by the poem.

The change itself comes at verse 7 which both breaks the sentence pattern and changes the subject matter. Verse 7 contains the only statement amongst the questions of these verses. In this way the poet highlights that all of the questions from the world of creation are intended to point to the behaviour of its creator, the *Sovereign Lord* (7), the Lord Yahweh. Just as a watchman's trumpet by its very nature strikes fear of impending bad news, just as a lion by its very nature roars at its prey, just as two people most naturally walk together by agreement, so it is in the very nature of God to act in ways that are revealed to humanity. All of the questions cumulatively build a sense of certainty that this is the case.

This is further reinforced by a subtle variation in the tenses. Tenses in biblical Hebrew differ markedly from the English tense system, in that they primarily indicate the nature of the action rather than when the action occurs. Time – past, present, future – is conveyed in other ways and often only by implication. There are only two tenses in biblical Hebrew, perfect and imperfect. Perfect is more likely to indicate time past and imperfect is more likely to indicate time future, but that is all that can be said with respect to time. More importantly for our purposes, the imperfect tense is normally used to indicate a generalization or ongoing state of affairs while the perfect tense is more likely to describe a definite action in space and time.[3] In the opening set of seven questions (3–6), the first six all use the imperfect tense, indicating generalization. The seventh question is different: *when disaster comes to a city, has not the LORD caused it?* (6). In this case, the second clause in that sentence, *has not the LORD caused it*, is in the perfect tense.

The effect of the change is twofold. First, it draws attention to the fact that all these questions point to the behaviour of the sovereign Lord. The primary interest of this piece of poetry is the nature and activity of God. We are intended to read the whole poem with this in mind. Secondly, the change of tense draws a distinction between the way of life of the various creatures referred to and the activity of God. It highlights that God acts in time and space with a particular intent and in particular ways. It is not enough to say that events occur because that is the way nature has been set up; particular things happen to particular people in particular places because God means for that to be the case. But that should not be thought of as exceptional. The poetic context of the asser-

---

[3] Another way of stating all this is that Hebrew tenses primarily indicate aspect rather than time.

tion of 6b, *has not the Lord caused it*, indicates that this happens all the time in human affairs. God is always sovereign over the temporal affairs of human society just as surely as God is the creator.

2. In the counsel of God

As we have seen, verse 6 switches the subject matter to the Lord. Verse 7 then follows with a statement, which, coming as it does in a sea of questions, stands out from the surrounding material. Now we come to the focus of the poem, namely, that *the Sovereign LORD does nothing without revealing his plan to his servants the prophets.* So far in this volume we have seen that God speaks,[4] that God's speaking is effective[5] and that the word of God may be relied upon.[6] Now we discover that God speaks through the agency of prophets. More than that, there is nothing that God does that may not be known by means of that agency. This is reinforced by another tense nuance in the Hebrew poetry. We have already noted the shift from imperfect to perfect in verse 6. Now we note that the second half of verse 7 should more properly be translated as a perfect, thus: 'unless he has revealed his counsel to his servants the prophets.' In the same way that God has brought disaster onto the city in verse 6, he has also revealed to humanity his intentions in space and time.

The word translated as *plan* (*sôd*) might also be rendered as 'counsel'. The focus of the word is more on the plan as the outcome of an assembly working together on something, rather than on an individually-conceived idea such as is conveyed by the English word 'plan'. See for example Psalm 111:1, which uses *sôd* to speak of a faithful assembly. And Proverbs 15:22 nicely highlights the distinction between 'plan' and 'counsel', the former being an individual idea that lacks the judgment of an assembled council (*sôd*). The use of that word in verse 7 does not paint a picture of God handing down something to the prophets who then transmit it; rather, it conveys a more collegial process in which the prophets are active. God does nothing without drawing his servants into the planning of it.[7] The Old Testament occasionally reveals a concept of a heavenly assembly over which Yahweh presides.[8] This verse appears to be saying that the prophets

[4] Ps. 19.
[5] Isa. 55.
[6] Prov. 30:1–9.
[7] A. Motyer, *The Day of the Lion: The Message of Amos* (London: IVP, 1974), p. 73, comments that *revealing his plan* could mean 'opening his fellowship'.
[8] Ps. 82 is the classic text in this respect.

become privileged participants in this assembly. In the process they glimpse and are able to convey to others the mind of God.

This is a remarkable statement in that it tells us three important things about the word of God. First, it speaks of transparency. God's intention towards his world may be known because he speaks with prophets who come to know the mind of God. He has no intention to hide his plans. Secondly, it speaks of participation. God invites his human agents, the prophets, into his thinking or counsel. In ways that we mostly barely understand, God takes us into his confidence. The words of the prophets, the text that we receive today as Scripture and the ability we have to read and interpret it all express the fact that God shares his mind with us. This is how the transparency of the word of God is achieved. There is much more to be said about this, and we will consider the role of the Holy Spirit in this process in the next chapter.

Thirdly, God's word is specific to particular times and places. It is grounded in human history. Just as God spoke to a particular people whose experience of him was then preserved in a text, so God through that text and its readers speaks into our own individual and collective moments of history. The tenses chosen by the writer of this poem reflect that. And the wisdom context reminds us that this dealing of God with history and place is inherent in his very nature. We could expect nothing other than that from the God revealed to us in Christ as witnessed to in the Scriptures.

Incidentally, the understanding of prophecy in these verses renders virtually irrelevant the debate over whether prophecy should be thought of as forthtelling or foretelling. By its very nature, participation in the mind of God entails a perspective that moves easily between the past, present and future. In our humanity we can only occupy one moment of time. From the perspective of that moment our glimpse into the mind of God in God's word will naturally entail variously past, present and future.[9] It is not so important to determine which as to discern God's perspective from the particular moment in history which we occupy.

3. The nature of prophecy

At this point, though, we need to clarify what we mean by prophecy. In the immediate context of the prophecy of Amos, this poem is a reflection on the vocation of particular individuals in the life of Israel, called out to prophesy. There is much debate over the extent

[9] Motyer, *Day of the Lion*, p. 73.

to which the social role of prophet was implicit or explicit at the time at which individuals prophesied. Were people such as Amos recognized by their peers or did that recognition come in the light of history?[10] However that question is answered, it does seem possible to say that the function of prophecy was well recognized within Israel, whether or not the writing prophets were recognized as such at the time they ministered. And a theological understanding also developed whereby prophecy was seen as part of God's provision of his word for Israel. Earlier in the book of Amos, the Lord through Amos reflects in condemnation of the people of Judah that, as well as his great salvation acts in the exodus and subsequent conquest of the land, he provided for the covenant people through chosen individuals whose lives and words signposted the will of God, namely, prophets and Nazirites.[11] Amos understood himself as one such person and in Amos 3 is reflecting on what he must do.[12]

Later on, in the famously enigmatic 7:14–15, Amos appears to draw a distinction between the person of the prophet and the task of prophecy. The enigma comes in the absence of verbs in the Hebrew with a consequent vagueness about time in the words of Amos. In 7:14 he literally says, 'I am/was neither a prophet nor the disciple of a prophet, and I am/was a shepherd and tender of sycamore-fig trees.' Has Amos ceased to be a shepherd and tender of sycamores and become a prophet? Or has he never been a prophet at all, but merely a shepherd and tender of sycamores who has been called by God to prophesy? It is not possible to know for sure. Perhaps the ambiguity is intended as a warning that there are some gifts from God that are inherently charismatic and cannot be reduced merely to institutional office, although they may be exercised by those who hold institutional office. What is clear is that Amos did not have any formal qualifications for prophecy other than that God called him to utter his words. In the calling comes the commitment expressed in verse 7 that God makes his mind known to his people.

In the twenty-first century of the Christian era the situation with respect to prophecy is a little different than in the days of Amos, although the commitment from God to speak is the same. How this is to be understood in the light of the life of Jesus and the New

---

[10] Note the discussion between A. G. Auld, 'Prophets through the Looking Glass: Between Writings and Moses', *JSOT* 27 (1983), p. 3–23, and T. W. Overholt, 'Prophecy in History: The Social Reality of Intermediation', *JSOT* 48 (1990), pp. 3–29.

[11] Amos 2:10–12.

[12] F. I. Andersen and D. N. Freedman, *Amos: A New Translation with Introduction and Commentary*, AB 24A (New York: Doubleday, 1989), pp. 371–372.

Testament which bears witness to him is a question that occasions some disagreement between Christians.[13] For the moment there are two things that may be said. The first is that, given the New Testament understanding of Jesus as the fulfilment of all the law and the prophets,[14] the witness to Jesus in the Scriptures is effectively a 'prophetic' witness.[15] As we will see further when we turn to 2 Peter 1:19–21 in the next chapter, the entire text of Scripture may therefore be thought of as prophetic.[16]

Secondly, we will also see in the context of our discussion of 2 Peter that the Old Testament perception of the Holy Spirit is primarily as the Spirit of prophecy. Within that Spirit of prophecy was found a divine promise of the democratization of the Spirit for all God's people.[17] The activity of the Holy Spirit in the production and reading and interpretation of the text along with the text itself is effectively the prophetic word of God. All Christians who read the text and are guided by the Spirit in doing so are ushered into the counsel of God that is promised by Amos 3:7.[18] In the text of Scripture we find the same transparency, participation and specificity that is a feature of God's relationship with his servants the prophets.

In terms of the Old Testament witness as a whole, verse 7 is yet another divine response to a regularly recurring anxiety on the part of the covenant people that the Lord may become inaccessible or unavailable to them. One spectacular example is in the events of Exodus 32 – 33. After the incident of the golden calf Moses and Yahweh engage in a frank exchange of views which culminates in these strange words from Yahweh to Moses: 'When my glory passes by, I will put you in a cleft in the rock and cover you with my hand until I have passed by. Then I will remove my hand and you will see my back; but my face must not be seen.'[19] All of this was in reassurance for Moses who at one point urges God, 'If your Presence does not go with us, do not send us up from here.'[20] He was not

---

[13] See the survey of views in M. Turner, *The Holy Spirit and Spiritual Gifts Then and Now* (Carlisle: Paternoster, 1996), pp. 185–220.

[14] Luke 24:27.

[15] This is the thrust of the argument by W. Grudem, *The Gift of Prophecy in the New Testament and Today* (Eastbourne: Kingsway, 1988), pp. 25–65.

[16] This raises the question of how the New Testament charism of 'prophecy' should be understood today, but that is beyond the scope of the present discussion.

[17] Joel 2:28–32.

[18] C. Hill, *Prophecy Past and Present: An Exploration of the Prophetic Ministry in the Bible and the Church Today* (Guildford: Eagle, 1989), pp. 70–72.

[19] Exod. 33:22–23.

[20] Exod. 33:15.

prepared to leave Sinai until he was assured that God would travel with the people. Similarly several centuries later Solomon prays at the dedication of the temple, pondering as he does so, 'But will God really dwell on earth? The heavens, even the highest heaven, cannot contain you. How much less this temple I have built! Yet give attention to your servant's prayer . . .'[21] In what would become an increasingly rare moment of humility for him, Solomon wonders if God could possibly be interested in any human creation, no matter how splendid. These are feelings that afflict all people of faith from time to time. Amos the prophet responds with this assurance that God's counsel is always available to God's people.

4. Prophecy, *torah* and wisdom

In the previous chapters we have noted the convergence in Old Testament thinking of the concepts of wisdom and *torah*. Both came to be thought of as agents of God sent forth to do God's will. And both came to be expressive of the word of God also in the accomplishment of God's purposes. As I write these words I see all around me in the Bethlehem district the almond tree blossoms, the first blossoms of the Judean spring, and am reminded of the words of Jeremiah. He sees an almond tree (*šāqēd*) and through a pun on the Hebrew word 'watching' (*šōqēd*) is reminded that God is 'watching to see that [his] word is fulfilled'.[22] God's word is God's agent and has a task to do.

Now we find that one way in which God's purposes which we see worked out in wisdom and *torah* and 'word' may be known to humanity is through the ministry of the prophets. For God admits them into his counsel. The work of God in the world may thereby be perceived and to some extent understood.

5. The context of the prophetic word

So far we have focused on verses 3–7 of the passage in question. Verses 1–2 and 8 provide bookends to the reflection on the inevitability and availability of God's word through the prophets. To what end might this be so? In the case of Amos, it is to the end that God might speak to a people who have grown proud and complacent in their achievements and status as God's people. They have enjoyed

[21] 1 Kgs 8:27–28.
[22] Jer. 1:11–12.

a period of prosperity in the first half of the eighth century BC unprecedented since the time of Solomon, but the glory days have passed and there are looming threats from an emergent Assyria. There is some evidence from the time (early to mid eighth century BC) of an economic 'stagflation', to use a word in currency some years ago. The creation of real wealth had slowed but those who possessed the wealth continued to live as if growth was the order of the day.[23] In times such as this, economic inequity becomes more and more of a feature, and that was certainly one of the complaints of the eighth-century prophets.[24] God's transparent word would not be a word of comfort, as the rest of the message of Amos makes clear. What can only be described as black humour reinforces the point. There will be a remnant that survives the impending judgment, just as there is occasionally a leftover limb once the lion has eaten the sheep.[25] Or what about those of you who like to be first amongst the notables? You can be first; you will be the first into exile, says the prophet.[26]

God speaks a word through the prophet that is *against* (1) or 'over' the people. To emphasize the point Amos notes that it is against *the whole family* (or more literally 'all the clans') that he has *brought up out of Egypt* (1). Amos is speaking at the royal shrines in the heart of the northern kingdom of Israel and so is at pains to re-inforce the message of the first two chapters of Amos, that the word of judgment applies every bit as much to Israel as to his native southern kingdom of Judah – and indeed as to the surrounding neighbours of both countries.[27] And it may not be a word of comfort. Verse 2b, *I will punish you for all your sins*, is explicit on that score.

At the other bookend, verse 8 returns to the rhetorical question-ing that has characterized verses 3–6. Having demonstrated that the inevitability of nature is a sign of the inevitability of the prophetic word of God, the poet reinforces the point with two more questions that also demand the answer 'no, of course not': *the lion has roared – who will not fear? The Sovereign Lord has spoken – who can but prophecy?* (8). Can a human being hear a lion roar without a fence between them and not feel a shiver of fear? Certainly not, in my experience. And can a prophet glimpse God's word and not speak it into his or her own situation? No. There is a divine constraint that is

---

[23] M. L. Chaney, 'Bitter Bounty: The Dynamics of Political Economy Critiqued by the Eighth-Century Prophets', in N. K. Gottwald and R. A. Horsley (eds.), *The Bible and Liberation: Political and Social Hermeneutics*, rev. ed. (Maryknoll: Orbis, 1993), pp. 250–263.

[24] For example Mic. 3:1–2; Isa. 1:21–23; Hos. 6:8–9.

[25] Amos 3:12.

[26] Amos 6:1, 7.

[27] Amos himself was from Tekoa, just a few miles from Bethlehem in the south.

as compelling as primeval fear. Contrary to the first six questions in this poem, the two in verse 8 are couched in the perfect tense, thus continuing the effect begun in the final clause of verse 6 that we have already noted. God's speaking to the prophet is seen as taking place in definite places and times and concerning particular matters; it is more than generality.

By returning to the opening metaphor in this poem, *the lion has roared* (8), the prophet reinforces that this word of God is not something that should be taken lightly. C. S. Lewis has achieved a powerful evocation of this effect in his portrayal of Aslan in the Narnia series: 'And Aslan stood up and when he opened his mouth to roar his face became so terrible that they did not dare to look at it. And they saw all the trees in front of him bend before the blast of his roaring as grass bends in a meadow before the wind.'[28]

But the figure of Aslan is also portrayed by Lewis as profoundly good. Again, he evokes this brilliantly: '"If there's anyone who can appear before Aslan without their knees knocking, they're either braver than most or else just silly." "Then he isn't safe?" said Lucy. "Safe?" said Mr. Beaver. "Don't you hear what Mrs. Beaver tells you? Who said anything about safe? 'Course he isn't safe. But he's good. He's the King, I tell you."'[29] In the same way, Yahweh's judging word comes against those whom he has *brought up out of Egypt* (1). Furthermore they are a people whom he still knows in a way that is unique (*you only have I chosen*, 2). The word that God compels his prophets to speak is almost too difficult to hear at times, but always it comes from within God's profound and unshakeable commitment to his people whom he brought out of the land of Egypt. The use of covenant language is not explicit at this point, but is strongly implied by phrases such as *you only have I chosen* (2). The verb in question is literally 'you only have I known', suggesting the intimacy of relationship between God and his people.

In previous chapters we have marvelled at the miracle of God's speaking. Now we are reminded that there is much more to this than the enjoyment of a wonderful sunrise or a purple passage in the Psalms. God's prophetic word is also to be treated with the utmost respect, and at times even feared. Those who read it and interpret it do well to remember that the encounter with God's word is not always fun. Jeremiah and Isaiah experienced this divine constraint in different ways. For Jeremiah, God's word spoke so strongly that he could not keep silent, while for Isaiah there was so much to say

---

[28] C. S. Lewis, *The Lion, the Witch and the Wardrobe* (New York: McMillan, 1950), pp. 133–134.
[29] Ibid., p. 64.

that he felt driven to silence.[30] But no matter how terrible the word of God might be, it emanates from the intimacy of God's knowing his people.

6. Scripture and imagination

The material we have been dealing with in this chapter is highly poetic. Writing poetry is an activity that requires the exercise of the imagination. Similarly, to appreciate poetry and the message of poetry also takes imagination. I do not derive a sense from Amos 3:3–8 of the accessibility of God's word by a series of proofs or theorems; instead I come to appreciate it because I see a bird caught in a trap, I feel my spine tingle at a lion's roar, I harness my observations of nature, I picture in my mind's eye meeting somebody on a road by prearrangement to travel with them. These are the things that draw me to a sense of God's word through his servants the prophets. I have deployed my imagination in interpretation. David repented of his sin with Bathsheba because his imagination had been captured by Nathan's story of the poor man with one little ewe lamb.[31]

There is a legitimate fear that the results of imagination in interpretation can be, in the words of John Goldingay, 'illusory or fanciful'.[32] Kevin Vanhoozer, for example, expresses it thus when he describes the process of Western culture and theology, beginning with an epigram invented by John Updike and used by Robert Funk: 'Priest, teacher, artist – the classic degeneration.'[33] To the priest reality is revealed, to the teacher it is rational, and to the artist, in the words of Vanhoozer, reality is 'marked by ambiguity, mystery, and irrationality'. While Updike's statement is used ironically it does express a commonly held sense that the more poetic and the less propositional and clear something is the less authoritative or certain it becomes. However, Goldingay does not stop with his hesitations about imagination. He reminds us that imagination is no more ambiguous a human faculty than reason when it comes to interpretation. Reason that is not submitted to the Holy Spirit is as likely to lead the interpreter astray as is imagination. Indeed, one might argue that the last two centuries of 'scientific' or text-

[30] Compare Jer. 20:9 and Isa. 42:14.
[31] 2 Sam. 12:1–14.
[32] J. E. Goldingay, *Models for Scripture* (Grand Rapids: Eerdmans, 1994), pp. 314–315.
[33] K. J. Vanhoozer, 'A Lamp in the Labyrinth: The Hermeneutics of "Aesthetic" Theology', *TrinJ* 8 (1987), pp. 25–56.

historical biblical criticism illustrate that point.[34] Imagination is equally 'the far-seeing and realistic ability to see what actually is there or actually is possible'. Far from being characterized chiefly by irrationality and a nature antithetical to a historical perspective, 'imagination is the point of contact between divine revelation and human experience'.[35]

Moreover, as has been illustrated by Amos 3, much of Scripture is couched in literary terms that lend themselves to an imaginative response. In particular it has been argued, I think rightly, that the Bible is cast primarily as story.[36] There are other forms within that: poetry, song, history, biography and propositional argument. They must be treated in their own terms. History should be dealt with in light of the ancient canons of history, poetry should be read according to the canons of Hebrew poetry, logical argument should be treated as such. But each of those forms is embedded in a story, the story of God and God's people. Too often our lack of imagination treats story as little more than something from which to distil morals. Scripture demands better than this of us. Along with reason and technical competence, a Spirit-filled imagination is a crucial tool in the interpretation of Scripture. Thus may God more powerfully admit us into his counsel in Scripture, and thus more competently may we convey that counsel to others. *The Sovereign Lord has spoken – who can but prophesy?* (8).

---

[34] This effect is more extensively explored in ch. 8 on Luke 1:1–4.

[35] Goldingay, *Models for Scripture*, p. 315. In a similar vein, see S. Barton, 'New Testament Interpretation as Performance', *SJT* 52 (1999), pp. 179–208.

[36] C. G. Bartholomew and M. W. Goheen, *The Drama of Scripture: Finding our Place in the Biblical Story* (Grand Rapids: Baker, 2004), pp. 15–27.

2 Peter 1:19–21
5. Through men and women moved by the Spirit

In my work with beginning theological students, I find that one of the most difficult questions that many of them face concerns the nature of Scripture as the word of God. It is difficult because it is characteristic of theological education that students come face to face with the humanity of Scripture in the course of their studies. Most, at least where I ply my trade, arrive with some real experience of God speaking to them through the Bible, and as a result have some clearly held if unexamined perceptions as to the divine nature of the Bible. They are entirely comfortable with the assertion by Agur that the word of God, which they equate with Scripture, is 'flawless' and complete.[1] But they have not thought very much about such questions as: the role of the church in the formation of the canon; the limitations imposed on Scripture by the time and space boundedness of its human authors; the inescapable fact that any reading and/or translation of the Bible, even one's own, is also an interpretation with its own limitations. Like most of us, they long for certainty and objectivity in the matter of communing with the divine and hope for the Bible to be an externally generated and objectively verifiable message from the Creator. It is difficult to discover that the ancient and ever-new set of documents we call the Bible has a long history of compilation and collection, a variegated track record of authorship, a diversity of perspectives, and a corresponding tendency to call forth competing interpretations from the ranks of its readers.

Such discovery generates a range of questions. One of the key questions is: how does one truly encounter the word of God in the midst of the human words of Scripture? One response is to ensure

[1] Prov. 30:5–6.

84

that the humanness of Scripture is not overdrawn in a way that causes faith to stumble. The Bible is also a miraculously coherent story of God's engagement with the cosmos and those who inhabit it, and its teaching is essentially self-consistent. That is an important assumption that I bring to this chapter.[2] At the same time, the human process behind the production and reading of Scripture can be a little distressing in its subjectivity. The concept of a so-called objective word of God appears elusive on closer study. And so students struggle.

Yet they need not. For the struggle usually arises from one of two inadequacies in understanding the way the Christian relates to the Bible. The first is, ironically, a desire to eliminate the need for faith in living the life of faith. If the Bible is conceived entirely as a divine word miraculously free from the fingerprint of humanity, whose meaning may be reliably discerned through the exercise of good method, then the need for faith is eliminated, or at least considerably diminished. The second closely-related deficiency pertains more directly to the point of this chapter, and it is what I would term an inadequate appreciation of the role of the Holy Spirit in Scripture. It is easy enough to assert in general terms that the Holy Spirit is active at the point of the 'inspiration' of the biblical writers,[3] but apparently much more difficult to conceive of the Holy Spirit as active and reliable at each operation through which the words of the Bible came to be and now are experienced as the word of God.

Such an appreciation requires a comprehensive sense of the Spirit of God pervasively active in God's word: when the writers wrote; when the editors edited; when the translators translate; when the early church discerned canonicity; when the scholars study and assemble data; when the commentators write; when readers read; and when preachers and teachers preach and teach. At each point the Spirit is at work bringing the word of God to life. Through the work of the Spirit, God is present in all the mundane realities of existence including the human uncertainty around the handling of Scripture. Just as the 'Word became flesh and made his dwelling among us',[4] so God's word takes on the raiment of humanity in the collection of texts known as the Bible, but never ceases to bring the word of God into the situations in which they are read. The answer to anxiety about the humanity of Scripture may be countered by a

---

[2] The validity of this assumption can be demonstrated in various ways. On a literary level, see the chapter on 'Composite Artistry' in R. Alter, *The Art of Biblical Narrative* (New York: Basic Books, 1981), pp. 131–154.

[3] What that might mean is considered in the context of a discussion of 2 Tim. 3:10–17 in ch. 18.

[4] John 1:14.

strong appreciation of the pervasive work of the Spirit at each point in the process, both historical and contemporary.[5] Peter's second epistle witnesses to this, especially at 1:19–21.

1. Several contested issues

Since several aspects of 2 Peter 1:19–21 are subject to debate, one's appreciation of their message is to some extent informed by the position taken on the contested issues. Indeed, there are few short portions of Scripture that potentially attract as much technical debate as this one. Without getting bogged down in these matters, then, I do need to declare my position on several key matters.

I am reading this letter as from the hand of the apostle Peter, the same author who wrote the stylistically quite different first letter of Peter.[6] Several other things flow from this that are relevant to an appreciation of Peter's message. First, in light of the strong tradition of Peter's death at the hands of the Romans in the mid 60s AD, the second epistle that bears his name would have been written shortly before that time.[7] Secondly, and as a closely related point, the letter reflects to some extent an early Christianity encountering the Gentile, and particularly the Hellenist world, something that must have been the experience of Peter's church in Rome by the mid sixties when Peter probably died.

This in turn brings into focus a third issue, the nature of the problem being addressed by this short letter. An early date calls into question the widely held assumption that the opponents of the writer were Gnostics, since Gnosticism was a phenomenon that arose somewhat later.[8] Richard Bauckham more recently has argued convincingly that Peter's opponents reflect pagan thinking arising from the church's interaction with Hellenism.[9] These people appeared to be sceptical about revelation from God being

---

[5] H. Thielicke, *The Evangelical Faith: Volume Three, Theology of the Spirit*, tr. and ed. G. W. Bromiley (Grand Rapids: Eerdmans, 1982), p. 192, characterizes this anxiety as a 'need to establish Scripture which does not dare any longer to seek God's Word in it with the help of the testimony of the Holy Spirit but in the passive attitude of a consumer [wanting] to find God's Word in book form'.

[6] See the detailed discussion by J. D. Charles, *Virtue Amidst Vice: The Catalog of Virtues in 2 Peter 1*, JSNTSup 150 (Sheffield: Sheffield Academic Press, 1997), pp. 63–75.

[7] M. Green, *The Second Epistle General of Peter and the General Epistle of Jude: An Introduction and Commentary*, TNTC (London: Tyndale, 1968), p. 129.

[8] E. Käsemann, *Essays on New Testament Themes*, SBT 41 (London: SCM, 1964), p. 171, famously argues for a Gnostic background.

[9] R. J. Bauckham, *Jude, 2 Peter*, WBC 50 (Waco: Word, 1983), pp. 154–157.

evident in the apostles' teaching. In response, the apostle Peter asserts that those responsible for the prophetic message *spoke from God* and were *carried along by the Holy Spirit* (21). Peter's Hellenist opponents also seem to have been casting doubt on the need to expect the return of Jesus, with an accompanying impatience with the ethical rigour that arises from that expectation in early Christianity.[10] As we will see, Peter's argument about the presence of the Spirit is accompanied both by an eschatological hope and by an interest in the expression of virtue in the lives of believers, and as such is a response to the challenges facing the church for which he wrote.

2. The word of the prophets

So from this need to confront doubt about the witness of the apostles and a corresponding concern to assert an eschatological hope and a call to live ethically in the meantime, Peter turns to consider the nature of the *prophetic message* (19). But what is this word and who are these prophets? The adjective *prophetic* is rare in the New Testament, its only other occurrence being in Romans 16:26, where it modifies the plural noun 'writings' (*graphai*), hence 'prophetic writings'. In the singular the same noun (*graphe*) may also be translated as *Scripture*, as it in fact is in verse 20 by most English translations. Which writings Paul exactly had in mind in Romans 16:26 may be debated, but it is generally accepted that he is referring to the authoritative witness of the written Hebrew Scriptures.[11] The phrase employed by Peter in verse 20, *prophecy of Scripture* (*graphē*), reflects the Pauline usage of Romans 16:26 in that it is likely also to apply to the prophetic message enshrined in authoritative writing. The phrase with which we began this discussion, though, *prophetic message* (19), is a little more wide-ranging. It may or may not indicate a written witness; in that respect the NIV's 'the word of the prophets' succeeds in conveying the possibility that the phrase may be understood as either a written word or a spoken or symbolic message.

The third reference to this type of material is simply to *prophecy* (21), a term that can encompass both the written and the spoken or symbolic. This may refer either to the prophet's speaking and acting or to the expression of prophetic activity in writing. What all of

---

[10] 2 Pet. 1:5–7.
[11] D. J. Moo, *The Epistle to the Romans*, NICNT (Grand Rapids: Eerdmans, 1996), p. 940.

this adds up to is an understanding of prophecy that includes both utterances spoken and actions enacted by particular individuals and the writings that arise from them. By including these two threads in his thinking, Peter affirms the activity of the Holy Spirit both in the writings that are described as *prophetic* (19) and in the speaking that leads to those writings. Both their production and their preservation in text are imbued with the Spirit. We will see further below the significance of this delicate dance between the prophet and the preserved authoritative word of the prophet, and a third element, *interpretation* (20).

Notwithstanding the analogy with Romans 16:26, this begs the question of what Peter may have intended by his use of the term *Scripture*. At the least, Peter is probably expressing a broad consensus on writings accepted as authoritative in the life of Judaism and hence of the earliest church.[12] Most commentators argue that the *prophetic message* (19) is a reference to the Old Testament rather than to prophetic activity in the church. It is highly unlikely that a Jewish Christian such as Peter would have yet seen the general prophetic impulse of the early church in the same light as sacred writings.[13] On the other hand, the apostle Peter does refer to the letters of 'our dear brother Paul' in the same breath as 'the other Scriptures',[14] again presumably the Old Testament writings. It is possible then that Peter has in mind some of the earliest Christian writings, such as those by Paul, which are beginning to be ascribed some authority by the believers. Just as for the Scriptures of the Old Testament, they too are subjected to interpretation. In short, we sense the beginnings of the formation of a wider collection of authoritative writings, which in due course the church came also to recognize as imbued by the Spirit, and themselves the outcome of people carried along by the wind of the Spirit in the writing of them.

This emphasis on the prophetic was probably the most natural way that Peter knew to consider the role of the Spirit with respect to the word of God. In the Old Testament, and indeed other Second

---

[12] There is an ongoing discussion about the existence or otherwise of a formal canon at the time that Peter wrote. R. T. Beckwith, *The Old Testament Canon of the New Testament Church and Its Background in Early Judaism* (London: SPCK, 1985), pp. 110–165, argues for an OT canon structured into its three parts and closed 'not less than 250 years earlier than the currently accepted date of AD 90' (p. 165), *contra* J. Barton, *Reading the Old Testament, Method in Biblical Study* (London: Darton, Longman and Todd, 1984), pp. 91–97, who probably represents a majority of scholars with his view that an early concept of canon is essentially anachronistic.

[13] D. J. Harrington, '2 Peter', in D. P. Senior and D. J. Harrington, *1 Peter, Jude and 2 Peter*, SP 15 (Collegeville: Michael Glazier, 2003), pp. 257–260.

[14] 2 Pet. 3:15–16.

Temple Jewish writing, the Spirit is mostly virtually synonymous with the 'spirit of prophecy' in the minds of the writers.[15] It would probably have been self-evident to Peter that the writing, the *graphē* or *Scripture*, has come into being through prophetic activity. And it would also have been self-evident that that prophetic activity was fuelled by the Holy Spirit. For that is how it has always been.[16] There could therefore have been no fine distinction made between the written words of Scripture and the prophetic activity at work prior to the fixing of that material into a text.

Inherent in such an environment of understanding is the possibility that the spirit of prophecy that brought the Scriptures into being and that informed the words of the prophets continues to be the Spirit behind the words and actions of Jesus and those who bear witness to him. As that witness gradually takes on, and is preserved in, written form, the expression of that Spirit-fuelled witness takes new shape. The beginnings of that process lurk in the background to this passage, and are reinforced by the hope of a *light shining in a dark place* (19).[17] Although what Peter is saying about the *prophetic message* (19) technically does not apply to what we now name the New Testament, the implicit possibility emerges that the *prophetic message* now embraces all of Christian Scripture.[18]

3. Made more certain

The prophetic word with which Peter is concerned is said to be *something completely reliable* (19), expressed in Greek with a comparative adjective. The NRSV translation, 'more fully confirmed', picks up the comparative sense. At the same time the Greek word order of verse 19 (literally 'we have more certain/sure the prophetic word') strongly implies a connection back to the mount of transfiguration and the revelatory experience that occurred there and that Peter alludes to in 2 Peter 1:16–18. It seems that the word of prophecy is being compared in some way to the revelatory experience of the transfiguration.

There is some debate as to how that comparison is being

---

[15] A. Hui, 'The Spirit of Prophecy and Pauline Pneumatology', *TynB* 50 (1999), pp. 93–115.

[16] D. E. Aune, *Prophecy in Early Christianity and the Ancient Mediterranean World* (Grand Rapids: Eerdmans, 1983), p. 86.

[17] This dynamic is more fully explored by J. B. Green, 'Narrating the Gospel in 1 and 2 Peter', *Int* 60 (2003), pp. 262–277.

[18] T. R. Schreiner, *1, 2 Peter, Jude*, TNAC 37 (Nashville: Broadman & Holman, 2003), p. 324.

conceived in the mind of the author. The debate is worth mentioning because it reflects differing understandings of Scripture with respect to the word of God. Some read that the witness of Scripture is more certain and enduring than the eyewitness experience of Jesus. Correspondingly, there is a body of opinion that places primary importance on the actual canonized text of Scripture as the locus of authority.[19] Others read here that the eyewitness account is what makes the written witness sure or reliable and the latter is diminished without the former. Similarly there are those who place a primary emphasis on the things to which the words of Scripture bear witness, and in particular on the one, Jesus, to whom they point.[20]

I suggest that the debate is not a particularly fruitful one, and that the ambiguity around *something completely reliable* (19) itself is meaningful. As we have already seen, Peter's use of the terms *Scripture*, *prophetic message* and *prophecy* suggests that he sees an interaction between the eyewitness and the text and the interpreter. In that vein, it seems that the comparison is working in two directions. Peter's reference to *something completely reliable* (19) functions to hold together the time-bound eyewitness revelation of Jesus – as in the allusion to the transfiguration experience – and the more enduring Scriptural witness of the prophetic word of God. The stories of Jesus witnessed to by the apostles and the Scriptures that foreshadow and preserve that witness together bring a prophetic word that is completely reliable in a way that neither could be on their own.

4. Above all

There is something that is of primary importance about this prophetic word known in Scripture and through the witness of the apostles. The Greek expresses this with the adverb translated in verse 20 as *above all* (*prōton*). The adverb is most likely to modify the verb that is translated as *understand* (20), so that what is understood is in some way primary. The term could refer to the first thing we understand, as in the sense of a primer, and it could refer to the

[19] Green, *The Second Epistle General of Peter*, p. 86; J. I. Packer, 'Inerrancy in Current Debate', in *Beyond the Battle for the Bible* (Westchester: Cornerstone, 1980), pp. 37–61.
[20] J. N. D. Kelly, *The Epistles of Peter and of Jude*, BNTC (London: Adam & Charles Black, 1969), pp. 320–321; K. Barth, *The Doctrine of the Word of God, Church Dogmatics* I/2, tr. G. T. Thomson and H. Knight (Edinburgh: T&T Clark, 1936), p. 514.

primary, or the most important thing that we understand. Both senses could be taken to apply to this context. In that case, Peter is about to say something very important about the prophetic message of Scripture whose importance may be thought of in two different ways that reflect the variability of *prōton*: first, that what is to follow is foundational to our appreciation of Scripture; and, secondly, that what is to follow is the first thing that needs to be said about this Scripture. Everything else flows from there. And so, having now got our attention, Peter turns to that foundational thing: the source and genesis of this prophetic word in the Holy Spirit.

5. One's own interpretation

He starts with a negative contrast: that the prophetic word is not by means of *the prophet's own interpretation* (20). In fact the word 'prophet' is not in the Greek, as a result of which the statement is more elliptical than the TNIV English translation leads one to believe. The NRSV captures it thus: 'no prophecy of scripture is a matter of one's own interpretation.'

However exactly it is translated, the phrase remains annoyingly out of focus in that it remains hard to articulate just what type of distinction between the *prophecy* itself and the *interpretation* is being made. Is prophecy the outcome of interpretation? Or are prophecy and interpretation considered to be two distinct operations, so that prophecy is what the prophet does while interpretation is what the interpreter does? If the former possibility is allowed for, then there is a contrast between interpretation in verse 20 and the work of the Spirit in verse 21. In the case of the latter possibility, there is a contrast between one's *own* (in Greek *idias*) interpretation and that of the Spirit; prophetic utterance is not idiosyncratic, not the product of a particular human, but owes its coming into being to the work of the Spirit.

Both possibilities could be illustrated from Scripture itself. On the one hand there is plenty of material that seems to arise directly as from an omniscient narrator, somebody who knows the truth of what he or she is writing. In that case, there is no evidence of a process of interpretation giving rise to the writing. Much of the Pentateuch is of that order. Interpretation lies in its reading; not its production. And much prophetic material is couched as the direct words of the Lord with little sense that the prophet is interpreting. Such discourse is marked by various Hebrew expressions that are translated as 'thus says the Lord' or similar. On the other hand, much apocalyptic material is explicitly about interpretation in that the task of the seer is to interpret events and symbolic messages with the help of heavenly 'messengers'. See for example Daniel's dependence on such messengers in his interpretation of visions.[21] This apocalyptic phenomenon of 'messengers' pushes back into the later prophetic material also. For example, there is a widely-held view that the name Malachi, of a prophet working in the post-exilic period, is as likely to be the term 'my messenger' (mal'ākî), as a proper name.[22] And another prophet of the restoration, Haggai, is also at one point referred to as a 'messenger' (mal'āk).[23] Even Amos, working two hundred years earlier than Haggai and Malachi, indicates that the role of the prophet is to sit in the counsel of God and then convey that counsel.[24] The language is not explicitly that of interpretation but the process is strongly implied.[25]

It seems best, therefore, to read the phrase the prophet's own interpretation as inclusive of the prophetic process rather than distinct from it. In that case, Peter is asserting that the prophet's message is not the result of a prophet's idiosyncratic ideas. In the context of his use of prophetic language noted above, the message is that the Scriptures do not arise merely from the unreliable imaginations of their human authors. The Spirit is active in the authors of Scripture, and the Spirit is active in overseeing the process by which their words come to be established as the authoritative word of God.

At the same time, both the Greek itself and the Old Testament background on which Peter was drawing permit the possibility that the phrase own interpretation is also an activity distinct from the prophecy that brought the Scriptures into being. In that case, this functions as a warning that there is no place for the interpretation of Scripture that is merely idiosyncratic. The classic response to this understanding is to distinguish between private and public interpretation with the emphasis that interpretation must be tested by the wider church. While that may be so, it is not necessarily the contrast that Peter is drawing. Rather, the distinction continues to be primarily between those who interpret idiosyncratically and those who interpret under the direction of the Spirit.[26] Of course, the differ-

---

[21] Dan. 7 – 12.
[22] See P. A. Verhoef, The Books of Haggai and Malachi, NICOT (Grand Rapids: Eerdmans, 1987), pp. 154–156.
[23] Hag. 1:13.
[24] Amos 3:7.
[25] J. H. Neyrey, 2 Peter, Jude: A New Translation with Introduction and Commentary, AB 37C (New York: Doubleday, 1993), pp. 181–182, illustrates how this would have been understood against the pagan Hellenist background which this epistle is addressing.
[26] Bauckham, Jude, 2 Peter, p. 230.

ence between the two types of interpretation needs to be discerned by the wider church. To that extent it is the case that public interpretation emerges over time to moderate private interpretations. But the key distinction is between that which is spoken in interpretation of the Scriptures by those bearing the Spirit and that which is merely human speculation and reasoning.

This highlights the role of the Spirit in the work of interpreters of Scripture as well as in those responsible for producing it. However, caution should be exercised here. That is not the same thing as equating the work of those who interpret Scripture with Scripture itself.[27] Correspondingly, it does not allow for the possibility that interpretive insights under the guidance of the Spirit may subsequently contradict the potential meaning of any portion of Scripture. It does, however, acknowledge that the literature in which Scripture finds itself is in many respects foreign and strange. There is technical work to be done in correctly discerning its possible meaning in its own day: language learning, historical discernment, philological study, genre appreciation.[28] At the same time, the words of Scripture themselves are rich in possibility and need rightly to be discerned from within various contexts. In that respect, there is a responsibility on the reader to understand how such passages speak meaning into to the lives of those around them. Both processes – the discernment of original meaning and the contemporary discernment of how they speak into a particular context – may be described as *interpretation*. And in both cases the word of God is truly conveyed as its interpreters are *carried along by the Holy Spirit* (21), and potentially distorted by work that is not under the direction of the Spirit.

Over time the church discerned under the direction of the Spirit what *prophetic message* came to occupy a place of priority and certainty or reliability, to use concepts from Peter's second letter. This we have come to know as Scripture. But the church has never lost a sense that these words must also be interpreted that they may continue to speak into the lives of individual Christians in all their unimaginable diversity of time and place. Just as the interpretive activity of the writers of Scripture was fuelled by the Spirit, so this responsibility to interpret is also fuelled by the Spirit.[29]

In terms of current debates around biblical interpretation, this

[27] The unique nature of Scripture is explored more fully in ch. 18 on 2 Tim. 3:10–17.

[28] This is the type of work that is often described as 'grammatico-historical'.

[29] For a systematic theological reflection on this point, see M. Welker, *God the Spirit*, tr. J. F. Hoffmeyer (Minneapolis: Fortress, 1994), p. 277.

means that the technical notion of reader-response must be taken seriously in the discernment of reading. Readers do have a responsibility to draw meaning from texts as they engage in interpretation. Under the direction of the Spirit, these interpretations must be tested over time and by the church, and must be constrained by the possibilities within the text, but that does not remove the responsibility for discerning reading. In such an environment, an interpretation is not merely something that comes from an external source; it is also discerned and experienced in the context of a Spirit-fuelled relationship with the God who speaks. Such work, if it is to bear the prophetic word of God into its own day, must be undertaken by people *carried along by the Holy Spirit* (21) reading the words of Scripture that in their turn are the outcome of prophets also 'carried along by the Holy Spirit'.

6. 'Carried along by the Holy Spirit'

But just what does it mean to be *carried along by the Holy Spirit*? The phrase should not be taken primarily to imply the ancient Greek notion of prophecy as an ecstatic activity in which the will of the speaker is taken over by a divine force of some sort. As a counter to that, Bede's comment from the eighth century still bears repeating: 'Some interpret Peter's words to mean that the Spirit inspired the prophets in much the same way as the flutist blows into his flute, so that the latter were no more than mechanical instruments in God's hands, saying what the Spirit told them to say without necessarily understanding it themselves. This is ridiculous.'[30] It is a commonplace that the phrase translated by TNIV as *carried along by* is a maritime metaphor of a ship being borne along by the wind.[31] It gives a picture of people who hoist their sails to catch the wind of the Spirit that the voice of God may be heard. The will and character and ability of the prophetic agent are fully engaged by the Spirit.

In that understanding there are three dimensions to the Spirit's involvement in the development of the prophetic word. First, the Holy Spirit engages in the lives of those who speak and write the words of Scripture, as people whose wills are set in obedience to God's Spirit. Verse 21 is quite clear that prophecy, this certain and primary prophetic word, comes about through the speaking of men and women being borne by the Spirit. It cannot in any sense come

---

[30] Cited in G. Bray (ed.), *James, 1-2 Peter, 1-3 John, Jude*, ACCS 11 (Downers Grove: IVP, 2000), p. 142.

[31] See for example Green, *The Second Epistle General of Peter*, p. 91.

into being apart from the human agents who speak it. All that they are as fallen and redeemed human beings is part of the prophetic word that they speak. That is why the interpreter must be aware of the life and limitations of each writer as well as the situation within which each one writes and speaks.

Secondly, though, and perhaps paradoxically, the *prophetic message* (19) does exist also apart from the prophets themselves. Once the prophets have spoken and the signs and symbols have been performed, something comes into being that then takes on a life and authority of its own. In a true sense it becomes the word of God, set free from the fallibilities of those who produced it. And it does so by means of the activity of the Spirit. It may then be spoken of as 'God-breathed'.[32] Inseparably related to this is the sense of Scripture coming into being, of its origin. This is found in two different Greek verbs, represented in the TNIV as *came about* (20) and *had its origin* (21). Each in its own way carries a sense of being created or formed or produced.[33] As the Spirit imbues the human authors of the words of Scripture, so also the Spirit imbues the very creative process by which these words come into being.

Thirdly, as we have seen, the Spirit is active in the process of interpretation of those prophetic words once they have been spoken and brought into being. Once the physical object that we call Scripture emerges God does not cease to be active. God through the Spirit works in those who read and interpret it.

We may be clear that the Holy Spirit was at work in the lives of those who wrote the words that we now know as Scripture, and we may be clear that there is a Holy Spirit quality to those words as they were subsequently preserved as the *prophetic message* (19). We may also be clear that the Spirit remains active in all that the church subsequently does to hear that message as the word of God: collection, preservation, translation, exposition. All of this may be gathered into the concept of *interpretation* (20). Our confidence rests in the all-encompassing activity of the Spirit as we read the words of Scripture whose very being is the product of the Spirit's activity. In the providence of God, this picture is not a tidy one. It does not yield a neat schema for the mechanics of inspiration, such as tends to emerge in systematic treatments.[34] Nor does it make a tidy status distinction between the inspiration of Scripture itself and

---

[32] 2 Tim. 3:16.

[33] Of the former verb, *ginomai*, one of its related nouns is 'genesis'.

[34] Green, *The Second Epistle General of Peter*, p. 91, has pointed out the telling fact that in this passage 'no interest should be displayed in the psychology of inspiration. The author is not concerned with what they felt like, or how much they understood, but simply with the fact that they were the bearers of God's message.'

the inspiration required for interpretation. There is an important distinction between the two, but not in this passage.[35] For now, we focus on the fact that the entire event of Scripture is soaked in the activity of the Spirit of God.

7. The wider environment of the work of the Spirit-borne prophetic word

As a result, the role of the Spirit in the development and hearing of Scripture impacts the past, present and future of the believer's life and the life of the church. All three are found in 2 Peter 1 as part of the context in which the role of the Spirit in Scripture is affirmed. The present context is seen in the often overlooked ethical concerns of 2 Peter 1:4–9. The apostle is at least partly interested in the daily life of the follower of Jesus. The Spirit engages with the ethical life of the Christian through the prophetic word of Scripture. The witness of Scripture also points into the past to the life and witness of Jesus himself as conveyed through eyewitnesses, such as Peter, and those who anticipate and reflect on him in Scripture.[36] The Spirit thus also engages with the historical memory on which the Christian faith is founded and brings it to life in the memory of the believer. Finally, within verses 19–21, the Spirit witnesses to the future hope of the believer. Scripture comes as a light into a murky place anticipating a time when *the day dawns and the morning star rises in [our] hearts* (19).[37] For now, we have this confidence that the Holy Spirit quickens the words of Scripture as well as their formation and reception, so that they become a divine word from yesterday about today and pointing into our future.

---

[35] But see ch. 18 on 2 Tim. 3:16.
[36] For further on this theme see the comments on John 2:18–25 in ch. 9.
[37] The eschatological nature of Scripture is treated more fully in ch. 15 on Rev. 5.

Part 2
God speaks in the written word

Exodus 19 – 20
6. The spoken word written

The Maori worldview in my country works extensively with the concept of *tapu*. It has this in common with most Polynesian and Melanesian cultures, and indeed with other indigenous cultures around the world. The idea is sometimes expressed in the West, usually somewhat uncomprehendingly, as 'taboo'. It is a concept that is difficult for the Western mind to grasp, and I remain puzzled by it. At one moment it seems to be a positive concept, such as in the Maori translation of the English word 'holy' as *tapu*, or in setting apart prominent leaders of the community as *tapu* or worthy of particular respect. At other times it has to do with separation and death. For example, when somebody drowns at a New Zealand beach, it is not uncommon for the local Maori elders to set a *rahui* over that place, which has the effect of making it *tapu*, and temporarily out of bounds until such time as the imbalance that has been created by the tragedy is put right. Until then any violation of the *rahui* places the violator in danger.[1]

I suspect the reason why the Western mind finds it difficult to reconcile both separation or destruction and high respect within the same concept is that it is founded on distinctions that are no longer made by the scientific worldview with its emphasis on the measureable world. In fact the idea of *tapu* has to do with setting something apart and in the process establishing boundaries that should not be crossed. If such boundaries are crossed the result is harmful. This is also closely related to two other distinctions that *tapu* cultures commonly make: between purity and impurity, and between the sacred

---

[1] On *tapu* see M. P. Shirres, *Te Tangata: The Human Person* (Auckland: Accent, 1997), pp. 33–49. On *rahui* see C. Barlow, *Tikanga Whakaaro: Key Concepts in Maori Culture* (Oxford: University Press, 1991), pp. 103–106.

and the profane.[2] The two distinctions are not identical but they are closely related. The violation of *tapu* partly has to do with confusion of the sacred with the profane, and also may result in impurity. Arguably a similar complex of ideas lies behind the Old Testament notion of *ḥērem* or 'ban'.[3] This term is often translated into English as 'devoted to destruction', as the NRSV in Joshua 6:17, but, like *tapu*, it in fact carries a more neutral sense of having been set apart or 'devoted' (the TNIV captures the neutrality better). Sometimes this is positive and sometimes, when there has been some kind of transgression, it heralds destruction.[4] The heart of the concept is the setting apart of something or somebody to the Lord, in the process of which the object or person acquires sacred status. Contact of the devoted thing with the profane or unclean compromises this sacred status and creates impurity and all the danger that that entails.[5] One outcome of this is a line drawn between the human and the divine which may only be crossed with great care and under strictly observed conditions.[6] Even when the concept of *ḥērem* (or 'ban') is not being explicitly applied, the Old Testament contains regular reminders that God is differentiated from God's creatures and his creation, and that the difference must be respected.

In the five chapters of Part 1 of this book, exploring the proposition that God speaks, I have been at pains to point out that God's speaking ought not to be mystified. It is down-to-earth, part of the realm that we as humans occupy on a daily basis. God makes himself available to the humanity that he has created. We noted also that God's word should not primarily be understood as a general principle so much as an explicit encounter between God and particular people, situations and contexts. Richard Hays captures the idea nicely when he writes of the 'palpable word' of God.[7] Indeed, the evocative picture of God walking in the garden looking for Adam and Eve in the cool of the evening at the end of a hot day somewhere in Mesopotamia conveys God's longing for that sort of communication with humanity.[8]

[2] M. Douglas, *Purity and Danger: An Analysis of Concepts of Pollution and Taboo* (London: Penguin, 1966).

[3] *NIDB* 1, p. 384. For a fuller explanation of this complex concept see J. P. U. Lilley, 'Understanding the *Herem*', *TynB* 44 (1993), pp. 169–177.

[4] Compare Lev. 27:21; Num. 18:14; Ezek. 44:29, with Deut. 7:26; 13:17–18.

[5] Douglas, *Purity and Danger*, p. 72.

[6] L. D. Hawk, *Joshua*, Berit Olam (Collegeville: Liturgical Press, 2000), p. 101.

[7] R. B. Hays, 'The Palpable Word as Ground of *Koinōnia*', in D. V. Henry and M. D. Beaty (eds.), *Christianity and the Soul of the University: Faith as a Foundation for Intellectual Community* (Grand Rapids: Baker Academic, 2006), pp. 19–36.

[8] Gen. 3:8.

At the same time, a cautionary note was sounded at various stages by the passages we have examined. The prophet Amos used the imagery of the lion to warn that the word of God should not be taken for granted.[9] Psalm 19 observed that the wonder of God's speaking leads to a plea for God's approval.[10] Proverbs 30 spoke of the purity of God's word with a corresponding warning against profaning that purity in any way.[11] But so far this aspect has been somewhat understated. Now the allusive roar of the lion in Amos becomes the full throated thunder of God at Mount Sinai. The sound and light of that desert mountain encounter presses an indelible imprint on those who pass near it. We are left in no doubt that the word of God should be treated with the utmost respect and caution. There are boundaries around the encounter encapsulated in the word of God that should no more be crossed than should *ḥērem* things or people be violated or misused. Or, as with the Maori concept of *tapu*, there are certain things that should be treated with great care lest misfortune befall. This we will discover as we read Exodus 19 and the chapters that flow from it. At the same time, we discover that this does not mean that God is forever set apart from humanity. Provision is made for a healthy and safe encounter. And part of that provision, as we are about to see, is through the paradoxical notion that the active word of God is preserved in the written text.

1. The speech-act of God

The encounter at Sinai flows from two important dynamics. First, there is a kind of dual initiative. After the scene- and time-setting details of the first two verses of Exodus 19, the first thing that happens is that Moses *went up to God* (19:3). We are not told why Moses went up to God or where or how he went (although in that mountainous setting the verb of ascent is suggestive), but what is evident is his availability. Almost at the same time, God also takes an initiative to declare something to the *house of Jacob* and *people of Israel* through Moses (19:3). It is not possible to discern either the actions of Moses or those of God as prior to the other. We are told first that Moses went up, and the use of the narrative tense indicates that God's speaking follows from that. So the action of Moses is important. Yet we know enough of God from episodes such as the

[9] Amos 1:2; 3:4, 8.
[10] Ps. 19:14.
[11] Prov. 30:5–6.

story of Balaam and his donkey[12] to know that God speaks when God chooses to speak. Somehow both parties in the conversation take initiatives in God's encounter with humankind. We saw something of this in the picture painted by Amos of the prophet sitting in the council chamber of God.[13]

Then, secondly, a dynamic of speech and act is set up. The people are reminded of all that they have seen God *do* in their escape from Egypt (19:4). And now they are to *hear* the voice of God (19:5). The people have seen the *act* of God and now they hear the *speech* of God. The grammatical link between these two statements highlights the conceptual link. Verse 4 begins with the emphatic pronoun 'you', translated as *you yourselves*, which reminds the people of the programmatic act of God in delivering them from the Egyptians. Then verse 5 begins with *Now*, denoting a link with what has gone before. What follows is a Hebrew idiom translated in the TNIV as *obey me fully*, but difficult to capture in English. It is in fact an emphatic form of the verb 'to hear' (*šāma'*). To hear something is to obey it; the verb, especially in the emphatic form used here, expresses more than the recording of an audible signal. The expression entails an emphatic hearing, and hence obeying, the 'voice' (*qôl*) of God. Now they will hear explicitly the speech of God following on from his act. In doing so they will hear what it means for them that they were delivered from Egypt.

In this way it becomes clear that God speaks with an intention to make things happen. First, there is a desire for obedience from the people of God. Not only are they to *hear* – that is, hear and obey – but they are also to *keep [God's] covenant* with them (19:5). The point could hardly be made more emphatically with its choice of verbs and verb forms here.

Then, secondly, as a result of their solicited obedience, the intention of God is that they be formed into *a kingdom of priests and a holy nation* (19:6). I take this to be indicating that they will acquire a clear identity, a stated purpose and an evident status. Their identity will be as a *nation*, one among other nations yet also distinct from others; indeed they will be clearly delineated by their status as *holy*. Their purpose will be as *priests* in that they will perform a priestly function with respect both to God and to the other peoples that God has made.[14] Their status will be *holy* and also a *treasured*

---

[12] Num. 22:21–30.

[13] Amos 3:7. See ch. 4.

[14] Leaving aside for the moment the exact nature of this priestly function. For the much debated possibilities see J. I. Durham, *Exodus*, WBC 3 (Dallas: Word, 1978), p. 262.

possession taken *out of all nations* (19:5) that God has brought into being.[15] God's speaking is to do with the formation of a people.

And so it was that obedience was promised by those to whom God spoke through Moses. The obedience is expressed as a mirror response to the speech-act of God to the people. God earlier spoke of what he *did to Egypt* (19:4) and followed that up with a promise to *speak* (19:6). Now the people acknowledge God's speech as what God *has said* and promise to act on or do what God has commanded (19:8). The verb translated as *do* (19:4) echoes that used of God's actions in 19:3. Thus the intention of God in speaking and acting is realized in the people's obedient response to God's words through Moses. Everything that follows is based on this dynamic of God's active speaking and the people's response there at Mount Sinai. The notion that God speaks and that God speaks in the text is founded on the relationship between God and God's people brought into being by the word and act of God. In that respect, these verses reflect the close association between word and covenant that we have seen emerging.

2. The limits of holiness

And so God prepares to speak his word to the people through Moses. That his speaking is within earshot of them (19:9) means that God expects that the people will participate in the reception of the word. When the third day comes they are led by Moses out of the camp *to meet with God* (19:17). But there are to be strict limits to that participation. These limits take on two aspects. First, there is a holiness limit. The people and their clothing are required to be *consecrated*, and symbolically they abstain from sexual relations (19:10, 14–15). They are dealing with that which is holy. And, secondly, there is a spatial limit. Moses *put limits* (19:23) around the mountain and forbade the people to approach or touch it. This boundary signifies to the people that the mountain itself has become *holy* (19:23). Here we have a holy people formed by God and a holy place wherein God speaks, and the two may not directly encounter each other.

[15] The closing phrase in v. 5, 'for all the earth is mine' (my translation) is most naturally read in the Hebrew as a modifier of what precedes it in v. 5 rather than as a preliminary to v. 6 as suggested by the TNIV punctuation. This means that the chosen ones ought not to take their status for granted. This word is for them but perhaps God has other words for other peoples. The prophets would later have cause to reflect on that possibility in the light of Israel's disobedience. See for example Amos 9:7–8; Isa. 56:3–6.

While the emphasis throughout Exodus 19 is on the holiness of the mountain, a subtle variation towards the end of the chapter indicates that the mountain itself is not intrinsically holy. In 19:23 Moses states that God has required him to set the mountain as holy and that any approach to the mountain is a transgression on that holiness. In the following verse the Lord's acknowledgement to Moses is that any forcing their way through to the mountain on the part of the people is in fact *to the Lord* (19:24). When they violate the boundary set around the holy mountain, they are effectively violating the holiness of the Lord himself. So the boundaries do more than separate a consecrated people from a holy mountain; they separate a consecrated people at this moment from the holy God who makes covenant with them.

That is why the danger to the people is that God – not the mountain – will *break out against them* (19:22, 24). The verb used (*pāraṣ*), is striking. It has the primary literal sense, as it has been translated here, of breaking out or bursting or breaking away, usually with quite a mundane object: a wall, a water container, a womb, for example.[16] It may also have the sense of spreading out,[17] which is a kind of subset of the semantic field. In a narrative context it is not commonly used with God as the subject.[18] That it is so used here draws attention to the concepts of purity and boundedness that lie at the heart of this encounter.

Another instance where the verb is used with God as the subject reinforces this. In 1 Chronicles 15:13 David is contemplating the risks of bringing the ark up to Jerusalem soon after he has established himself as king. He remembers an earlier attempt to transport the ark from Kiriath Jearim. On that occasion Uzzah reached out to steady it on the cart when the oxen stumbled, and was killed by God. The attempt was then abandoned, and the ark was deposited with Obed-Edom the Gittite instead.[19] Now, as David anticipates a second attempt to bring the ark to Jerusalem, he urges the Levites to consecrate themselves properly this time so that God will not 'break out' against them.[20] A boundary had been violated and the result

---

[16] Gen. 38:29; 2 Chr. 24:7; Mic. 2:13; Neh. 2:13; 2 Kgs 14:13.

[17] Exod. 1:12.

[18] Although that usage occurs more often in metaphorical contexts. See for example Isa. 5:5; Job 16:14; Pss. 60:1; 80:12.

[19] 1 Chr. 13: 5–14. On these verses see S. Japhet, *I & II Chronicles: A Commentary*, OTL (Louisville: Westminster John Knox, 1993), pp. 280–282. The guardianship of Obed-Edom was presumably established on one or both of two premises: that God was less likely to break out against a non-Israelite, and/or that if he did it would not matter so much! One cannot help feeling a little sorry for Obed-Edom, and very sorry for Uzzah.

[20] 1 Chr. 15:12–15.

was as destructive for Uzzah as it potentially was for the people gathered at the foot of Mount Sinai as Moses received the law.

3. Encountering the holiness of God

Despite that, the holy God of the covenant cannot make a covenant without encountering the covenant partner. There are several devices put in place to facilitate this encounter across the boundaries of holiness. We have already alluded to one of them, namely, the role of Moses. As we have noted, Moses finds himself in the counsel of God and from there becomes responsible for shuttle diplomacy between the people and God. Through him God is persuaded of the people's intent towards obedience, and through him the people hear and accept God's requirement of a strictly observed holiness (19:7–8). In short, Moses is fulfilling what may be described as a prophetic function in the participatory way that we saw it described in Amos 3:7. The dynamic that we observe in these chapters is the prophetic process writ large.[21] As we saw in our discussion of Amos 3:1–8, that is one of God's provisions for making his word available to his people.[22]

A second provision of God is the establishment of the people as a *kingdom of priests and a holy nation* (19:6). Moreover, this kingdom and nation is to be *for me* (19:6), says God. By speaking thus, God declares that they are to be a people of the covenant. This is enormously significant, but need not be laboured as we have seen throughout Part 1 that the phenomenon of God's speaking is inevitably to do with the establishment of relationship with the people whom God has made. However carefully the encounter needs to be managed, there is always the intention on God's part to establish relationship.

4. The presence of God

Thirdly, there is a particular aspect of the relationship that emerges during the encounter at Mount Sinai. To find it, we need to read beyond chapter 19. With one or two interruptions, Exodus 20 – 31 constitute one account of the contents of the law given by God to Moses on Mount Sinai. Then comes the vivid account of the

---

[21] It is no accident that Moses was regarded by the Deuteronomists as the archetypal prophet. See Deut. 34:12.
[22] Amos 2:11.

people's unfaithfulness in the matter of the golden calf and the robust response of God to this unfaithfulness (Exod. 32). This leaves a large question hanging in the air: will God go with the people once they move on from Mount Sinai, as God tells them they must do?[23] At the start of Exodus 33, while commanding them to move on, the Lord declares that he will not be going with them. While God's words appear to be in reaction to the failings of the people, they were heard in the context of an assumption in those primitive times that the gods of people belonged to particular places. Safety is found in remaining within the jurisdiction of one's own tribal god. The group of tribes following Moses out from Egypt and towards the promised land were susceptible to this form of thinking, notwithstanding the demonstrations of God's power over Egypt.[24] Indeed, the claimed motivation for the golden calf itself was the desire for a god the people could take with them.[25] Moses brings the anguish of the people to the Lord and wrests from him a promise that he will in fact travel with them.[26]

God's faithfulness in that respect is demonstrated by several phenomena which are ultimately inexplicable, and of which we have little choice but to accept the biblical account. They seem to relate to the presence of God's 'glory' (kābôd). This remains a difficult concept but the actual Hebrew term used contains a cluster of concepts: weightiness, honour, splendour, physical manifestation of the presence of God. The first manifestation of God's presence is the strange experience of Moses in God's response to his request at the end of chapter 33 to see God's glory. God says that all of his 'goodness' will pass before Moses but he may not see his face; he may not see God in all his fullness. And so God covers Moses with his hand and allows him only to see his back. Although he cannot be fully viewed, the character of God is on display: his goodness, his mercy, his compassion.[27]

Strangely, at the same time that God is putting Moses in a cleft of the rock and covering him with his hand, he permits him to enter the 'tent of meeting' and speak with him 'face to face'. Although the people are excluded from the encounter, they too see the evidence of God in the pillar of cloud and in the radiance of Moses' face,[28] in

---

[23] Exod. 33:1.
[24] Note the view of the Arameans in 1 Kgs 20:23. See also M. L. Coloe, *God Dwells with Us: Temple Symbolism in the Fourth Gospel* (Collegeville: Liturgical Press, 2001), pp. 34–39.
[25] Exod. 32:1.
[26] Exod. 33:4–6, 15–17.
[27] Exod. 33:19–23.
[28] Exod. 33:7–11; 34:29–35.

the same way that Moses was permitted to see God's back and his goodness. Finally, the evidence of God's ongoing presence with his people as they travel towards the promised land is seen in the pillar of cloud and of fire over the tabernacle.[29] Indeed, that very pillar of cloud and fire is indicative of the glory of God.[30] Although the encounter of God with his people is constrained by God's otherness and his holiness, there is still a connection between the two parties, seen in the effects of God's glory.

5. God's presence in God's word

Each of those interventions between the holiness of God and the holiness of his people – the prophetic ministry of Moses, the establishment of covenant, and the presence of God at Sinai and on the journey – are programmatic for the ongoing life of the people of God. While these events and phenomena anticipate the ongoing involvement of God with his people, they are also to some extent transitory and local. They remain captured in history. There is however one further instrument of encounter between God and his people, and that is the word of God both spoken and written. This word is able to transcend the original encounter.

Just as Moses' meeting with God in chapter 33 has to do with the glory of God, so the word of God also has to do with the glory of God. There is a broad hint in that direction within the strange episode of the cleft in the rock that we have just been looking at. It concerns the statement that God, in passing before Moses and giving him a glimpse of his glory, will 'proclaim [his] name, the LORD, in [Moses'] presence'.[31] Several verses later, on Moses' return to the mountain to receive the re-chiseled tablets, we are told that 'the LORD came down in the cloud and stood there with him and proclaimed his name'.[32] Then follows the word of God enshrined in writing. The coincidence of vocabulary between Exodus 33:19 and 34:5 is striking and serves to alert the reader to the link between the glory of God and the fact that God speaks.[33] In the first chapter of this volume, I argued from Psalm 19 and also from Isaiah 40:5 that the glory of God is most fully revealed in the word of God, in the fact that God speaks. It is surely no coincidence that the acute

[29] Exod. 40:36–38.
[30] Exod. 40:35.
[31] Exod. 33:19.
[32] Exod. 34:5.
[33] For more on the character of God see R. A. Cole, *Exodus: An Introduction and Commentary*, TOTC (London: IVP, 1973), p. 228.

concern with holiness and glory of these chapters is associated with an episode of God's speech that overshadows all others in the Old Testament. For all of the thunder and power of that encounter at Mount Sinai, what actually happened was that *God spoke all these words . . .* (20:1).

Embedded into the details of the law given as God spoke[34] are details of the dynamics around the reception of those words: Moses' intervention with and on behalf of the people, the episode of the golden calf, the broken tablets and their subsequent re-issuing, and the process by which these words became written. This embedded material evinces an obvious concern with the preservation of the words of God. The incredible care taken in the boundary-setting of Exodus 19 sets a tone such that the reader is looking for something really significant when finally *God spoke all these words* (20:1). Then we find that God has 'written' these things for the instruction of the people.[35] Notwithstanding the hint that the contents of the second set of tablets is the 'ten words',[36] the nature of these stone tablets and their contents will forever remain a mystery. It seems hardly likely that even Moses, who was obviously a very fit man, could have carried enough stone tablets up and down the mountain to contain all the speech of God in Exodus 20 – 31. So the focus of Scripture at this point is not so much on the tablets as on the fact that the word of God is written.

And it was very important that it be written. This is evident from God's desire to replace the tablets that Moses smashed in his anger at the unfaithfulness of the people around the golden calf.[37] The content of the tablets is summarized as 'the words of the covenant',[38] for it was around the writing of the two new tablets of stone that God made a covenant with the people whom Moses was leading.[39] The link between 34:28 and 34:29 makes clear that 'the law' at this point in the narrative becomes shorthand for the words of the covenant spoken and written by God. Then the text of Exodus moves into a long description of the specifications for the tabernacle.[40] The details need not detain us, but it is important to note that one of the functions of the tabernacle is to contain 'the law',[41] and that the tabernacle's journey with the people of Israel

[34] Up to Exod. 35:19.
[35] Exod. 24:12.
[36] Exod. 34:28.
[37] Exod. 32:19; 34:1.
[38] Exod. 34:28.
[39] Exod. 34:10.
[40] Exod. 35:1 – 40:33.
[41] Exod. 40:5. The word 'covenant' in TNIV is not present in the Hebrew.

signifies to them God's ongoing presence as promised to Moses at Mount Sinai.[42]

The outcome of all this is that the written text has an ongoing function as the word of God in the life of the covenant people. The words transcend the context of their initial utterance while also establishing the importance of that utterance for the ongoing life of the people. With respect to the particular needs of that group of people in the Sinai wilderness late in the second millennium BC, the text also becomes part of God's spoken assurance of his enduring presence with his people. It becomes a means by which a consecrated people may safely encounter a holy God on an ongoing basis.

In the wider witness of Scripture as a whole, there is more to say about the written word of God; the environment of *ḥērem* (the 'ban') and of holiness and danger in which the word is received is not the only type of encounter.[43] But the message of Exodus 19–40 is an important part of the biblical witness. It reminds us that relationship with God is a call to holiness or 'consecration'; that sometimes God may 'break out' of his holiness in anger and destruction; that God's word written is a great gift in safely encountering this God; and that even God's written word reflects God's character and so should be regarded as holy. All of this is part of the formation of the covenant people of God. And it still calls forth the type of obedience which seems to have motivated Moses to write down what he had received.[44]

6. Words, writing and responsibility

In conclusion, the production and nature of the written 'law' or 'words of the covenant' (taking the two terms to refer to the same thing) deserve a moment's reflection. As we have seen, the starting point is the encounter of Moses with the God who speaks and acts. The written version encapsulates the words and deeds of God and enables them to continue with the people of the covenant as they move on from Mount Sinai. The biblical text is sufficiently vague about the actual form the written word took to suggest that this is secondary to the ongoing availability through the text of encounter with God. Nevertheless, it is located in a particular place (the ark

[42] Exod. 40:36–38.

[43] See for example ch. 12 on Hebrews 1:1–4, where we reflect on Jesus as the one who 'suffered outside the city gate' (Heb. 13:12) and paradoxically thereby '[entered] the inner sanctuary behind the curtain' (Heb. 6:19). He thus became a boundary-crosser on behalf of the covenant people.

[44] Exod. 24:3–4.

of the covenant in the tabernacle) and is accordingly worthy of the same respect as any other place or object that is associated with the encounter between God and people. The boundedness of God evident at Mount Sinai also applies to God's presence as expressed in the preserved text.

There is also a paradox of responsibility in the production of the text. We noted at the start of this chapter that there was a kind of dual initiative exercised by both Moses and God towards the reception of God's word at Sinai. Correspondingly, there is also a kind of dual responsibility exercised in the production of the written version of the 'law' or 'words of the covenant'. First, Moses took it upon himself to write everything that God had said on the mountain.[45] Although the words were God's, the initiative to preserve them initially seems to have been from Moses. Then God tells Moses that he will receive on behalf of his people tablets of stone that contain 'the law and commandments [God has] written for their instruction'.[46] This material is a little later vividly described as having been 'inscribed by the finger of God'.[47] This time the agency is entirely God's. That initiative continues with God as he commences a process for replacing the smashed tablets. He commands Moses to 'chisel out two stone tablets' so that he 'will write on them'.[48] But then, after some time hearing God speak, Moses writes down the words.[49] And the words he writes are the 'ten words',[50] yet God has just been talking about something else. Are the work of Moses and the work of 'the finger of God' the same thing? Do they hold the same status? Is there is a distinction between what God wrote and what Moses wrote, which is reflected in the canonical text?

These questions are not resolvable by exegesis of the biblical material. What they finally leave us with is a sense of a particular set of dynamics behind the written word of God. First, the paradox around the holiness of the text and the holiness of what it represents warns us against too readily imposing formulae about the exact nature of Scripture. These chapters of Exodus permit us to distinguish between the word of God and the written witness to the word of God. At the same time, just as the mountain is holy and dangerous because God is holy and dangerous and demands the same respect that God demands, so the preserved words of God in

[45] Exod. 24:4.
[46] Exod. 24:12.
[47] Exod. 31:18.
[48] Exod. 34:1.
[49] Exod. 34:27–28.
[50] Exod. 34:28, TNIV 'Ten Commandments'.

the text ask to be treated as the very words and activity of God and not merely a representation of them. Any formulation of the nature of Scripture must be generous enough to contain both sides of this paradox.

Secondly, the ambivalence of aspects of these chapters of Exodus warns against simplistic formulations about responsibility for the text of the word of God. How much of Moses is in what we receive and how much is 'the finger of God'? The text is in no doubt that the preserved material comes from God and is at God's initiative. At the same time, Moses also displays initiative and seems to take on a responsibility for writing that is distinct from that undertaken by God. The words and actions of God in the exodus event and the formation of a covenant people at Sinai are carried forward in the text because of the work of both Moses and God. There is a delicate dance described by the interaction between God and God's servants responsible for the production of the written text of Scripture.[51]

[51] For further, see K. J. Vanhoozer, *The Drama of Doctrine: A Canonical-Linguistic Approach to Christian Theology* (Louisville: Westminster John Knox, 2005), pp. 44–46.

Deuteronomy 4:1–20
7. The covenant remembered

As I write this chapter I look from our apartment in Beit Jala on the occupied West Bank across to the main Bethlehem ridge and, on a clear day, to the hills of Moab. Perhaps if I knew where to look I could see Mount Nebo where Moses once sat, looked across the Jordan rift and realized that he would never tread on the land he saw.[1] It was a land that God was giving to the people Moses had led for all those years. But not to him. Did he struggle with the unfairness of it all or did he die with a sense of a job well done? I suspect Moses found himself somewhere between the two. Perhaps he thought alternately of the *iron-smelting furnace* of *Egypt* and the *inheritance* of Canaan that he had mentioned in an earlier speech to his people (20).

The land to which he looked and its inhabitants still find themselves caught between the furnace and the anticipated inheritance. For the Jewish people of Israel, the road to the state of Israel has been a long furnace culminating in the *Shoah* and the struggle for a Jewish homeland. There may be some sense of an inheritance achieved, but, from whatever angle the Jewish people view the current conflict, the furnace is still throwing out heat and the inheritance remains elusive. For those committed to the achievement of a greater Israel on the map, then possession and dispossession remain incomplete. For those to whom the role of occupier is a denial of the essence of what Israel should be, realization of inheritance remains just as elusive.[2] Yet a yearning for peace never recedes entirely.

For the Arab people, who lived in the land of Palestine more or

<hr>

[1] Deut. 34:1–4.
[2] For a marvelous account of the diverse phenomenon of modern day 'Israel' see D. Rosenthal, *The Israelis: Ordinary People in an Extraordinary Land* (New York: Free Press, 2003).

less continuously for many generations up until the 1948 war, the furnace is an ever-present reality while the inheritance seems to have been plucked from them.[3] Suffering and irony and indignity continue to pile up, both at the hands of the occupier, Israel, and as a result of an increasing fragmentation of Palestinian identity.[4] Yet a yearning for peace never recedes entirely.

Those who are Christians in a land that is now predominantly either Jewish or Muslim, sometimes describe themselves as caught between two fires.[5] Messianic Jews constantly face doubt as to their loyalty from their compatriots, and must struggle to hold a commitment to the state of Israel with a loyalty to Jesus.[6] For Palestinian Christians there is a very real sense of being caught in the crossfire. They are subjected to the same restrictions of occupation as any other Palestinian while also battling to remain faithful in an increasingly dominant Muslim majority culture. For them the furnace just seems to get hotter.

I have only touched on one place in the world where these types of issues are played out, albeit one that is particularly sharply etched and more rife with theological freight than most. But there are numerous indigenous struggles for identity in the face of persecution, and injustice against their own people by corrupt regimes. There are millions of Christians whose loyalty to Jesus is taken as disloyalty to their neighbours. Each one is similarly able to speak of looking from the furnace to the inheritance.

These issues are also present in Western democracies that remain relatively free of corruption and blatant injustice, at least for educated members of the majority culture. Yet we in the West are bemused by apparently increasing levels of violence, dysfunction in relationships and alienation from the social infrastructure, and wonder what is bringing it about. The West faces a furnace of identity of its own, and the question of inheritance is a live one for our cultures and for those who find themselves as disaffected outsiders in various ways.

For all such peoples the vision of a covenant that draws people from the furnace of oppression or alienation into an inheritance is

---

[3] A. Awad, *Palestinian Memories: The Story of a Palestinian Mother and Her People* (Bethlehem: Bethlehem Bible College, 2008), pp. 91–108.

[4] M. Rees, *Cain's Field: Faith, Fratricide, and Fear in the Middle East* (New York: Free Press, 2004), pp. 9–120.

[5] J. Kincaid, *Between Two Fires: The Untold Story of Palestinian Christians* (Gainesville: Banner, 2002).

[6] D. Stern, 'The Land from a Messianic Jewish Perspective', in L. Loden, P. Walker and M. Wood (eds.), *The Bible and the Land: An Encounter* (Jerusalem: Musalaha, 2000), pp. 37–54.

deeply attractive. And, as we will see, it is a covenant that is conveyed in the written word of God and in the transmission of that word.

1. Remember the day

In the previous chapter we thought about the establishment of a covenant people around the great events of Mount Sinai. The memory of those events and the covenant itself were preserved in the text.[7] As a result, as we saw, the preserved words of God from that time continue to be the word and words of God. They continue, in the terms we suggested then, to function also as the word by which God acts. But that does not happen automatically, hence the plea from Moses that the people remember the words and convey them to their descendents: *watch yourselves closely so that you do not forget the things your eyes have seen or let them slip from your heart . . . Teach them to your children and to their children after them* (9).

This plea is set in the context of a document, the basis of the book of Deuteronomy, that was probably formed some time after the events around Mount Sinai.[8] Much has happened since that time. The land has been apportioned to the tribes, the chaotic period of the judges has been negotiated, the glory days of the united monarchy now lie in the past, and a divided kingdom struggles to hear the words of God. The encounter between Moses and God, in which the people participated, has become a distant memory. Then, in the six hundreds BC, a startling discovery is made during renovation of the temple, a discovery which strengthens the hand of the prophets and provides the impetus for a reform movement under the leadership of King Josiah. This movement, occasioned by the discovery of the book of the law, ultimately would be unsuccessful, but an enduring outcome was the preservation of the law and the important historical memories that have come to be known as the deuteronomist history.[9]

Deuteronomy 4 should be read in that context of a rediscovered memory. A central point in these verses is the plea that the people of the law not let the words of God *slip from [their] heart* (9). We could imagine the word 'again' echoing between the lines, as the words

---

[7] Exod. 24:3–4.

[8] The book of Deuteronomy, literally the second law, is likely to have originated in the reforms under Josiah related in 2 Kgs 22 – 23, around 622 BC, although it contains material that was much earlier. See *NIDB* 2, p. 105.

[9] For an introduction see T. Römer, *The So-Called Deuteronomistic History: A Sociological, Historical and Literary Introduction* (London: T&T Clark, 2007).

are an implicit reminder of how heedless the people had become by the time of King Josiah. Then the writer through Moses reminds the people of those great events at *Horeb* (10, 11, 15), another name for Sinai. He also remembers that the words of God were written down at that time, using the shorthand term seen in Exodus, 'the ten words' (13), and that they constituted the heart of the covenant between God and his people (13).

But there's more. It is not enough simply to remember, it is not enough to note that all this once happened. If the written word of God truly is to continue to be God at work it must be nurtured and passed on. This entails remembering and teaching. Thus we find that it is in the nature of God's word written that it is meant to be read. That seems like a statement of the obvious, but contemporary Christian practice suggests that it is still a point that needs to be made. In the previous chapter we noted that there is a sense in which the very text itself of God's word is holy, but that its importance is realized in its becoming the active word of God as it is read. It should be treated with great respect for what it is, but it must also be taken off the shelf and appropriated. Only then will God be heard to speak again.

In the Christian tradition this act of reading entails a whole gamut of activities that may be summed up in the command to *remember* (10) the great saving acts of God. On this occasion the memory is explicitly of Horeb/Sinai, but there are a range of key events that Scripture enjoins us to remember. As a culmination of all of them and supremely we remember both the death and resurrection of Jesus and the command of Jesus to remember.[10] This memory is maintained as the message of God's word, the Scriptures, is maintained.

2. What should be remembered?

And the memory of the saving acts of God is conveyed through teaching. This dynamic was inherent in the first giving of the law. Moses recalls how at the very time that God gave the covenant and it took on written form he was directed *to teach* all that it contained (14). The act of teaching is inherent in this dynamic whereby God continues to speak and act into the lives of those who encounter his word in the text. Many years later, having faced the danger of losing the covenant through ignoring the call to remember, a new generation hears the call to teach succeeding generations.

[10] Luke 22:19.

The content of that teaching is couched in suggestive terms. The TNIV translates it as *the things your eyes have seen* (9). The plural noun translated as *things* (*dĕbārîm*) usually means 'word', but can sometimes be translated as 'matter' or 'subject' or 'thing'. The things which the people have seen are therefore also potentially 'words'; they are to recall the words that they have seen. The language shows the closeness of the link between the words and the action of God. This blurring of the distinction between the visual and the verbal, and a consequent linking of them, is also commonly found amongst the prophets. Amos, for example, was commanded to speak the 'words' which he 'saw' as a 'vision'.[11] By teaching later generations the people do more than convey the contents of a text; they enable the words of that text to be heard and seen again as the active word of God at work among later generations.[12]

3. The nature of remembering

This call to *teach* (9) or, more literally from the Hebrew, to 'make known' or 'cause to know', may refer to a variety of activities. It should not be thought of only as the classroom-based practice with which we today associate the term 'teaching'. Most basically, it entails a responsibility to preserve and transmit the text that contains these things. Both Christianity and Judaism have attended to this with varying degrees of diligence through the centuries. Peaks may be identified wherein particular efforts have been made. One thinks, for example, of the work of the medieval masoretic scribes,[13] or Jerome's rediscovery of the significance of the Hebrew text to Christians,[14] or the burgeoning of textual work in the wake of the Enlightenment.[15]

Secondly, both Judaism and Christianity have exhibited a lively sense that the preserved text, if it is indeed to be the speech-act of God in a later day, must somehow be appropriated into the contemporary context. Christianity has done that through formulating

---

[11] Amos 1:1.

[12] M. E. Biddle, *Deuteronomy*, SHBC (Macon: Smith & Helwys, 2003), pp. 83–84.

[13] The Jewish scribes in the early medieval period who took responsibility to preserve and copy the text of the Hebrew Bible with extraordinary accuracy and whose work still forms the basis of the best Hebrew text today, known as the Masoretic Text.

[14] Jerome, 347–420 AD.

[15] See for example the account of the work of the Renaissance scholar, Erasmus, on the Greek text of the New Testament in R. H. Bainton, *Erasmus of Christendom* (London: Collins, 1969), pp. 164–172.

theological responses to the text. Kevin Vanhoozer has described this process as 'the drama of doctrine' in a book so entitled.[16] For him it is the dramatic or lived process whereby exegetical insight of the text is lived out in a way that is faithful to the canon of Scriptures but is more than merely an anachronistic reproduction of them.[17] In contrast to Christian responses, the Jewish appropriation of Scripture has been less about theological formulation, and more about telling and living within the story.[18] There has not been the same drive to systematize, but there has been a similar recognition of the need to appropriate. This may be seen in such things as the Aramaic targums, and the development of the immense literatures of the Mishnah and the Talmuds.[19] All are done with the aim of keeping the word of God in the text alive in future generations.

As a closely related point, Andrew Walls has argued that the Christian faith is a faith that translates.[20] Constantly that which is seen and heard is incorporated into new contexts and generations. This translation is both literal and metaphorical. It is literal in that the text is constantly being translated into the equivalence of other languages, such that the words and acts of God are encountered just as truly in the translation as in the original linguistic forms that the text may have taken. Metaphorically, translation also expresses the way that culturally appropriate forms are devised of living out the faith. While early Celtic monks and medieval theologians and European reformers and twenty-first-century African Pentecostals devised modes of worship and ethical responses to the faith that are quite distinctive from one another, all are appropriating the same text, the same speech-acts of God, in doing so. All seek to obey the command to pass the words of God onto subsequent generations,

---

[16] K. J. Vanhoozer, *The Drama of Doctrine: A Canonical-Linguistic Approach to Christian Theology* (Louisville: Westminster John Knox, 2005).

[17] See his exploration of this as a 'turn to context' in K. J. Vanhoozer, '"One Rule to Rule Them All?" Theological Method in an Era of World Christianity', in C. Ott and H. A. Netland (eds.), *Globalizing Theology: Belief and Practice in an Era of World Christianity* (Grand Rapids: Baker Academic, 2006), pp. 92–115.

[18] It is no accident that a rediscovered appreciation of biblical narrative has been led by Jewish scholarship. See for instance A. Berlin, *Poetics and Interpretation of Biblical Narrative* (Winona Lake: Eisenbrauns, 1994), or S. Bar-Efrat, *Narrative Art in the Bible* (Sheffield: Almond, 1989).

[19] The targums were paraphrases of the Hebrew text into Aramaic to enable understanding by ordinary folk for whom Hebrew was no longer their mother tongue. The Mishnah and Talmuds are collections of rabbinical material concerning key passages and themes in the Law, dating up to about 600 AD.

[20] A. F. Walls, *The Missionary Movement in Christian History: Studies in the Transmission of Faith* (Maryknoll: Orbis, 1996), pp. 3–15.

and so to continue hearing and seeing the word of God active in different times and places.

The musical metaphor of transposition is slightly different from translation, but further clarifies the point being made. Transposition involves preserving the same harmony and melody of a piece of music while playing it in a different key. When this concept is applied to the process of living the text, 'the aim is to preserve the same figure and form of Christ . . . in different cultural keys'.[21]

All of this sounds rather theoretical, but these things cannot be left to the academy and academics. Theology, translation and transposition are merely the underpinning of everyday Christian practice whereby succeeding generations are incorporated into the faith. Some of it, what we might call Christian education, is formal. Some of it is more informal, such as when parents are examplars of the faith for their children. Whatever form it takes, though, it must be intentional. The text means nothing unless this responsibility to pass it on and apply it in fresh contexts is grasped by its readers and by the church as a whole.[22]

4. The responsibility to remember

Still focused on verses 9 and 10, the effects of remembering through the words of Scripture are twofold. First, the people are to *be careful, and watch yourselves closely* (9). The noun that TNIV has rendered as *yourselves* (*nepeš*) may be variously translated, but central to its meaning is the essence of a person as encapsulating body, mind and spirit. It would not have occurred to the Hebrew mind to make that sort of division within the person, but it is difficult to explain it otherwise to an English-speaking mindset. The whole person is in view. Remembering and sustaining the word of God is a necessary part of being a whole functioning person. Where the word of God ceases to be a living memory, when the story of God's work is not interacted with on a regular basis, the effect is damaging to the person.

Secondly, Moses enjoins the people not to forget these things or *let them slip from your heart* (9). The English translation makes the forgetting sound like a gentle process of omission. In fact a literal translation is rather more active than that: 'lest they [the words which your eyes have seen] turn aside from your heart.' On that reading, the words and acts of God play an active part in absenting themselves from the heart of the one who forgets. Too much should

---

[21] Vanhoozer, *Drama of Doctrine*, p. 254.
[22] For more on this see ch. 20 on 2 Thess. 2:13–17.

not be made of this point, but it is a timely reminder that a long neglect of something important can develop its own momentum that becomes harder and harder to reverse. And we should note also that the Hebrew word *heart* is used to reflect the seat of the will. When the will is not regularly fed with the sights and sounds of God's activity, obedience to the word that enshrines those sights and sounds becomes more and more elusive.

This is a sobering thought for individual believers. But it is an even more sobering thought for the community of faith, because the immediate context of this utterance is the command to teach succeeding generations. Where this is not done a corporate forgetting can occur that becomes harder to reverse with each succeeding generation. The church must heed that call. Already in the West we see the corporate memory of the great Christian events receding rapidly. It will be drastic indeed if the church also loses its memory and hence its ability to call society towards a Christian ethic and practice.

5. The effect of remembering

The loss of memory will be drastic because a community that is soaked in the word of God, in whom God's speech remains active, bears certain characteristics. First, it is a community that demonstrates *wisdom and understanding* (6). These two words are both established wisdom terms. They are both multifaceted and hard to pin down to an exact definition, but between them they speak of skill, competence, knowledge and an appreciation of what to do with those things. The term translated as *wisdom* (*ḥokmâ*) also brings a spiritual dimension, in that a sage or wise person is one who discerns well the things of God. In all, they speak of a community that intentionally seeks to live in the light of God's revelation. In the context of Deuteronomy, such people are those who appropriate the word of God.[23]

Secondly, this wisdom and understanding is noticed by other *nations* (6); it becomes a witness. And it is a witness not to the wondrous wisdom and understanding of the people themselves but to the source of that wisdom, namely, *the Lord our God* (7). The remembering of God's word thereby becomes a continuation of the activity of God in the world.

A third effect of this remembering is that any form of idolatry

---

[23] This is hardly surprising in light of the link between wisdom and *torah*, noted in the previous chapter.

becomes inappropriate (15–19).[24] Remember that for all the pyro-technic splendour of the giving of the law at Sinai,[25] the focus remained firmly on the word of God. The glory of God rested not in the physical effects but in the fact that God spoke.[26] This is encapsulated in Moses' comment, *You saw no form of any kind the day the Lord spoke to you . . .* (15). A wise people are a people who focus on the God who comes in God's word. Anything less is not good enough; anything less is a denial of the command to convey this word so that God's activity may continue to be manifest. Almost anything, from our trade to relationships to liturgical practice, may become a *form* that diverts us from the glory of God in the word of God. When we are so diverted not only is our witness compromised but our ability to convey the faith to other generations and places is also diminished.

6. Inheritance

Finally, our reading is framed by the concept of inheritance. Inheritance is the context in which the covenant that is brought into being by the word of God is remembered and passed on. Verse 1 speaks of *[taking] possession of the land* that God *is giving* to the people. Then verse 20 refers to the *inheritance* of the people. As the word of God is appropriated and passed on the people come into possession of the inheritance that God is giving them. In the deuteronomic vision this inheritance is the land that has been promised. As a result of the word of God they have been led from the *furnace* of *Egypt* into a landed *inheritance* (20).

Deuteronomy typically draws these links between possession of and inheritance in the land and the covenant.[27] The particular link with the land is problematic and will be explored in detail in the following section. Nevertheless, leaving that aside for the moment, it is a profound truth that the word of God, in which we experience the ongoing activity of God, is indispensably connected to the formation of the people of God. As children of the covenant our identity and connection with others, as well as our experience of the blessings of God, is found in the word of God. We may say that in two senses. First, the word of God is the story and memory that

[24] R. Brown, *The Message of Deuteronomy*, BST (Leicester: IVP, 1993), pp. 68–70.
[25] Exod. 19.
[26] Exod. 20:1.
[27] See for example Deut. 15:4–5.

bind us together. Secondly, the word of God is the ongoing activity of God by which we continue to be formed and bound to one another.

This is contrasted with the experience of slavery in Egypt. There the identity of the people was in danger, the blessings of God seemed far distant and they had no place to stand. The covenant formed by the *decrees and laws* (1) given at Mount Sinai formed the basis on which to address those lacks. They became the means whereby the people could become a witness of God's glory to the surrounding nations. As I commented at the start of this chapter, still today people and people groups experience the furnace of alienation and marginalization. Still today God offers a covenant formed by the words and acts of God that may produce an inheritance of identity and hope.

But there is a surprising twist in the tail of verse 20. The phrase *the people of his inheritance* is interesting in two respects. The first is that it is open-ended as to whether the inheritance is something that the people are or something that they have. From elsewhere in Deuteronomy it is clear that the people do have an inheritance from God. At the same time, it is also legitimate to read the phrase as indicating that the people themselves are an inheritance. This raises the question, whose inheritance? One possible answer is that the people whom God has brought into being become God's inheritance. A second possibility is that the *people of inheritance* become the instruments of inheritance, that is, the means by which God holds out a place in the covenant to others.

With respect to the first ambiguity, the wider context of Deuteronomy leads us to accept that the covenant people are beneficiaries of an inheritance confirmed by a place in the land. At the same time, the subtle turn of phrase also allows the intriguing possibility that God is also a beneficiary of the word of God,[28] and thus indicates that the covenant relationship is something in which God rejoices and of which God is a part. With respect to the second ambiguity, once again the people are inheritors of blessing; we know that from elsewhere in Deuteronomy. At the same time, the people brought into being by the word of God potentially become the source of blessing for others.[29] They are the means by which others also come into God's inheritance.

Thus the word of God as the text that enshrines the covenant-making activity of God continues to function as the lively word

[28] See also ch. 2 on Isa. 55:11 wherein God is himself a beneficiary of the ever-reliable word of God.
[29] See Gen. 12:1–3.

of God when the text is read and appropriated and passed down through the generations.

7. Reading Deuteronomy today

All of this raises the question of how the Old Testament should be read in the light of Jesus. A non-observant Jewish peace activist once observed to me that the first six books of the Bible essentially constitute a chronicle of genocide. I countered that Genesis 1 – 11 set the universalist framework against which covenant and possession/ dispossession should be read, but he was not convinced. And he had statistics on his side. He was also justified in thinking that the book of Deuteronomy closely ties the idea of covenant to the possession of the land and hence the dispossession of the earlier inhabitants of that land.[30] This is a central plank in the identity of the covenant people. My friend could also have noted how often – more often than is necessary to make the point – Deuteronomy describes the land as that which God has given the people for them to *take possession* (1, 5) or 'occupy'. Indeed, the book of Deuteronomy alone accounts for about one third of all uses of the verb translated as 'take possession' or 'occupy' (*yāraš*). And this possession/dispossession seems to be a zero-sum game; in order for somebody to possess, somebody else must be dispossessed, and Deuteronomy is unapologetic about this. It is the essence of *yāraš* that one requires the other.

From our perspective, it is an uncomfortable fact that Deuteronomy 4 ties the word of God and covenant closely to possession of the land. This need not trouble us too much while we read the Old Testament primarily as an allegory whose deeper meaning is the important one, or even as a typology of the message of Christ. But it becomes more difficult when the Old Testament is read with an eye on the call for justice by the classical prophets and the universal love of God in Jesus for all peoples. Then the fate of the Canaanites seems unfair because they too have a stake in the inheritance of God.[31] It becomes even more difficult when the very same piece of land is still subject to the same zero-sum attitudes. Once again the inhabitants of the land, now the Arab people of Palestine/Israel,[32] many of them Christian, are being dispossessed

---

[30] I avoid referring to the 'original' inhabitants as there is almost nowhere in the world where such a denotation could be made with confidence. Almost everybody has displaced somebody else.

[31] Amos 9:7.

[32] Terminology is difficult, but I use 'Palestine/Israel' to refer to the swathe of land covered by the political entities of both the state of Israel and the occupied

to make way for a homeland for the Jewish people. The results are no prettier than they were when the Canaanites were being dispossessed. And just as grieving to the heart of God. At the same time there are some Christian readers of Deuteronomy who endorse the present-day programme of possession/dispossession as if the state of Israel equates to the people formed around the covenant made with Moses at Sinai. In the light of all that, it is extraordinarily hard for some Christians to receive Deuteronomy 4 as the word of God.

By way of response I begin by acknowledging that the whole episode of the conquest is problematic from this side of the cross. And it is doubly difficult for those who themselves have been dispossessed of land at the hands of others claiming a divine imperative. That will always be part of the struggle to read Deuteronomy well. But there are several more positive points that may be made in response. First, Western readers need to understand the nature of land 'ownership'. To the Western mind ownership or possession of land relates to a commodity that can be bought and sold like any other possession. To the hearers of these words possession is closely tied to the notion of inheritance. It concerns what the people are entitled to by virtue of who they are. Possession of land, and conversely dispossession of other people from the land, is only legitimately undertaken in the context of coming into an inheritance.[33] And these verses are about the inheritance of the people of God rather than about a simple mandate for territorial expansion.[34]

Secondly, notwithstanding my friend's objections, the universalist vision of Genesis 1– 11 must be a key to our reading of the exodus, covenant and conquest. The point of transfer from the cosmic story of Genesis 1 – 11 to the story of the patriarchs and their descendents in the form of Israel is Genesis 12:1–3. Therein the promises to Abraham and his descendents are given so that 'all peoples on earth will be blessed'. In that light, the ensuing story of God's covenant people is in implementation of the dreams and hopes of God for all humanity, dreams and hopes and possibilities

West Bank and Gaza. Therefore the Arab people I refer to include present Arab citizens of the state of Israel, those who live in and are confined to the occupied territories and those who formerly lived in Palestine but no longer do so for whatever reason. For further on the current situation in Israel/Palestine, see J. Halper, *An Israeli in Palestine: Resisting Dispossession, Redeeming Israel* (London: Pluto, 2008).

[33] W. Brueggemann, *The Land: Place as Gift, Promise, and Challenge in Biblical Faith*, 2nd ed., OBT (Minneapolis: Fortress, 2002), pp. 45–50.

[34] N. Wazana, 'From Dan to Beer-Sheba and from the Wilderness to the Sea: Literal and Literary Images of the Promised Land in the Bible', in M. MacDonald (ed.), *Experiences of Place* (Cambridge: Centre for the Study of World Religions, 2003), pp. 45–85.

that have just been expressed in Genesis 1 – 11.[35] I referred above to 'the universal love of God in Jesus'. While God's love is supremely realized in Jesus, it is there from the creation of the world and permeates the pages of the Old Testament. Therefore, as has been well put by one particular Palestinian Christian, the intercontinental land bridge known variously as Palestine or Israel, like any other piece of land on the planet, 'belongs to God', not inalienably to any single group of people, whether Palestinian or Israeli.[36]

Reading the book of Deuteronomy in that light is reinforced by two other important points, both of which counter errors that are frequently made by Christians. The first entails an important principle of reading that says historical accounts in Scripture should not necessarily be taken as models of action to be undertaken by later readers.[37] It therefore does not follow that the command to conquer the Canaanites is a prescription for later generations of believers or manifestations of states called 'Israel'; the most that can be said is that this was something that happened once under the sovereignty of God. That it happened does not suspend the moral requirements of a just and merciful God who is concerned for all nations. Indeed, the words of the prophets uttered probably from the same era as that in which Deuteronomy was formed make it impossible to replicate the possession/dispossession of land as integral to a covenant inheritance.[38]

Secondly, a reading that draws parallels between the conquest of the Canaanites and the rights of the state of Israel today – whether the reading be pro or anti the state of Israel – makes a false assumption that modern Israel is equivalent to the people formed by God around the covenant in those far off days on the Sinai Peninsula. Furthermore, it is patently not the case that the modern state of Israel equates to the Jewish people *per se*.[39] Therefore great care should be taken in reading: for those who want to justify current Israeli conquest or colonization, not to assume that support can be drawn from the book of Deuteronomy for the contemporary dispossession of land and housing; and for those who are reacting against this, not to reject Deuteronomy on the equally mistaken assumption that it somehow supports injustice against disenfranchised peoples. It is no more the case that the state of Israel equates to the covenant

---

[35] C. J. H. Wright, *The Mission of God: Unlocking the Bible's Grand Narrative* (Leicester and Downers Grove: IVP, 2006), pp. 456–461.

[36] Y. Katanacho, 'Christ is the Owner of *Ha-aretz*', *CSR* 34 (2005), pp. 425–441.

[37] J. E. Goldingay, *Old Testament Theology, Volume Three: Israel's Life* (Downers Grove: IVP, 2009), pp. 580–582.

[38] Isa. 56:1–8, for example.

[39] Awad, *Palestinian Memories*, pp. 51–59.

people led by Moses than it is the case that the modern state of Italy equates to the Roman Empire.

Finally, Deuteronomy should be read for what it is, a story about an inheritance from God, enshrined in and remembered and re-implemented by means of the text. The inheritance of land had to be appropriated, but this was only possible because it was ultimately a gift from God. And it was an inheritance that only remained in place at the pleasure of God and conditional on the faithfulness of the people. That is why there was an exile.[40] Integral to that inheritance was the covenant made between God and his people, and the ongoing remembrance of that covenant.

As we are faithful to the command to teach these things to *[our] children and their children after them* (9), in the light of Jesus, we see that Israel has not been replaced as covenant partner but that the covenant has now expanded to provide an inheritance to all those for whom Christ died.[41] By this means the people of Abraham truly become instruments of inheritance in the form of a blessing for 'all peoples on earth'.[42] Ultimately the book of Deuteronomy is part of a story that belongs to all those families. And so it is part of a story that is much bigger than possession of one particular parcel of land, although that is a part of the story that remains important to people of Jewish and Christian faith, albeit in different ways.[43] It is a part of the story that is to be remembered and handed down, for it records and continues to enact the work of God. And in doing so it continues to lead God's people, wherever they may be, from the *furnace* to the *inheritance* (20).

---

[40] 1 Kgs 9:6–9; 2 Kgs 24:20; Ezek. 36:18–19; Jer. 22:8–9.
[41] 1 Pet. 1:3–9.
[42] Gen. 12:3.
[43] Brueggemann, *The Land*, p. 198.

Luke 1:1–4
8. The written word as witness

In the previous two chapters we have been concerned with God's speaking in the establishment of the covenant, and the written record and transmission of those events so that they continue to speak as the voice of God to subsequent generations. Essentially, the result is a text that is at least partly an historical record. In order to read it well we need, among other things, to come to terms with history.

We are creatures of our times and we live in a post-Enlightenment age with all the advantages and drawbacks that that entails. One of the difficulties is what one eighteenth-century scholar, in a memorable phrase, termed the 'ugly ditch' that has been dug between theology and history.[1] At the risk of over-simplifying a highly nuanced question, two characteristics of modern historical enquiry contribute to this ditch. First, historical enquiry is reliant in the first instance on eyewitness accounts of something that happened. That does not mean the eyewitness account is accepted; assessment and testing of the account is part of doing history. But it does mean that historical enquiry concerns events that human experience indicates are inherently plausible. Secondly, modern historical enquiry is only able to respond to events and phenomena and their accompanying human behaviour on the basis of previous experience of those same events, phenomena or behaviour. Where something new has occurred or been responded to, an historian needs to find enough therein that is already familiar or plausible in order to be able to give an historical account of it.

Herein lies the 'ugly ditch' between history and theology. As we

---

[1] Gotthold Ephraim Lessing (1729-81). Cited in J. C. O'Neill, *The Bible's Authority: A Portrait Gallery of Thinkers from Lessing to Bultmann* (Edinburgh: T&T Clark, 1991), p. 18.

have seen, the historical record within the text of Scripture is an integral part of the ongoing speech-act of God. From a Christian perspective, the resurrection of Jesus Christ is the central act of God to which the Scriptures bear witness. And yet, in the modernist terms indicated above, it is not an event that yields to historical enquiry. Notwithstanding investigations of the human response to belief in the resurrection of Jesus of the type made famous by books like *Who Moved the Stone?*,[2] nobody saw the actual moment of resurrection, and the alleged significance of the event is in a category of one. There is simply no similar experience or set of phenomena around which to base an historical investigation. And yet, to paraphrase Paul, without the resurrection our faith is in vain.[3] The ongoing experience of our faith draws on the history of the acts and words of God, and yet the central act in that story is supposedly excluded from historical investigation.

I see three possible responses to this problem. Each of the first two sets up camp on one or other side of the 'ugly ditch'. The first is to draw a line between historical conclusion and declaration of faith. In that case, even when the resurrection is affirmed as true, it is affirmed as a type of truth that does not yield to historical enquiry. The problem with this is that any interpretation of historical events in the light of God becomes problematic, and we become unsure of God's involvement in history. A further result is that we end up hardly knowing how to talk about the incarnation, even though it is at the heart of God's involvement in history.[4] We thereby settle on the history side of the ditch. A second response is to privilege statements of faith without troubling ourselves too much with historical questions, thereby camping on the theology side of the ditch. This seems like a more 'faithful' response but its results are not too different from working from the other side of the ditch. Faith becomes confined to the 'supernatural' and detached from the everyday; we become similarly unsure about the work of God in history, and we focus more on God at work primarily in terms of personal faith. In this response we choose theology over history.

A third approach is more courageous and difficult than either of the first two, but if we are to be true to Scripture and as open as we possibly can be to its message, it is the necessary approach. It entails redefining the nature of history and historical enquiry, such that

---

[2] F. Morison, *Who Moved the Stone? A Skeptic Looks at the Death and Resurrection of Christ* (Grand Rapids: Zondervan, 1958 [1930]).

[3] 1 Cor. 15:14.

[4] See M. Rae, *History and Hermeneutics* (London: T&T Clark, 2005), p. 20, on the Jesus Seminar as an example of one such approach.

history is not centred on a method that can work only with observable data. Instead, it takes as its focus the entire Christ event, which lies at the heart of God's engagement with humanity in history.[5] It learns to deal with the possibility of a one-off event, such as the resurrection, which is just as historical as other events; it looks at everything through the prism of what has been revealed by God in Christ.[6] It adopts an epistemology, a way of knowing, that recognizes that belief has to do with knowledge and that this applies as much in history as it does in scientific knowledge.[7]

Turning to the Bible itself on this matter, Moses would probably not have defined himself as an historian, as moderns understand the term, and the tradition that has preserved the memory of him certainly does not do so. Moses was understood essentially as a prophet; indeed he came to be seen as the fountainhead of the prophetic tradition.[8] That same tradition refers to the historical material in the Old Testament (Joshua – 2 Kings) as the 'former prophets', suggesting that the early Jewish conception of history had in common with their understanding of prophecy that both discern the word of God speaking into humanity. Therefore, to the Hebrew writers of Scripture, the understanding and retelling of historical events is prophetic in that it entails discernment of God at work in space and time. The recovery of Jesus Christ as central to historical enquiry similarly conceives of history as the venue of God's speaking in Christ the incarnate Word.

Steeped as he was in both the 'mode of OT biblical history'[9] and his own contemporary Graeco-Roman categories of 'ancient historiography',[10] Luke, the writer of the third Gospel and the book of Acts, was acutely aware of the place of Jesus Christ in history. He was concerned to express the importance of those

[5] For more on this rich and important theme see L. Newbigin, *The Gospel in a Pluralist Society* (Grand Rapids: Eerdmans, 1989), pp. 103–115, on 'Christ, the Clue to History'.

[6] Rae, *History and Hermeneutics*, p. 48.

[7] See the chapter on 'Knowing and Believing: Faith in the Past', in I. Provan, V. P. Long and T. Longman, *A Biblical History of Israel* (Louisville: Westminster John Knox, 2003), pp. 36–50.

[8] J. E. Goldingay, *Old Testament Theology Volume One: Israel's Gospel* (Downers Grove: IVP, 2003), pp. 432–433.

[9] J. A. Fitzmyer, *The Gospel According to Luke (I–IX)*, AB 28 (New York: Doubleday, 1981), p. 290.

[10] J. B. Green, *The Gospel of Luke*, NICNT (Grand Rapids: Eerdmans, 1997), pp. 2–6. While there is some debate as to the exact genre being written by Luke, most agree that a recognizable form of historical writing is being undertaken. On the debate, see B. Witherington, 'The Preface of Luke-Acts and Historiography', *NTS* 31 (1985), pp. 576–581.

great historical events around the life of Jesus as the speech and acts of God, and to gather those events into a text in a way that would convey their power to later generations of readers. The brief preface with which he opens his Gospel addresses the very issues that have been outlined above. As one who has been described as 'historian and theologian',[11] his preface in Luke 1:1-4 is crucial to an understanding of the nature of the written record of God's work in history.

1. Stages of witness

A sense of time, the very stuff of history, is woven through the grammar of these few verses. In Greek, as similarly in English, the perfect tense stands in the present and looks back to a completed process. The perfect participle *that have been fulfilled* (1) speaks of past events that are operative at the moment that Luke writes. This present reality has its roots in the past in that it concerns things that *were handed down to us* (2). Here the tense is no longer perfect but aorist, that is, more likely to be related to completed actions in the past. The two verses (1 and 2) are linked by the comparative conjunction *just as* (2). One effect of this link is to equate the things that impact Luke's readers at the time of his writing (1) with a word that was previously passed down (2). Finally Luke shifts his focus again, this time onto Theophilus and his need to know the truth about *the certainty of . . . things* (4). Luke's sentiments towards Theophilus are couched in the present, but in fact now have a future cast. Luke's implicit desire is for Theophilus to carry into the future a truth that is presently held as a result of the witness of those in the past. As we will see further below, the present truths are of a kind with that which was *from the beginning* (3). In this way, what is written becomes a vehicle of the very acts to which the text bears witness.

2. The object of witness

There are several terms used to refer to what Luke is writing about: *things that have been fulfilled* (1); *the word* (2); *everything* (3); and *things* again (4). The Greek distinguishes between *pragmata* (*things*, 1) and *logoi* (*the word* and *things*, 2 and 4), and they are not quite the same as each other. The NRSV rendering for *pragmata*, 'events', is somewhat better than 'things', but still does not quite capture the

---

[11] I. H. Marshall, *Luke: Historian and Theologian* (Exeter: Paternoster, 1970).

implications of the word. The term has the sense of deeds or acts or ongoing states of affair. It generally conveys activity. For example, Luke's only other use of the term refers to the action of Ananias in lying about the proceeds from his field.[12] James 3:16 uses the word as part of a phrase translated as 'evil practice'. And several occurrences in the book of Hebrews refer to a range of divine activities or even 'realities'.[13] By using the plural noun *pragmata* Luke has taken us into the realm of activity, implicitly the activity of God.

At the same time the conjunction *just as*, which as we have seen links verses 1 and 2, also has the effect of equating *pragmata* with *logoi*. The 'events' or 'activities' that have been seen and experienced are summed up by Luke in verse 2 as *the word*. And so, with the equation of *pragmata* and *logoi*, we are back into speech-act territory. The word of God has been effective in bringing about certain actions and events in history. This identification of word and act is arguably inherent in the range of meaning of *logos* ('word') itself; Luke has effectively reinforced it by his parallel use of *pragmata* ('things' or 'events'). The task of the Gospel writer is to enshrine those actions by writing about them. Therein lies the task of the historian, according to this account. Not only does he or she provide a narrative of events and actions; he or she, like the prophetic witness of old, also discerns the activity and voice of God in what has been observed and experienced.[14]

3. The witnesses

This dynamic of encapsulating the speech-act of God is reinforced by a further equivalence between verses 1 and 2 around *just as* (2). The *eye witnesses and servants of the word* (2), who have thus far been handing down the word, are also equated with those who *have undertaken to draw up an account* (1). At this point it is important to clarify the meaning of the word translated as *servants*, *hypēretai*. In its ordinary sense it is a custodial term. Outside of Luke the Gospels use the term to refer to the guards or temple police.[15] Indeed, Luke himself also does so at Acts 5:22. Mostly, though, Luke uses the term to imply a guardianship of or support for a tradition or body of knowledge or set of texts. Jesus hands the scroll to a

---

[12] Acts 5:4.

[13] For example Heb. 10:1.

[14] D. L. Bock, *Luke Volume 1: 1:1–9:50*, BECNT (Grand Rapids: Baker, 1994), pp. 62–63.

[15] Matt. 5:25; 26:58; Mark 14:54; John 7:32; 18:3; 19:6.

hypēretēs after he has read from it;[16] John Mark is a *hypēretēs* to the proclamation of Saul and Barnabas;[17] Paul is so designated in his role as one who witnesses to what God has done.[18] Paul also links the function of *hypēretēs* to caring for the mysteries of God.[19] By means of this word, the eyewitness testimony to the acts of God appears to be linked to the care of the memory created by the eyewitnesses.[20]

Whether or not the care of that memory is a written one cannot be definitively determined by the word *hypēretēs* on its own. However that *eye witnesses and servants* (*hypēretēs*) (2) are paralleled with those who *draw up an account* (1) suggests that the written record is integral to the stewardship of the memory. From earliest times, the words and acts of God are both seen and recorded. As a result the acts of God in history continue on as the acts of God in the *word* that has been *handed down* (2).

4. The subject of witness

Talk of the acts of God brings us to the subject of this witness. What is it, according to Luke, that the recorded word of God is about? What are the acts for which the written historical record becomes a vehicle? First, they are *things that have been fulfilled* (1). As with several terms in this brief prologue, it is difficult to pin down what exactly is in mind with the word translated as 'fulfilled'. The TNIV plumps for 'have been fulfilled' but in a precautionary footnote wonders about 'been surely believed'. The term is only used five other times in the New Testament, and each of those cases entails certainty in the faith.[21] The one occurrence that is more like the Luke 1:1 usage is 2 Timothy 4:17, wherein the 'message' is 'fully proclaimed'. The meaning range of the Greek word used (*plēroō*), as much as it can be discerned from this small and rather diverse sample, is of something having come to fruition or arrived at a settled state. In this context, the 'events' (*pragmata*) about which Luke is writing a narrative have come to fruition in some way.

As a result of this emphasis, the narrative, or *account* (3), which Luke seeks to compile is not only of a particular group of events. He is also concerned to connect those events or acts to an earlier and longer story. Supposing that the *things* or events *among us* (1)

---

[16] Luke 4:20.
[17] Acts 13:5.
[18] Acts 26:6.
[19] 1 Cor. 4:1.
[20] J. Nolland, *Luke 1–9:20*, WBC 35A (Dallas: Word, 1989), p. 7.
[21] Rom. 4:21; 14:5; Col. 4:12; 2 Tim. 4:5.

are represented by the contents of the ensuing Gospel, we may take them to be the life and significance of Jesus, including his resurrection.[22] The history or account that Luke compiles then recognizes that Jesus brings to completion other events or acts of God. What that might include is subject to interpretation, but it is enough to note that part of the role of the written witness is to connect other events in human history to the programmatic event of the life, death and resurrection of Jesus Christ. So the Gospel is not only a life of Jesus; it sets a trajectory for an interpretation of history in the light of Jesus.

At this point the little hinge conjunction, *just as* (2), comes back into play. So far we have seen it serve to draw parallels between verses 1 and 2. Just as there are *things that have been fulfilled among us*, so also the *word* has been *handed down* by those *who from the first were eye witnesses and servants* (2). We have discussed the function of these *eye witnesses and servants*; now we can say a little more about who they are. On the face of it, they are the people responsible for maintaining a memory of the life of Jesus. But there is more to it than that, because the word *handed down* potentially includes the long record of the acts of God with the covenant people, such as those that we have looked at in the previous two chapters. Therefore, the early *eye witnesses and servants* were responsible for the memory of that which has been fulfilled by the presence of Jesus among us. As a result that memory, through its fulfilment in Jesus, becomes part of the ongoing word and work of God.

5. The nature of Luke's witness

Luke then decides that he too should write about Jesus. In the light of our discussion so far, there are several things to note about his approach to the task. First, although he uses different vocabulary, Luke's account is both in continuity and in discontinuity with what has gone before. He contrasts his own account as in some way discontinuous with those that others have *undertaken* (1) to write. The verb in question is a little too generously translated by TNIV as 'undertaken'. Luke is the only New Testament writer to use it, and then only on two other occasions.[23] Each time the verb clearly describes a failed attempt at something, and so it should probably be read here.[24] The recent narratives that have so far been drawn up

---

[22] R. H. Stein, 'Luke 1:1-4 and *Traditionsgeschichte*', *JETS* 26 (1983), p. 423.
[23] Acts 9:29; 19:13.
[24] Fitzmyer, *The Gospel According to Luke*, p. 291.

by others are considered by Luke to be unsatisfactory. On the other hand, he regards his account as in continuity with the word that has been *handed down* by the *eye witnesses and servants* (2). The verb 'to hand down' or 'to hand over' (*paradidōmi*) is a neutral one in that it can describe a handing over that is either negative or positive.[25] Luke sees his account as building on the memory and texts of the acts of God that have previously been passed down, however inadequately, and shaping them into a historical account that makes them available to his readers.

This continuity is further expressed in the distinction between the two phrases *from the first* (2) and *from the beginning* (3). The term translated as *from the first* is relatively straightforward. It carries a chronological sense and refers to the textual record to which Luke had access. However, the term used in verse 3, *from the beginning* (*anōthen*), is not a common adverb and is harder to pin down. Probably it refers not so much to a starting point as to the source or context of the account that Luke seeks to write. Often it is translated as 'from above' as if from God or heaven,[26] although it also may be used in a mundane sense.[27] Luke's single other use of the word has Paul telling Agrippa that his Jewish opponents have known him *anōthen*.[28] Although the easiest way to translate in that context is with 'from the beginning', it links with the more wide-ranging sense of the term in that it conveys that they have known Paul in the widest possible context.[29] In the same way, the account that Luke is setting out to write for Theophilus is an outcome of an investigation that tries to understand the events in question as fully as possible, in terms both of their connections with what has gone before and of the divine action that they encapsulate. Thus, an important feature of the history that Luke seeks to write is that it takes into account the divine encounter with the human.

Verse 3 also contains several words that describe the nature of Luke's investigations and his relationship to the events under examination. There are two adverbs, *akribōs* and *kathexēs*, which are hard to separate and together suggest *an orderly account*. They

---

[25] In a positive sense note from the LXX Gen. 27:20 and from the New Testament Matt. 25:14. But see Matt. 26:2 where it is used of handing over Jesus in betrayal. See 1 Cor. 15:3 for passing on the tradition. Nolland, *Luke 1–9:20*, p. 8.

[26] For example John 3:3, 7, 31; 19:11; Jas 3:15, 17.

[27] For example Matt. 27:51; Mark 15:38.

[28] Acts 26:5.

[29] L. Alexander, *The Preface to Luke's Gospel: Literary Convention and Social Context in Luke 1.1–4 and Acts 1.1*, SNTSMS 78 (Cambridge: Cambridge University Press, 1993), p. 130, suggests that the word '[conveys] a general impression of complete and thorough knowledge'.

describe an approach that is orderly and thorough and accurate.[30] It is anachronistic to read back into the verse what is today regarded as good practice in historical investigation, but Luke seems to be interested in producing something that can be relied upon (on which see more below). It will be an account that discerns what is important, that is comprehensive and that is useful because it explains in a way that is careful and accessible.

But this is more than simply the work of a good journalist. Luke's report emerges from having *investigated* (3) his subject. Like so much of Luke's vocabulary in this section, the Greek word in question (*parakoloutheō*) is infrequently used, but together the three other instances of the word imply accompanying or following or observing.[31] Its use suggests that Luke the historian is reporting on something that he has come to know thoroughly from the inside, and to which he has a deep personal commitment. For Luke there is no 'ugly ditch' between theology and history. His account of the life and significance of Jesus is as thorough and careful and comprehensible as it can be, with a concern to connect what he finds with all that is already known, just as any good modern approach to history should be. At the same time it is earthed in a deep commitment to what he is writing about. His is a way of knowing that understands instinctively what postmodernity is helping us rediscover, that knowing is earthed in commitment and belief; and that history is always 'interested' in the sense that it is always undertaken from a particular point of view. Whatever else it may be, history for Luke is an account of the acts of God.

6. The result of witness

The result of the process of witness that Luke describes is, first, personal. It is an account *for you, most excellent Theophilus* (3). All the careful recording of the witness to Jesus and what he fulfils is with a view to connecting a particular individual with these events. The emphatic form of expression with both the personal singular pronoun *you* and the name of Luke's reader reinforces this. The work of Luke and other *eye witnesses and servants* (2), along with the narratives they have formed and the memories they have handed down, enable later individuals to encounter the events and words that they have preserved. As we have seen, this entails encountering

---

[30] See the extended discussion by Fitzmyer, *The Gospel According to Luke*, pp. 298–299, on the force of these two words.
[31] Elsewhere in Mark 16:17; 1 Tim. 4:6; 2 Tim. 3:10.

the word and actions of God for themselves. As for Theophilus, so is our experience of the words of Scripture.

Like Theophilus, we are in a later generation of readers for whom the encounter with Jesus specifically, and with the activity of God generally, is by means of the text. Luke understands that for such readers, a random sample of oral memories passed on by particular individuals is not enough. Even allowing for the operation of the Holy Spirit in such transactions of memory,[32] this state of affairs does not create *certainty* (4). Luke is concerned that Theophilus know this certainty. The word translated as *certainty* (*asphaleia*) is another uncommon word, used only on one other occasion by Luke and once by Paul.[33] In Acts it speaks of a securely locked prison door, and Paul uses it to describe the complacent 'safety' of those unready for the day of the Lord. It conveys the type of certainty that comes from feeling secure and out of danger as much as from being in possession of the truth. This is the sort of security that Luke desires for Theophilus. For those who read Luke's text in the generations that followed Theophilus, the words of Scripture provide security against what Peter calls 'the prophet's own interpretation of things'.[34] Idiosyncratic interpretation is a constant danger when our ongoing encounter with the work and words of God is not through the careful ordering of the memory and the acts of God of the sort for which Luke is striving.

From that early consciousness of a programmatic encounter with God at the foot of Mount Sinai, the people of God understood the responsibility to preserve that encounter for others.[35] They also understood the responsibility to transmit what was preserved as a means by which later generations could have the same encounter.[36] The security that comes with knowing God truly, in Luke's understanding, partly entails this transmission or, in his terms, teaching or catechesis (4). But the teaching is not sufficient of itself. As time moves on from the events of which the eyewitnesses have spoken, it is important to test the teaching constantly against what has been written *from the first* (2) and *from the beginning* (3). Together the teaching and the written record bring a *certainty* or 'security' within which the very words and acts of God in history become the word and act of God in the life of later readers. The placing of the Greek word *aspheleian* (*certainty*) at the end of the long complex sentence

[32] See ch. 5 on 2 Pet. 1:19–21.
[33] Acts 5:23; 1 Thess. 5:3.
[34] 2 Pet. 1:20.
[35] See ch. 6 on Exod. 19.
[36] See ch. 7 on Deut. 4:9.

that comprises Luke 1:1–4 emphasizes the importance of this outcome in Luke's mind.[37] In this way, theology and history work together to discern the work of God in human affairs.[38]

[37] Fitzmyer, *The Gospel According to Luke*, p. 300.
[38] I. I. du Plessis, 'Once More: The Purpose of Luke's Prologue (Lk 1 1–4)', *NovT* 16 (1974), p. 271, concludes that Luke is concerned to deliver 'a true report of *God acting in history*' (emphasis original).

John 2:13–25
9. The Scriptures and the resurrection of the Word

In the course of Christian life we often encounter things that are difficult to understand. In light of the sovereignty of God, are human beings truly free? If God is the creator of all things, how can evil be explained?[1] These are but two examples of questions for which the Bible seems not to provide neatly packaged answers. There are also technical questions that remain essentially inscrutable or subject to historical debate with godly people on both sides. Who wrote the letter to the Hebrews? How many times did Jesus cleanse the temple, and if once was it at the beginning or end of his earthly ministry? But perhaps the most puzzling of all are the more personal questions that arise when human experience does not seem to square with Christian teaching. Where is the love of God when a young bride is diagnosed with cancer on her honeymoon and dies within two months of her marriage? In light of the sanctity of marriage, why do some people blossom in Christian service in the wake of a divorce? How do I respond to a friend or relative whose devotion to Jesus is as real as mine and who has come to accept that being gay is part of his discipleship? Sometimes the Bible seems silent in the face of such things. At such moments, 'divine discourse', the notion that God speaks and may be understood by human beings is reduced to a theoretical concept.

When I was beginning my theological study, a wise mentor encouraged me to open a mental 'suspense account'. He anticipated in me a youthful inclination, when encountering things I did not understand or could not reconcile with my own opinions, to rush to

---

[1] I am doing a final revision of this chapter as the death toll from an earthquake in Christchurch, the city of my roots, is steadily rising towards 200. At such a time hard questions are the order of the day.

inadequate explanations or too readily to reject people or ideas that I did not understand. A suspense account is a way of putting problems into storage against the day when life experience and greater maturity may eventually bring peace about some of life's puzzles. Rather than rush to conclusions, my mentor was saying to me, sometimes it is best to allow the questions to mature and to wait for greater understanding in God's time. It is also a way of acknowledging that there are some things that we, as finite human beings, will never fully explain until we meet Jesus face to face, which in itself is another reason for humility in the face of life's big questions.

Another way of thinking about this search for understanding in conversation with the Scriptures is through the linguistic category of relevance.[2] Relevance Theory is a branch of pragmatic linguistics which looks at the place of inference in human communication.[3] Essentially this theory proposes that in order for successful communication to occur, relevance must be achieved. One of the requirements for relevance is the existence of an optimum amount of shared knowledge between the speaker/writer and listener/reader. If a communicator is telling me nothing that I do not already know, or is not reframing my knowledge in some way, then I stop listening. On the other hand, if a communicator is speaking in terms that are too much at odds with my own experience or understanding, I will then stop listening also. In neither case will relevance have been achieved, and so successful communication will not have occurred. A listener perceives relevance when there is enough in common with the speaker for the discourse to be comprehensible or acceptable, enough shared knowledge for the listener to be able to *infer* the speaker's intent, but also enough that is new for the discourse to be interesting or useful.

There is a two-way responsibility for achieving relevance. The speaker or writer must communicate in a way that is accessible to his or her audience; at the same time, the listener or reader has a responsibility to connect as much as possible to the world out of which the speaker or writer speaks or writes. Even when those responsibilities are exercised, however, there are times when understanding is not achieved. This is sometimes the case in the reading of Scripture. Indeed, it is the nature of the case that there is always

---

[2] I have previously promised not to burden the reader with linguistic theory, but seek forgiveness for this brief interlude in Relevance Theory.

[3] On this concept see A. Pilkington, 'Introduction: Relevance Theory and Literary Style', *Language and Literature* 5 (1996), p. 157. On Relevance Theory as a whole and its applicability to Scripture see S. W. Pattemore, *The People of God in the Apocalypse: Discourse, Structure, and Exegesis*, SNTSMS 128 (Cambridge: Cambridge University Press, 2003), pp. 13–50.

further understanding of the words of God just out of reach of our human capacity. God is not inaccessible, as we have seen, but there is always more to know. When relevance in communication with God is not achieved through Bible reading, this does not necessarily mean the subject matter of a communication is not relevant. Rather, it is time for the suspense account, until the time when the hearer or reader finds sufficient shared knowledge or experience to reconnect with what has been puzzling.

In their encounters with Jesus, the disciples had many occasions on which to use a suspense account. They encountered many things that they did not understand, and that only became clear to them in the light of the resurrection. One such occasion was the cleansing of the temple, which John's Gospel records at the start of the public ministry of Jesus.[4] That event and its functioning as a *sign* (23) is interesting and instructive in a range of ways, but in the context of this volume our focus is on the immediate aftermath in which the disciples process what they have seen, since that has implications for our understanding of how Scripture functions as the word of God.

1. An anatomy of belief

Jesus' cleansing of the temple no doubt resulted in some annoyed merchants, confused birds and livestock, and possibly some happy looters as the gathered crowd vacuumed up the scattered coins. But the significant upshot from John's perspective was belief. After all that transpired, *then they believed* (22). The account of the incident concludes with the author's postscript on the nature of belief (23–25).

There seem to be four elements working dynamically together to induce the belief of the disciples. First there is the *sign* of the cleansing itself. Then there is the fact that Jesus was *raised from the dead* (22). The next thing that is mentioned is *the Scripture* (22), and finally *the words that Jesus had spoken* (22). This is the order in which they appear in the Gospel account.

The impact of each on the disciples themselves would have been in a different order. We may assume first a long acquaintance with the Scriptures to which John refers. The group of disciples brought varying degrees of prior religious observance with them to their acquaintance with Jesus. Nathaniel, for instance, seems to have

---

[4] The Synoptic Gospels place such an event at the end of Jesus' ministry rather than at the start, which has occasioned some debate. For a succinct summary of the issue see C. Kruse, *John*, TNTC (Leicester: IVP, 2003), p. 98.

been a devout man, but Matthew the tax collector was perhaps more worldly wise. Whatever the case, for some of the disciples at least, the words and actions of Jesus must often have called to mind readings they had heard in the synagogue, or commentary on those readings from a targum[5] or a local rabbi. We could suppose that they must have been constantly processing what they observed in the light of the religious tradition in which they lived, and that this would have been happening at an individual and group level. What we now call the Old Testament and the tradition of its interpretation would have been vital in this process. The disciples encountered both the words and signs of Jesus in the light of that prior knowledge. At any given instance, such as the cleansing of the temple, they would have had cause to recall both Jesus' words and the Scriptures that were then available to them. On the evidence of this passage, this created some puzzles. What on earth did Jesus mean when he said he would *raise [the temple] again in three days* (19), for instance? There was nothing in Scripture that they knew of to shed light on this. Understanding only dawned later once the significance of the fourth element in the anatomy of belief, the resurrection of Jesus, became apparent. Together the signs and words of Jesus, the reading of Scripture, and finally the resurrection brought belief. Or, in the linguistic terms suggested above, relevance in communication was achieved.[6]

2. Jesus and Scripture

This process is further elucidated by two pairings that are implicit in the postscript to the event: first, the sign of Jesus' action and the words of Jesus; and, secondly, *the Scripture* and *the words that Jesus had spoken* (22). We will look at the second pair first. TNIV has used the plural *words* to translate the singular *logos*,[7] but the problem with the plural is its implication that the message of Jesus in which the disciples believed is confined to his particular words about the

---

[5] The synagogue readings of Scripture were always in the Hebrew of the Bible, which was no longer spoken as mother tongue in the Palestine of Jesus' day. The targums were explanatory translations into the Aramaic spoken by most ordinary Jews in Palestine, and were read alongside the formally appointed portions of Hebrew Scripture.

[6] This emphasis on communication could sound like another example of the Christian habit of talking too much and doing too little. But remember that we have been thinking of the word of God as a speech-act. So when I talk about communication I am assuming something that leads to action.

[7] Compare NRSV: 'the word that Jesus had spoken.'

sign of the cleansing of the temple.[8] The singular *logos* ('word'), on the other hand, may imply the message or wider import of all that Jesus was about. We have seen already that the 'word' in Hebrew often carries that broader sense of 'matter' or 'thing'. Although the most immediate context of 'the word' of Jesus is his enigmatic reference to destroying the temple (19), the narrator's use of *logos* potentially includes a more comprehensive reflection on the dynamic whereby Scripture and the message embodied by the entire life and work of Jesus together lead to belief.[9]

Neither Scripture nor the personal encounter with Jesus on their own achieved belief, in the sense of a true connection between the word of God and those who encounter it. As we have seen, the intention of scriptural text was always that it become a vehicle of the very speech-act of God to those who encounter it.[10] And the New Testament reinforces this expectation. It is also true, though, that the words of the text have the potential to become trapped by the text itself, to become simply an object rather than a living partner in the discourse between God and humanity.[11] Much of Jesus' struggle with the Pharisees of his day was around that very issue, but the problem was not new or unique to the late Second Temple period. It had been anticipated by the writing prophets who called for a religion as much of the heart as of the book. Jeremiah for example envisaged a new covenant of the heart. This would be a covenant within which all God's people would 'know [God], from the least of them to the greatest'.[12] It would be a knowing not by means of a covenant of the book, which the covenants of Moses and David had become for those to whom Jeremiah spoke. The call for a covenant of the heart is not merely as a result of human hardness of heart. It also reflects the constant tension felt by believing readers of Scripture between confidence that in the text itself we find the very words of God and realization that the text is not effective unless the God of the text is encountered by means of the text.

Looking at the other side of the Scripture/word of Jesus pairing – the word of Jesus – the Gospels illustrate over and over again that simply encountering Jesus in the flesh did not achieve belief. This is perhaps most explicitly addressed in Jesus' struggles with his

---

[8] The assumption of most commentators. See for example A. J. Köstenberger, *John*, BECNT (Grand Rapids: Baker Academic, 2004), p. 110.

[9] H. Ridderbos, *The Gospel According to John: A Theological Commentary*, tr. J. Vriend (Grand Rapids: Eerdmans, 1997), p. 121.

[10] See particularly ch. 7 on Deut. 4:1–20.

[11] J. K. A. Smith, 'The Closing of the Book: Pentecostals, Evangelicals, and the Sacred Writings', *JPT* 11 (1997), pp. 49–71, explores this effect.

[12] Jer. 31:31–34.

opponents. When the Pharisees ask for a sign, he remarks that a sign on its own is not necessarily sufficient to induce belief.[13] An earlier remark of his implies that Jesus' presence among the people is itself a sign that may be wilfully ignored.[14] Hence neither the words of Scripture nor the work of Jesus are guaranteed to put people into communication with God. In the terms that we have been using over the last few chapters, neither the speech of God (the Scriptures) nor the act of God (as the incarnation of God in Jesus) on their own are necessarily effective.

3. Signs and words

The pairing that I identified as the first that emerges in the Gospel writer's reflection is captured in the phrase, *After he was raised from the dead, his disciples recalled what he had said* (22). In this instance, the phrase *what he had said* suggests the more specific reference to Jesus' words concerning the destruction of the temple and his raising it in three days (19). The other half of the pair, Jesus' actions in the temple, is implied by the context of the author's reflection. Jesus has just released the animals and poured out the money changers' coins onto the floor of the temple court. Next there was an exchange about the significance of his actions, which leaves everybody flummoxed by Jesus' promise to raise a destroyed temple in three days. Then we are told that the disciples remembered his words after his resurrection, with the implication that at that point they made sense of his earlier actions in the temple. So this comment draws together both the words of Jesus and his actions. Verse 23 refers to the *signs* that Jesus *was performing*, and in this context I read the cleansing of the temple as one of those signs.[15] This takes us back into speech-act territory. The words of Jesus and the enacted sign in this instance come together to form the active word of God. Yet at the time neither the words of Jesus nor his actions made much sense to the disciples in the state of their knowledge and experience to that point.

---

[13] Matt. 12:38–42.

[14] Matt. 11:16–19.

[15] In John's Gospel a sign need not be miraculous. It is any action or event that serves as a signpost to God. The cleansing of the temple was one such. F. J. Moloney, *The Gospel of John*, SP4 (Collegeville: Liturgical Press, 1994), p. 84.

4. The resurrection

In both the pairings that we have looked at above the missing link is the raising of Jesus from the dead. In the first pair examined, the more general point is made that the Scriptures and the message of Jesus are together believed once Jesus has been raised. Secondly, the particular disjunction between the sign enacted by Jesus in the temple and his subsequent words of explanation is now resolved in light of the resurrection.

Part of what is going on is a subtle, and typically Johannine, play on words. The verb used of the raising of the temple is *egeirō* (19, 20). While this verb could be used in classical Greek of the erection of buildings, it is never so used by the New Testament writers. It is occasionally deployed to speak of a person being aroused or awakened,[16] but it is overwhelmingly used when speaking of the resurrection of Jesus, and indeed of raising others from the dead also.[17] As a result, the writer's use of *egeirō* with reference to rebuilding the temple is an unmistakable literary identification of Jesus with the temple itself.[18] That is part of what is going on in these verses with reference to the resurrection.

But the link between relevance or understanding and the resurrection is more than a literary play on words. The pairing of the 'word' of Jesus and the Scriptures serves to lift the significance of the resurrection from this particular exchange into the realm of the word of God more generally. In the light of Jesus' resurrection from the dead, the message of his life and the words in the text of Scripture work together as the word of God. The resurrection, according to John's Gospel, is the clincher in this process. The resurrection enables true discourse to occur between God and those who encounter Jesus and the text that bears witness to him. In the light of the resurrection, relevance is achieved in the sense that the personal encounter with God made possible by that event creates a shared environment within which the words of Scripture may be understood. This point is reinforced by the authorial aside in John 20:9.[19] Peter and John reach the empty tomb but 'they still did not understand from Scripture that Jesus had to rise from the dead'. Once a personal encounter with the living Lord is established then the Scriptures are able to speak fully. There is then enough that is shared by both text and reader for the word of God to communicate with the disciples.

[16] For example Matt. 1:24; 2:13; Mark 2:9.
[17] Several examples among many are Mark 14:28; Acts 13:30; 1 Cor. 15:4.
[18] G. M. Burge, *John*, NIVAC (Grand Rapids: Zondervan, 2000), p. 97.
[19] In similar vein see also John 12:16.

In the vision of the Gospel writer this dynamic is intimately associated with belief, a link to which we turn below. But first, a brief excursus on history is in order. As we saw in the previous chapter, for Luke history is an account of the acts of God, acts which have come to be encapsulated in the text in such a way that the text becomes a means by which God may continue to act and speak with later readers of the text. It is a history written from the standpoint of belief and in the light of the resurrection of Jesus. The Gospel of John takes this a step further in at least two ways. First, it does so with its focus on the resurrection as the defining moment in the history of God's involvement with humanity. In the light of the resurrection everything begins to come into focus. The words of Jesus, the signs that he did, and indeed the fullness of his life as a whole and the Scriptures that have so far foreshadowed him and will go on in the New Testament to record him, all of these are brought to coherence by God's raising of Jesus from the dead. The resurrection enables an encounter between the living Lord and humankind, such that the words and word of God now achieve relevance in the minds and hearts of those who read the Scripture.[20]

In terms of the ugly ditch between theology and history, with which I began the discussion on Luke 1:1–4,[21] if this ditch is to be traversed by an appreciation of history as a discernment of the acts of God in the world that God has made, then the resurrection is indispensible. It cannot be somehow factored out as beyond historical enquiry. For it is only in the light of the resurrection that history can be appreciated in terms of the acts of God. Furthermore, the personal encounter with the risen Lord made possible through the resurrection introduces people to a plane of experience that enables a new type of relevance to be achieved, a relevance that can glimpse the hand of God in people and events. In light of the shared experience that this encounter brings, the resurrection itself becomes inherently plausible and therefore a necessary part of the historical endeavour to understand the world and our part in it. As we live and grow in the light of the resurrection of Jesus, we find that our commonality with the text of Scripture also grows, and increasingly we are able to hear the voice of God in the text of Scripture. In the process, gradually the items on our suspense accounts are dealt with.[22] Or, to put it another way, Scripture

---

[20] The presence of the Holy Spirit is a crucial element in this process. For further on this aspect, see ch. 19 on John 14:15–26.

[21] See ch. 8.

[22] This is not a neat linear process, of course. The suspense account continues to take deposits as well as issue withdrawals throughout our lives.

becomes more and more relevant in the light of the experience of the resurrection.

5. Belief

As we have noted, in the passage under examination the outcome is belief. However, belief in John's Gospel is varied in expression. On one hand, the goal of the Gospel writer is 'that you may believe'.[23] On the other, there are numerous examples of inadequate belief. Many who once believed turned away in the face of Jesus' hard teaching.[24] We might suppose that some of those were among the many who saw him overturn the money changers' tables and release the livestock, and consequently *believed in his name* (23). The text is clear that their signs-based belief could not be enduring.[25] At the same time, the Gospel writer himself knows that the production of his text on its own cannot ensure belief any more than witnessing a spectacular sign is able to do so. That is why we have these occasional asides on the range of factors that together create life-giving faith, crucial among which is the resurrection of Jesus.

So far in this volume the focus has been on the written text of Scripture as both the word of God and vehicle for the word of God. With the Gospel writers a shift begins to occur towards consideration of the living Word of God, Jesus. Now a partnership begins to emerge between Jesus and the text. The Scriptures remain vital but their vitality is inseparable from the one whom they foreshadow and to whom they bear witness. Gradually we are being drawn to the third proposition of this volume, which is that God speaks in Christ. Before turning to that proposition, however, we will look in the next chapter at the practice of Jesus himself in handling Scripture. In doing so, we will witness something of the dynamic that occurs when the written word of God encounters Jesus, the incarnate Word of God.

---

[23] John 20:31. There is an unresolved debate as to whether this entails drawing people into new belief or nurturing them in an existing belief. Both readings work and both should be entertained by the reader. R. E. Brown, *The Gospel According to John XIII–XXI*, AB 29A (New York: Doubleday, 1970), p. 1056, presents both views.

[24] John 6:66.

[25] Köstenberger, *John*, p. 116.

Matthew 12:1–21
10. The Scriptures interpreted and fulfilled by Jesus

'The law is an ass,' said Mr Bumble in Charles Dickens' tale of *Oliver Twist*. Mr Bumble's remark was in response to the proposition that 'the law supposes that your wife acts under your direction'.[1] His riposte was that the law must be a bachelor if it thinks that! There are occasions when what probably began as a sensible law has, under changing conditions, gradually lost contact with the realities of day-to-day experience or begun to create unintended effects. Mr Bumble is reflecting how the traditional English common law of coverture (the merging of a woman's legal rights with those of her husband) hardened into later systematization of relationships between the sexes. In my own country, privacy legislation seems to have unintended effects when one is attempting to act as next of kin or advocate for somebody in the clutches of some aspect of the public system. Sometimes interpreters and enforcers of the law are as much asses as the law itself. Yet everybody – legislator and implementer – means well, and nobody would dispute that privacy laws and property laws and all sorts of other laws are necessary to the ordering of a peaceful and just society. The trouble is that human life has a transcendent dimension that can never be fully expressed in a set of written rules, and so cannot be satisfactorily implemented merely by an unimaginative application of those rules.

This same paradox appears in the human encounter with the divine. We can only connect to God by means of various institutions that are at least partly the product of human enterprise. Christians are called into community, and human beings cannot help but give this calling institutional expression in the form of congregations and denominations and parachurch organizations and the hierarchies

[1] Charles Dickens, *Oliver Twist* (London: Chapman & Hall, 1858), p. 420.

that go with them. All of these things are necessary, yet each can become an end in itself. When that happens the institutional expression of faith can become a diversion from engagement with the call of God, rather than a means by which that call is expressed. One common response is to reject all institutional expression of the faith, but that fails to take into account that God meets us in our humanity and not in some unearthly dimension. We must constantly hold together commitment to God through allegiance to human expressions of that commitment, with a recognition that the human expressions themselves are conditional and temporary.

This struggle is also discernible in the dynamics around the text of Scripture as the word of God. We have seen a variety of motivations behind the formation of the text, and have suggested that together they add up to the ongoing availability of the word and action of God for subsequent generations of believers. We have also begun to see that inherent in the process of turning the word of God into a text is the ironic human potential to take the text *per se* as an end in itself, and in so doing to reduce the word of God to something less than it was ever intended to be. It can become the object of academic historical and antiquarian study (and in the process a vehicle for realizing academic ambition). It can become a family heirloom. It can become a set of rules used to prescribe behaviour. It can become an instrument of oppression. Or, on the other side of the same coin, it can become a licence for undisciplined and egotistical behaviour. Whenever this happens, the text that is the very word of God, the Bible, is placed in danger of muting the voice of God. Much of Jesus' earthly ministry involved confronting this phenomenon. One example was his running battle with the Pharisees over Sabbath observation. Matthew 12:1–21 contains one such incident, which can be read as indicative of Jesus' response to those who lose sight of the speech-act of God within the institutions that are intended to contain it.[2]

1. The Pharisees' position

The Pharisees began with the noblest of intentions. There is debate over their roots but it is likely that they could trace their

[2] Language is always tricky when these things are being discussed, and it is the nature of divine-human encounters that language is never quite adequate. In this context I am discussing dynamics arising from the distinction between the Bible and the word of God and so I speak of Scripture *containing* the word of God. This is not to deny what I have argued also in earlier chapters, that Scripture *is* the word of God.

spiritual ancestry back to the reaction against the excesses of the later Hasmonean rulers of Judah who emerged in the wake of the successful Maccabean revolt against their Greek overlords in the second century BC.[3] In implementing their highly nationalist vision of Judaism, these rulers took the high priesthood under their control, thus violating a long-held principle that the offices of king and high priesthood should be separate.[4] It would be anachronistic to equate this with modern notions of the separation of church and state, for the king was always responsible for the health of the religious system generally and the interests of its officers in particular. Yet there was always a sense that there were affairs in which the king should not interfere, an idea that arguably reaches as far back as God's refusal to allow David to build the temple.[5] In reaction to Hasmonean nationalism, the *chasidim*, the precursors to the Pharisees, responded with a call to return to the *torah* as a much truer connection with Yahweh than that offered by the Hasmonean regime. The Pharisees retained this focus on the priority of preserving the integrity of the *torah*. By the time of the period covered by the Gospels, the opponents of that approach were the Sadducees, who had become highly politicized and interested in the preservation of political power through accommodation with their pagan occupiers.[6]

Ironically, this impetus to get to the heart of the law resulted in a range of provisions that could be as unyielding and distracting as the nationalism the Pharisees sought to counter. I say 'could be' because it is clear that there were some Pharisees who remained true to a quest for relationship with the God of Israel. Nicodemus and Gamaliel are examples.[7] We see more of the other in the Gospels, though, because their opposition to Jesus is so much a part of his own self-definition.

One area that absorbed much Pharisaic energy was the keeping of the Sabbath.[8] It is hardly surprising, then, that it becomes a point of contention with Jesus, and the Pharisees' grievance about Jesus' approach to the Sabbath symbolic of larger wedges between the two

---

[3] *NIDB* 4, p. 491–492.

[4] L. L. Grabbe, *Judaism from Cyrus to Hadrian* (London: SCM, 1994), pp. 308–311.

[5] 2 Sam. 7.

[6] Grabbe, *Judaism*, pp. 484–487.

[7] John 3:1–9; 19:39; Acts 5:34.

[8] For examples of Pharisaic law on the Sabbath see C. Rowland, 'A Summary of Sabbath Observance in Judaism at the Beginning of the Christian Era', in D. A. Carson (ed.), *From Sabbath to Lord's Day: A Biblical, Historical and Theological Investigation* (Grand Rapids: Zondervan, 1982), p. 48.

parties. In the passage we are looking at, the presenting incident is a trivial one. The disciples are walking through the fields and *began to pick some ears of corn and eat them* (1). Although the writer prefaces the action with the note that they *were hungry* (1), presumably they could have done without the grain. At the same time, there is no hint of any wrongdoing apart from the Sabbath issue. In a society where agriculture was a clan-based and communal enterprise, this was quite normal behaviour.[9] Nevertheless, in such a society there are also few secrets and the Pharisees quickly hear of their action and decide to interpret it as Sabbath-breaking.

Their position roughly is that any work on the Sabbath, with some clearly delineated exceptions around saving life and protecting one's family, breaks the *torah*.[10] Later on Jesus presses them on this point with a much less trivial instance when the Pharisees effectively challenge him to heal on the Sabbath (10). His reputation as a healer is by now well established in the locality, and when the Pharisees spot a disabled man in the synagogue on the Sabbath in the presence of Jesus they press the point. Jesus unhesitatingly picks up the challenge and heals the *man with a shriveled hand* (10, 13). Indeed, the easily-overlooked pronoun *their* (9), as in *their [the Pharisees'] synagogue* implies that Jesus may even have gone looking for a more substantial confrontation over the Sabbath issue than that provided by the grain-picking incident, one that would better illustrate the call to mercy.[11] He found that in the opportunity to heal the disabled man at the home ground, so to speak, of his Pharisaic opponents. In any case, he could presumably have waited until sundown and the end of the Sabbath to heal the man; it was not a life-or-death matter. But he chose to make the point.[12] Having by now run out of arguments, the response of the Pharisees nevertheless makes their disapproval of Jesus' action unmistakable: they *went out and plotted how they might kill* him (14). To them, neither human welfare nor the fundamental purpose of the Sabbath is a relevant consideration. The important thing is the definition of what constitutes work on the Sabbath day. In this way the institution has become more important than the essence.

---

[9] Deut. 23:25.

[10] J. M. Hicks, 'The Sabbath Controversy in Matthew: An Exegesis of Matthew 12:1–14', *Restoration Quarterly* 27 (1984), pp. 79–91.

[11] See for example D. A. Hagner, *Matthew 1–13*, WBC 33A (Dallas: Word, 1993), p. 333.

[12] B. Witherington, *Matthew*, SHBC (Macon: Smyth & Helwys, 2006), p. 242.

2. The paradox of religious institution

Part of Jesus' response to the problem of the Sabbath is to illustrate the paradox at the heart of its observance. The Sabbath is a day of rest in response to a command of God to keep it holy 'to the Lord your God'.[13] Yet how can the holiness of the Sabbath 'to the Lord' be expressed without some form of associated religious observance? And how may this observance occur unless the priests, in the words of Jesus, *desecrate the Sabbath* (5) by working to enable the people to worship? It is not possible, as even the Pharisees are compelled to recognize. The Sabbath cannot be kept by most people unless it is broken by some people. There are other similar paradoxes, albeit from a different direction. If the Sabbath must be broken to be kept, there are other commandments that may be broken while still being kept.[14] People like the rich young man can observe all the provisions of the *torah* and yet be no closer to God.[15] Others can keep the ten commandments to the letter yet still harbour the seeds of murder and lust in their hearts; their observance has not drawn them one jot closer to God,[16] despite the law's intent in that direction.

This links back to something we observed at the start of this section on God's word in the text (ch. 6). While the law was being given at Mount Sinai there was an interesting dynamic occurring at the base of the mountain, centred on the Hebrew concept of the 'ban' (*ḥērem*), which we likened to the concept in some cultures of what the Maori term *tapu*. The people of God were required to make themselves holy, to set themselves apart for the encounter with God in the giving of the law.[17] At the same time the mountain itself was holy in a way that expressed the holiness of God.[18] The two were not to come together. Somehow, though, once again paradoxically, despite the otherness of God from God's people, a covenant was made between the two parties. The set apartness or holiness of each was overcome. Yet the inner contradiction so created did not go away. The difference between God and the *torah* which is expressive of God kept intruding into the covenant between God and his people. As a result, the law may be observed in a way that actually violates the covenant relationship, and the law sometimes needs to be broken in the service of that same relationship.

---

[13] Exod. 20:10.
[14] See in ch. 13 on the so-called antitheses of Jesus in Matt. 5.
[15] Matt. 19:22.
[16] Matt. 5:21–30.
[17] Exod. 19:10–12.
[18] Exod. 19:23.

3. The response of Jesus

Jesus responds to the Pharisees by recognizing that the conflict is at least partly around how the Scriptures should be read. Twice he uses the phrase, *haven't you read?* (3, 5). He also comments, *If you had known what these words mean . . .* (7). The Pharisees' approach to Sabbath-keeping arose from their reading of Scripture. As it evolved, this reading placed a priority on the literal maintenance of the holiness of the day without regard to other reading that paid attention to the reason that the Sabbath was given as a gift to humanity. Jesus points out that there are things they have missed in their reading. In particular he refers them back to Hosea 6:6, in which God says through the prophet: *I desire mercy, not sacrifice* (7). The point being made by the prophet is that the Israelites' observance of the law, which was intended as a bridge, had become a barrier between God and the people. The people had lost sight of its purpose, which was relationship, not ritual for its own sake. This is summed up by Jesus in the epithet, 'mercy, not sacrifice'. The Pharisees had allowed their reading of the text to distract them from the very purpose of the text, which was encounter with the speech and action of God and hence relationship with him.

At one level, the debate between Jesus and the Pharisees was a hermeneutical one. In such debates, each side habitually claims that their reading is the one that best captures the heart of the matter. For the Pharisees the heart of the matter was the holiness of the Sabbath day. For Jesus, it was the human and relational purpose of the Sabbath. Each side also has a principle of reading backing their interpretation. For the Pharisees it was the integrity of the religious system given by the *torah*, everything that is encapsulated in the 'sacrifice' side of Jesus' 'mercy, not sacrifice' epithet. For Jesus it was everything encapsulated by the 'mercy' side of the epithet, for which he claims scriptural backing from the prophet Hosea.

So the scene is set for Jesus to meet the man with the withered hand. The Pharisees ask, *Is it lawful to heal on the Sabbath?* (10) Jesus responds with the simple agricultural example of a valuable animal that gets into trouble. Would a farmer deal with the sheep down a pit, even on the Sabbath? Of course he would. And so, Jesus concludes, *it is lawful to do good on the Sabbath* (12). Not to do so would be a denial of the holiness of the Sabbath to the Lord, for it would be a denial of the character of the God who is being honoured on that day. Earlier Jesus had referred to an incident in the life of David when the priest Ahimalek gave him some of the *consecrated bread* (4) from the shrine of Nob because there was no other available to feed David and his men. In the original account, this action is justified on the grounds that David and his men are already ritually pure.[19] The point that Jesus makes is the more general one that the Sabbath is routinely compromised in the cause of the greater good to which the Sabbath points, in this case the well-being of God's servant David. And so how much the more should this principle apply for the healing of a human being.

All of this is a sobering reminder that although God speaks in the written word, God's voice may be silenced by readers of that same word. The paradox inherent in the Pharisees' response to the Sabbath continues through into the very text of Scripture itself. It can be read in such a way that, instead of ushering its readers into God's presence, it conceals God.

4. Something 'greater than the temple'

This is more than a debate over whose reading is best, though. It is also about the very nature of the word of God in the written words of Scripture. In his response to the Pharisees, Jesus implicitly extrapolates out from the Sabbath issue into the much wider question of his relationship to the religious system of the day. That extrapolation is inherent in his assertion that *one greater than the temple is here* (6). The word translated as *one greater* (6) is a neuter adjective, hence more literally 'a greater thing' (*meizon*). By using this particular turn of phrase Jesus turns attention to something more than the person named Jesus present on the day in which and at the place where this conversation takes place. He points his hearers to the broader phenomenon of the incarnation, the incursion of God into the life of humanity and the world in which God has set humanity.[20] Jesus thereby implies that if the significance of the person of Jesus was truly understood, then this would guide their reading of the Scriptures. All that is represented by the physical *temple* (6) is no longer the guiding paradigm.

But still there is more. If that was all there was to say, then Jesus would be no more than the winning contestant in a game of hermeneutical chess. But he is not only *greater than the temple* (6); he, as the *Son of Man*, is also *Lord of the Sabbath* (8). The significance of this for reading is that an understanding of how to keep the Sabbath as 'to the Lord your God'[21] is arrived at by knowing Jesus as Lord of the Sabbath. This is also tied up with how the Scriptures that are

---

[19] 1 Sam. 21:1–6.
[20] L. Morris, *The Gospel According to Matthew* (Leicester: IVP, 1992), p. 303.
[21] Exod. 20:10.

about the Sabbath are read. If they are read in the light of the incarnate Jesus then they truly are revelatory of God's word.[22]

The point is reinforced as Jesus withdraws and continues his healing ministry away from the limelight of official interrogation (15). This leads to a narrative aside from Matthew to the effect that in his actions Jesus embodies that which is anticipated by the prophet Isaiah in the first servant song (18–21).[23] He is the one who brings to fruition the hopes of the Old Testament for God's engagement with humanity in justice and peace and healing and mercy.[24] Jesus is the one to whom Scripture points and in the light of whom Scripture makes sense. Of course, Jesus is also the liberator of humankind, the enabler of justice for all people, the gentle pastor of his flock and much more. But for our immediate purposes, he is the one in the light of whom all Scripture is now read. As the fulfiller of the temple,[25] Jesus truly is one *greater than the temple* (6).

5. Jesus as the essence of the law

We began this chapter by reflecting on the paradoxical nature of the encounter of God with humankind, mediated as it is through human institutions. Because the encounter is between both a God and a people whose very natures set them apart from each other, the meeting is tricky.[26] Things can go wrong. One of the things that can go wrong is that the institutions of encounter can develop unintended and even contradictory effects. The Scriptures themselves – or at least the results of reading them – are not immune from this phenomenon. As God made incarnate among us, Jesus is uniquely placed to provide a meeting between God and humanity. In Jesus is resident the pure intent of the various mediating institutions within which God and people meet each other. This includes the Scriptures. When the Scriptures are read through the eyes of Jesus then there is the least likelihood of misreading and the greatest possibility of encountering through them the work and word of God. This was the experience of the two friends on the road to Emmaus, whose 'hearts [burned] within' them as a result of the Scriptures being opened for them by Jesus.[27]

[22] Witherington, *Matthew*, p. 242.
[23] Isa. 42:1–4.
[24] J. H. Neyrey, 'The Thematic Use of Isaiah 42:1–4 in Matthew 12', *Biblica* 63 (1982), pp. 457–473.
[25] John 2:19–21.
[26] See ch. 6 on Exod. 19.
[27] Luke 24:30–32.

When Jesus challenges the Pharisees on the understanding of the Sabbath that their reading has led them to, he is not intending to suspend the law. Rather, he is encapsulating the essence of it in his own person, and calling for all Scripture to be read in the light of Christ. A variety of things can happen when this is achieved. Sometimes the Scriptures are easier to incorporate as a result; sometimes they are harder. In the case of the Sabbath, a refocus onto the true nature of Sabbath rest frees people from a dehumanizing legalism. On the other hand, a refocus onto the love and purity of the God who gave the law may challenge a libertarian approach to discipleship. The rich young man is no closer to God through keeping the commands, because he has not understood the costly love of Christ into which God is calling him.[28] Keeping the Ten Commandments is similarly no guarantee of Christ-like purity when the heart remains lustful or murderous in intent.[29] When the Scriptures are read in the searching light of Christ then most truly the word of God is encountered. This is both a glorious freedom and an impossible challenge. Let the interpreter beware.

All of which leads into part 3 of this study and the proposition that 'God Speaks in Christ'.

[28] Matt. 19:21–22.
[29] Matt. 5:21–30.

Part 3
God speaks in Christ

John 1:1–14
11. The Word made flesh

Our former Prime Minister recently resigned from Parliament to take up a key role with the United Nations. As a result, only six months after a general election, at the time of writing there is a parliamentary by-election in a nearby urban Auckland seat. The campaign has created much interest, both because it is the first electoral test of a new government and because of some cantankerous local issues, all spiced up by an uncertain economic environment. In the midst of all this one candidate, who at least until yesterday had a real chance of pulling off an upset, in the pressure of a bad-tempered local meeting made an unthinking aside about another sector of the city. I am pretty sure she did not mean what she said, but the gaffe will haunt her and has probably destroyed her electoral chances. The incident has reminded me again of what James said nearly two millennia ago, that words have extraordinary power for good and ill.[1]

Philosophers spend a great deal of time thinking about how this actually works, around issues like the nature of language, the location of meaning and the dynamics of discourse.[2] Despite all the mental firepower that has been poured into those discussions through the centuries, language remains a mystery, and the human capacity to communicate despite the potential for misunderstanding remains something of a miracle. In spite of the complexities, though, one thing is unavoidable: somehow language is central to human knowing and relating. The biblical witness makes clear that language is also central to our knowing and relating to God and God's knowing and relating to us. Even more, as we read Scripture

---

[1] Jas 3:1–12.
[2] As an example, see A. C. Thiselton, *New Horizons in Hermeneutics* (Grand Rapids: Zondervan, 1992), pp. 35–38.

we sense that language is foundational to the architecture of the universe itself, and the means by which God relates to the *kosmos*, to use the Greek word used by John's Gospel (9, 10). That is why this volume so often finds itself drawn by the biblical text to what has been called the speech-act of God. We ought not to be surprised, then, that words can determine the result of elections.

And we should be even less surprised that the central event of God's involvement with his *kosmos* is conveyed at least partly as a language event.[3] Nowhere is this more explicitly spelled out than in the prologue to John's Gospel (John 1:1–14). In God's becoming flesh in Christ, it is the Word, the *logos*, that *became flesh and made his dwelling among us* (14).[4] So far we have seen that the world's encounter with God is made possible in that God speaks. Furthermore, the ongoing acquaintance with God's acting and speaking is enshrined in the text of Scripture. We have also begun to sense that the Scripture itself and the Word of God that dwells with humanity in the person of Christ are intimately associated with each other. Now, as we turn to the prologue to John's Gospel, we think further about the nature of God's speaking in and through Christ, and the implications of that for understanding the nature of God's word.

1. In the beginning

The first word in the Hebrew Bible means 'in the beginning' (*bĕrē'šît*).[5] In the Septuagint this is translated into Greek as *en archē*. The opening Greek words of John's Gospel are identical, *en archē*, *in the beginning* (1). The effect is unmistakable. What John is about to talk about is as fundamental as what is expressed by the opening of the book of Genesis. The English translation 'beginning' at the start of Genesis has never been an entirely satisfactory translation of the Hebrew, linked as it is to the word *rō'š*. This has the sense of chief or top or first or fundamental. The range of meaning carries the idea of the essence and origins and primacy of something.[6] The opening phrase of the book of Genesis is therefore much more than a chronological statement, although chronological priority is con-

---

[3] As expressed by F. J. Moloney, *The Gospel of John*, SP 4 (Collegeville: Liturgical Press, 1998), p. 42: 'In the end the Johannine use of *logos* is determined by the universal truth that a word is essentially about communication.'

[4] On the background to the concept of *logos*, see G. R. Beasley-Murray, *John*, WBC 36 (Dallas: Word, 1999), pp. 5–10.

[5] Gen. 1:1.

[6] *TWOT*, 2:825–826.

tained within the meaning of the word. In Genesis 1:1 the source and the very nature of the created order is that 'God created'. No more fundamental or primary statement can be made about the nature of the world than that God created it; this is the ultimate cosmological fact. The Greek translation of the Hebrew *rē'šît*, *archē*, has similar limitations to the English 'beginning', although slightly less so. It is strongly chronological, but the Septuagint's consistent use of it, along with its relation *aparchē*, to translate *rē'šît* means that for the New Testament writers *archē* bore something of the sense of the Hebrew *rē'šît*. Therefore when John opens his Gospel with *in the beginning* (*en archē*), he too wants to say something about the source and very nature of the created order. In his case it is *the Word* (1). If the ultimate cosmological fact is that God created, it is thus because the Word is at the heart of that creative process. For without the Word, *nothing was made that has been made* (3). All things stem from God's speaking.

2. The Word was with God

Now comes a surprising turn of phrase. While it is true that both God[7] and *the Word* (1) are said to be in the beginning, the two are distinct from each other in that there is a relationship between the two. The preposition chosen to express the link between God and the Word is a giant hint in this direction. English translations mostly say that the Word was *with* God (1). This English preposition at least tells us that the Word and God are distinguishable from each other, but it expresses little more than coincidence; it is essentially a static notion. But that is not the sort of preposition that the Greek writer has chosen, even though one almost exactly equivalent to the English 'with' was available to him. Rather, the writer speaks of the word being *pros* God. The idea of movement is a dominating part of the meaning of *pros*. A better translation into English, albeit a somewhat clumsy one, would be 'towards': 'the Word was towards God'. The effect is to convey an active relationship between God and the Word.[8]

It is never a good idea to ask a preposition to bear too much of an exegetical load. Nevertheless, the hint of relationship introduced right at the start of John's reflection on Jesus, and then repeated for emphasis, bears thinking about. To start with it shows relationship

[7] Gen. 1:1.
[8] A. J. Köstenberger, *John*, BECNT (Grand Rapids: Baker Academic, 2004), p. 27.

at the heart of the Godhead. That is why we can say that it is of God's nature to seek relationship with his creation. At the same time, the fact that the word is not only *with* God but also *is* God indicates that language is also at the heart of the Godhead. That is why we can also say that it is of God's nature to express relationship through language. Since creation came into being by means of the active word of God, God's relationship with creation is pursued by the same means.[9] In the vision of John's Gospel, God is seen supremely as a W/word who may be heard, understood, replied to.

In the previous chapter we considered the paradoxical nature of the text as both the word of God and containing the word of God. One ironic outcome of this paradox is that the text as God's word may be used in such a way that it becomes a denial of the very word that it contains. We suggested then that God's response to this problem is to define his word in the person of Jesus, and thus to tie the interpretation of the textualized word to Jesus the incarnate Word.

In the light of the Johannine prologue we glimpse that this paradox is an inevitable outworking of the nature of God's relationship with God's Word. For, immediately after the first phrase in the Gospel asserting the foundational and primary nature of the Word, we read in verse 1b: *the Word was with God, and the Word was God.* The Word, who is incarnate in Jesus, is at the same time both God and the agent of God. In the same way, the text of Scripture is both the very word of God and the carrier of that word. As the agent, its message may be distorted by its interpreters. That is why it is so important that the incarnate Word of God, Jesus, who himself straddles both agency and identity with respect to God, be the ultimate interpreter of God's word.[10]

This point is reinforced by the reference to *John* the Baptist (6-8). John's presence in the prologue is often thought of as an interruption to the flow of thought about the Word made flesh. But in the context of our present line of thinking about Jesus as the *Word*, we might think of John as one of those interpreters of the word of God referred to above.[11] John came as a *witness* to the *light* (7). In case the reader misses the point the first time, the Gospel writer emphasizes that *he himself was not the light; he came only as witness to the*

---

[9] This is a profoundly important point for understanding the manner in which God and humanity relate. For a detailed reflection, see G. Ebeling, *Introduction to a Theological Theory of Language* (London: Collins, 1973), pp. 43–53.

[10] This relates closely to the role of the Spirit in interpretation, on which see ch. 5 on 2 Pet. 1:19–21.

[11] D. A. Carson, *The Gospel According to John* (Leicester: IVP, 1991), pp. 120–121.

light (8). There is only one whose witness is truly grounded in the essence of that concerning which he testifies. And, for all his qualities as catalogued by the Gospel writers, it is not John the Baptist; it is Jesus, who comes as the Word of God. If this point had to be made of the archetypal forerunner of Jesus, how much more should other interpreters of the word of God respect their otherness from that word, and do their work in the 'light' of the Word incarnate. That is also why this exposition of the theme of the word of God in Scripture must also take account of the fact that God speaks not only in the text but also in Christ.

3. Life and light

The Gospel writer then explores the Word's interaction with humanity through three key themes, one before the interlude in verses 6–8 and two after: light (4–5), birth (12–13) and glory (14). Each recalls aspects of the word of God in Scripture that we have already encountered in the Old Testament material, and so each reinforces the link between the Word incarnate and the word of God in the text.

We begin by looking at the theme of light. One of the outcomes of the Word's involvement in creation is that all life flows from him. In the case of the human part of creation, this is expressed as *light* (4). All people who have been created by the Word of God in some way are enlightened by that Word: *that life was the light of all people* (4). This is reinforced a few verses later when we are told that *the true light that gives light to everyone was coming into the world* (9). Moreover, that light was not *overcome* by the darkness (5).

There are at least two echoes of the Old Testament creation tradition in this. First, note that the enlightening effect of the Word is particularly directed to *all people* (4) rather than *all things* that *were made* (3). This recalls that in the second account of creation the detail is added that the Lord God 'breathed into [man's] nostrils the breath of life'.[12] The link between the breath of *life* in Genesis 2:7 and the *life* that is the *light of all people* (4) is suggestive. Just as the breath of the creator brought life to those first humans so the enlightening effect of the Word made flesh is itself life-giving.[13]

Secondly, the life-giving light of the opening verses of John is engaged in a struggle with the powers of darkness, and finally the

[12] Gen. 2:7.
[13] Köstenberger, *John*, pp. 31–32.

darkness could not *overcome* it (5).[14] This recalls the ancient struggle against chaos that seems to have been part of the creation memory of the Old Testament. This is not so obvious in Genesis, outside of the reference to the earth being 'formless and empty',[15] but emerges in places like Job 38:4–15. In those verses we see God, as well as being the craftsman of Genesis 1, also as a creator wrestling with the forces of chaos represented by the sea, and setting limits on malevolent powers. Indeed, according to Job, in the context of God's creative work the wicked are brought to light and their power broken. All of this recalls the enigmatic comment that the darkness was not able to *overcome* the enlightening Word that is both God and *with* God (5). Cumulatively, this has the effect of grounding the Word in the creative speech of God to which the *kosmos* owes its very being, and echoing the text that has preserved those speech-acts thus far.

4. Children of God

The Word of God made flesh also enables birth into the family of God; those who receive him become *children of God* (12). The writer is not now talking about the Word's involvement with the creative process. That is made clear by the comment that these *children* are not those who are the natural product of processes set in train by the creation of humanity. Children constantly are born *of natural descent, of human decision* and as a result of *a husband's will* with his wife (13). The interpretation of this verse is debated, but it is most likely to be drawing an emphatic distinction between the formation of the covenant and the creation of humankind as a whole.[16] It is a reminder that, as well as bringing the *kosmos* into being, the Word made flesh also forms a covenant people. This is an outcome of God's speaking that we have already observed in our discussion of Exodus 19 – 20 and more particularly in Deuteronomy 4.[17] There we noted that an important effect of the word of God in the text was the formation of a covenant with the people of God and, in the case of Deuteronomy 4, the wherewithal by which the covenant could

---

[14] The Greek verb translated by TNIV as 'overcome' (*katalambanō*) is often translated into English as 'understood' (e.g., NIV). That is one small section of the semantic field of the word, in that something that is understood may be said to have been 'grasped' or 'seized upon', but the TNIV translation, 'overcome', better captures the sense of struggle contained within the Greek verb. See C. G. Kruse, *John*, TNTC (Grand Rapids: Eerdmans, 2003), p. 65.

[15] Gen. 1:2; in Hebrew *tōhû wābōhû*.

[16] Moloney, *John*, p. 38.

[17] See chs. 6 and 7.

be sustained by means of its transmission to subsequent generations. Once again, the Word made flesh is grounded in the words of God in bringing the covenant and the covenant people into being. The Word made flesh epitomizes what the text has sought to do. Now this is expressed as the entitlement of *children of God* (12).

5. Glory of God

Finally, the Word made flesh reflects the aspirations of the text of the word of God in that he too is a manifestation of *glory* (14). There are several aspects to this theme as it is expressed in the extraordinarily rich verse 14. First, the theme of glory harks back to a phenomenon that we observed in our discussion of Psalm 19,[18] that the glory of God may be understood in the fact that God's word is available to humanity. This also emerges, as we saw, in Isaiah 40:5, where 'the glory of the LORD' is depicted as that of which 'the mouth of the LORD has spoken'. There we argued that the glory of God, a notion that is difficult to define, lies primarily in the fact that God has spoken. This is a simple idea but profound in its implications. The Word made flesh in Jesus cannot be other than glorious, for he is the visible expression of the fact that God speaks with and acts among us.

To the first readers of these verses this would have also raised echoes of the wilderness tabernacle. The Greek verb translated as *made his dwelling* (14) is *skēnoō*, which reflects the Hebrew verbal root *škn*, also meaning 'to dwell'. From this was derived the Aramaic word *šĕkînâ*, a technical term for God's presence with his people which came by extension to mean 'glory'. The ancient Aramaic paraphrase of Exodus 25:8, for example, equates the glory of God's presence with the wilderness tabernacle by paraphrasing thus: 'I shall cause my *šĕkînâ* to reside among them.'[19] We saw with respect to Exodus 19 – 20 that the encounter with God at Sinai was fuelled to some extent by Moses' anxiety that God would continue to be with the people even as they journeyed on from Sinai.[20] God eventually promised that that would be the case.[21] We noted then that this presence would be expressed through the intertwined concepts of God's word and God's glory. Those who first heard or

[18] See ch. 1.
[19] R. E. Brown, *The Gospel According to John I–XII*, AB 29 (New York: Doubleday, 1966), pp. 33–34.
[20] See ch. 6.
[21] Exod. 33:17.

read the prologue to John's Gospel would have been put in mind of God's glory and presence and of the physical expression of both in the form of the tabernacle. They would also have been challenged to see God's glory and presence now in the incarnate God, Jesus the Word as a tabernacle amongst humanity.

And it is characteristic of this presence of God that it is *full of grace and truth* (14). This phrase also takes us back to the provision of the *torah*, the active word of God in written form, in that the law was given by a God 'abounding in love and faithfulness'.[22] The Hebrew word there translated as 'faithfulness' is *'emet* while that for 'abounding love' is *ḥesed*, God's irresistible covenant loyalty and love. The linking of the two terms is not uncommon in the Old Testament portrayal of Yahweh.[23] It is likely that the phrase *full of grace and truth* (14) reflects this linking.[24]

In that case the Word made flesh is associated with the giving of the *torah* through Moses, and the accompanying assurance of God's presence with his people by means of the word of God.[25] If this link is only implicit in verse 14, the reference to Moses in verse 17 makes it explicit. In the words of Raymond Brown: 'The great exhibition of the enduring covenant love of God in the OT took place at Sinai, the same setting where the Tabernacle became the dwelling for God's glory. So now the supreme exhibition of God's love is the incarnate Word, Jesus Christ, the new Tabernacle of divine glory.'[26] And, we might add, the incarnate Word is the ultimate speech-act of God.

---

[22] Exod. 34:6.

[23] See for example Pss. 25:10; 61:7; 86:15; Prov. 20:28.

[24] For more on this link see T. J. Meadowcroft, 'Christ and Creation in the Johannine Prologue', *Stimulus* 7, no. 3 (1999), p. 36.

[25] See E. J. Epp, 'Wisdom, Torah, Word: The Johannine Prologue and the Purpose of the Fourth Gospel', in G. F. Hawthorne (ed.), *Current Issues in Biblical and Patristic Interpretation* (Grand Rapids: Eerdmans, 1975), pp. 138–141.

[26] Brown, *John I–XII*, p. 35.

Hebrews 1:1–4
12. In these last days God has spoken

In 140 AD Marcion, from Pontus on the Black Sea and already well into middle age, arrived in Rome. Little is known of him prior to that time. One tradition has him as a wealthy ship owner who endowed the congregation in Rome on his arrival; another as the son of the bishop of Sinope, in what is now modern Turkey.[1] Whatever the case, it seems that Marcion was 'haunted by the problem of evil and suffering',[2] an affliction common to both sons of bishops and ship owners. As often happens, his theology responded to his experience as he sought increasingly to distance the God revealed in Jesus from any involvement with human suffering or evil. As also occasionally happens to a theology strongly driven by human experience, he seems to have lost sight of the bigger picture.

For Marcion there was a sharp discontinuity between the God of grace and love disclosed by Jesus, his son, and the vengeful and evil god of this world. He associated one with the New Testament and the other with the Old Testament. Along with his rejection of the vengeful and evil god came a rejection of the Scriptures that he believed belonged to that god, namely, the Old Testament. Justin Martyr refers to Marcion as 'teaching his disciples to believe in some other god greater than the Creator'.[3] To Irenaeus this entailed

---

[1] K. S. Latourette, *A History of the Expansion of Christianity. Volume 1: The First Five Centuries* (Grand Rapids: Zondervan, 1970 [1937]), p. 345. See also Tertullian (160–225), *A Prescription Against Heretics*, ch. 30, <http://www.ccel.org/ccel/schaff/anf03.iv.iii.xxx.html>.

[2] W. Walker, *A History of the Christian Church*, rev. ed (Edinburgh: T&T Clark, 1959 [1918]), p. 54.

[3] Justin Martyr (*c.* 114–*c.* 165), *Apology* I.26, cited in J. Stevenson (ed.), *A New Eusebius: Documents Illustrative of the History of the Church to A.D. 337* (London: SPCK, 1960), p. 98.

'dividing God into two, maintaining one to be good and the other judicial'. The outcome, in his view, was that Marcion had 'put an end to deity'.[4] Effectively, this entailed, according to Tertullian, 'the separation of the law and the gospel'.[5]

Although the movement headed by Marcion was briefly strong, ultimately it could not bear the weight of the flawed thinking on which it was based. Nevertheless Marcion's name has survived in the adjective 'Marcionite', used still to describe those who make a particularly sharp discontinuity between the Old and New Testaments and their respective portraits of God, and who find it difficult to view the Old Testament as Christian Scripture. The term still crops up because the church today is not free from Marcionite tendencies. Although their attitudes are largely unexamined, many Christians see the Old Testament as about law and the New about grace, and seriously under-read the Old Testament. Mostly this is a relatively harmless misreading, although it does somewhat blunt the potential of Scripture as the word of God. And it is often sustained by the notion of progressive revelation, the idea that God is progressively revealed through the Scriptures and that the Old Testament portrait, especially in its more troubling hues, is at best incomplete. It is only a short step from there, though, to the view that the Old Testament is inadequate or even wrong in its understanding of God. From there it is another short step to a settled suspicion or even rejection of the Old Testament as the reliable word of God.

This may be illustrated from one particular context where reading the Old Testament is fraught with difficulty for Christians. In propounding a Palestinian theology of liberation, Naeem Ateek worries that:

> [the Old Testament] cannot be fully comprehended apart from its completion and fulfilment in Christ . . . Without Christ, the Old Testament is not only incomplete, it can be, in some of its parts, a very dangerous document that calls for ethnic cleansing and can produce fanatical actions by fanatical people.[6]

In a sense it is unfair of me to quote Ateek, who lives and works in the crucible of a very difficult struggle to read the Bible well with a Christian community who are experiencing daily systemic injustice

---

[4] Irenaeus (d. 202), III.40.2, cited in Stevenson, *A New Eusebius*, p. 99.

[5] Tertullian, *Against Marcion*, I.19, cited in ibid.

[6] N. Ateek, 'Putting Christ at the Centre: The Land from a Palestinian Christian Perspective', in L. Loden, P. Walker and M. Wood (eds.), *The Bible and the Land: An Encounter* (Jerusalem: Musalaha, 2000), p. 56.

at the hands of a people who bear the same name as the people of God in the Old Testament. His views as a Palestinian Christian are understandable, and in fact not as radical taken as a whole, as is implied by the above quote.[7] But he does illustrate the potential impact of holding too great a discontinuity between the Testaments. Indeed, many Christians, with much less excuse for doing so than Ateek, are inclined to exclude the Old Testament from their reading in response to the difficulties it presents.[8] They effectively work with an unexamined 'canon within a canon'[9] that results in a loss both of appreciation of the word of God and of God himself. It is a loss that would deeply disappoint the writer of the book of Hebrews, with whom this chapter is concerned.[10]

1. At the end of these days

The book of Hebrews begins with two contrasts, particularly as the first two verses are normally translated into English. The first is a contrast of time – *in the past* (1) and *in these last days* (2) – and the second is a contrast of the means by which God spoke/speaks: *through the prophets* (1) and *by his son* (2). There is a third implied contrast around the twinned adverbs *at many times and in various ways* (1), namely, the implication that God previously employed a range of means of speaking while today his speaking is through the son. However, the sense of discontinuity between the past and the present age is not quite as clear cut as most English translations lead us to expect.[11] I suggest that the first two verses are better translated thus: 'The God who spoke at many times and in various ways in the past to the fathers by the prophets has spoken at the end of these days to us in a son . . .'

There are several things to note about this. First, the structure of the first two verses around the forms of the verbs *spoke* (1) and *has spoken* (2) emphasizes the activity of the subject of the verb, God,

---

[7] See an appreciation of his work and comment on its potential weakness by another Palestinian theologian, Y. Katanacho, 'Palestinian Protestant Theological Responses to a World Marked by Violence', *Missiology* 36 (2008), pp. 292–294.

[8] This issue is addressed in the short study of the problematic Josh. 11 by W. Brueggemann, *Divine Presence Amid Violence: Contextualizing the Book of Joshua* (Eugene: Cascade: 2009).

[9] A shorthand term for the process of privileging some parts of Scripture over others.

[10] For a good summary of the issues around the mystery of the authorship of Hebrews see P. Ellingworth, *The Epistle to the Hebrews*, NIGTC (Grand Rapids: Eerdmans, 1993), pp. 3–21.

[11] A. C. Mitchell, *Hebrews*, SP 13 (Collegeville: Liturgical Press, 2007), p. 36.

and the continuity between the two acts of speaking. This God who spoke to the ancestors through the prophets is the same God who spoke by means of the son. Moreover, the two verbal forms of 'speak' are both in the aorist tense. This could indicate that the speaking through the prophets was prior to the speaking through the son, but it potentially also conveys that the two verbs together form a snapshot of God speaking, without being particularly concerned with the order in which the speaking occurs. It is sufficient for our purpose to note that the syntax of the long complex Greek sentence that constitutes verses 1 and 2 does not make a distinction in type between God's speaking through the prophets and God's speaking through the son. The voice we heard through the prophets is the same voice we hear in the revelation of God's son.

The Greek form of the phrase *these last days* (2) also softens the distinction between *these last days* (2) and *the past* (1). The phrase is probably better understood as 'at the end of these days'. But that then begs the question: to what does 'these days' refer? The phrase could refer to the culmination of a season during which God spoke through his son, but given the particular past tense in the Greek this is unlikely.[12] It would be more natural to read 'these days' as the time during which God spoke. Therefore the revelation of God in his son is the culmination of the various times and ways in which God has spoken. The two speakings are not fundamentally different in kind.

It is also important to note with respect to both the points just made, that the *but* which appears in many English versions as the first word of verse 2 is not represented at all in the Greek. As a result there is a continuity expressed between what has occurred before and what is now occurring in the end through the son. The word of God spoken *through the prophets* (1) is likely to refer to the witness that is drawn together in the Old Testament.[13] To be sure, as we have seen in the last three chapters, this word as text has not been sufficient on its own; it reaches its culmination in the Word of God manifest in his son, Jesus. Nevertheless, these verses do not support Marcion. The God who speaks in Jesus is the same God who has always spoken, and the word of the prophets preserved in the text is still the word of God as much as the Word in Christ which has been revealed 'at the end of these days'. We may debate how to read the Scriptures in the light of Christ, and even more what exactly we

---

[12] For further on the grammatical issues raised, see D. B. Wallace, *Greek Grammar Beyond the Basics: An Exegetical Syntax of the New Testament* (Grand Rapids: Zondervan, 1996), pp. 554–557, 614–615.

[13] G. H. Guthrie, *Hebrews*, NIVAC (Grand Rapids: Zondervan, 1998), p. 46.

should do with the Old Testament in the light of the New, but we cannot doubt that in all the Scriptures we hear the voice of the God who is father of Jesus.

At the same time there is some level of discontinuity between Jesus and what has gone before him. The discontinuity comes in that Jesus is presented as the culmination of God's speaking.[14] This concept of Jesus as the culminating, but not the contradicting Word, runs through the book of Hebrews. It could be illustrated at a number of points, but the beginning of Hebrews 2 is as good a place as any. There the writer warns his or her readers to 'pay the most careful attention'[15] to what has been heard. An earlier message, a message 'spoken through angels',[16] was binding and could be disobeyed only at peril of punishment. How much the more, then, should the salvation announced by Christ be embraced, is the logic in Hebrews 2:1–4. The link with the angelic message expresses a continuity while also acknowledging that something new has happened as a result of the coming of the great High Priest, God's son.[17]

2. Heir and creator of all things

Arguably the remainder of the letter to the Hebrews explains why it is appropriate that God should *in these last days* have *spoken to us by his Son* (2). Much of that argument focuses on the nature of the Son through whom God speaks. The essence of that part of the argument is found in these first four verses. Having declared that God has now spoken *by his Son* (2), the writer indicates something of the nature of the Son who makes this speaking possible.

First, the Son is the *heir of all things* and the one through whom *[God] made the universe* (2). These two phrases should be read together, but we will take them one at a time and see how they inform each other. First, Jesus is the *heir*. The term used has a straightforward sense of one who comes into an inheritance. This is how it is used by Jesus in the parable of the tenants.[18] The epistle writers use the word in a spiritual sense of those who inherit the promises of the faith.[19] This is usually the case in the letter to the

---

[14] E. V. McKnight and C. Church, *Hebrews–James*, SHBC (Macon: Smith & Helwys, 2004), p. 29, express this as the 'eschatological speech of the Son'.
[15] Heb. 2:1.
[16] Heb. 2:2.
[17] L. T. Johnson, *Hebrews: A Commentary*, NTL (Louisville: Westminster John Knox, 2006), pp. 65–67.
[18] Matt. 21:38; Mark 12:7; Luke 20:14.
[19] Rom. 4:13; Gal. 3:29; Jas 2:5.

Hebrews also.[20] Nowhere else do we read of Christ being an *heir*, with the possible exception of Romans 8:17, where Paul speaks of believers being 'co-heirs with Christ'. There he is speaking of sharing the sufferings of Christ, which is not quite the emphasis in Hebrews. So the concept of the Son as *heir*, although it is a natural extension of the commonly used offspring image, is unique to this verse.[21] It means simply that Christ inherits all that the Father has. That being the case, the Son cannot be heir to less than *all things* (2).[22] In the context of this present study, this presumably includes the fact that the Son shares in God's speaking.[23] That would seem to be the case in the light of John's concept of Jesus as Word.

Of course the notion of the Son of God as the heir of God is problematic. An heir is somebody who enjoys a present status but awaits a future realization of an inheritance that is due. Since God and God's Son are both eternal, the status and the future inheritance must, at any given moment, already be realized. If the Son is the *heir of all things*, then he presumably shares in all that it means to be God and has always done so. Indeed, we are told in verse 4 that the Son of God *has inherited* from God and so already bears the name that indicates that status. That is why the son is also the one through whom God *made the universe* (2). The Son of God, the means of God speaking, has always been and will always be. He was and will be present and active at those two moments that remain unimaginable to time-bound humanity: the beginning of all things (creation) and the end of all things (inheritance). And, by implication, everywhere in between. In short, he is 'the Alpha and the Omega'.[24]

In speaking of Christ, that he has inherited all things and that he participated in the creation of the universe cannot be separated. The two ideas are twinned concepts, and, in the manner of Hebrew thought through parallelism, the two ideas inform each other. In that case, the terms *all things* and *universe* (2) explain each other. In that respect the Greek word translated as 'universe' (*aiōn*) is an interesting one. It is the word most commonly used by the Septuagint to translate the Hebrew *'ôlām*, which can denote either the universe or eternity. It suggests all of time and all of space and matter. While the Greek term *per se* is primarily reflective of time, its use in the Septuagint means that it has come to include a spatial element. It connotes the idea of both all of time and all of space or

[20] Heb. 6:17; 11:7.
[21] Although it is strongly implied by the pre-eminence of the 'Son' as 'firstborn over all creation' in Col. 1:15–17.
[22] R. Brown, *The Message of Hebrews*, BST (Leicester: IVP, 1982), pp. 29–30.
[23] Mitchell, *Hebrews*, p. 40.
[24] Rev. 1:8.

matter. There can be no more comprehensive statement of the scope of God's rule than as the one who is so described. Everywhere and everything and always is God's. That is likely also to be the idea behind the author's use of the word *aiōn* here and which the TNIV and other English translators are trying to express with the word 'universe'.

As a result the term *universe* is a kind of clarification of what is meant by *all things* earlier in the sentence. Christ, the one through whom God speaks, the one who now has *sat down at the right hand of the Majesty in heaven* (3), exercises an influence as vast and as all-encompassing as it is possible for human beings to imagine.[25] By so doing he brings God's word within the hearing of finite human beings. And because of the nature of the one who brings and is this Word, it is thoroughly reliable both in itself and as the interpretive key of the expression of that word in the text.[26]

3. The radiance of God's glory

As this long Greek sentence continues, the qualifications of the Son as the one through whom God has spoken at the end of *these last days* (1) continue to pile up. Now we find that he is *the exact representation of [God's] being* (3). This could hardly be a stronger affirmation that the one who has inherited all things from God is in fact virtually indistinguishable from God at the deepest core of his being. The phrase translated as *representation* does not quite capture the closeness of identification inherent in the word which it translates, the Greek *charaktēr*. The word is here unique in the New Testament, but in classical Greek has the sense of an engraver's tool or the mark or style that is characteristic of a particular artist. As a result the word can indicate both a reproduction or impression of something else and the distinctive nature of something. By extension, in its use by the writer of Hebrews, the *charaktēr* or *representation* is more than a reflection of another, although it is that.[27] Linked as it is to God's very *being* (3), it expresses an unimaginably strong identification between God and the Son of God.

That terminology can be read as expansive of the fact that the Son is *the radiance of God's glory* (3). When we look at the Son we see God's glory in all its fullness, not as a reflection with all the loss of identity with the original that is part of any copying process. At

---

[25] Johnson, *Hebrews*, p. 67.
[26] See ch. 10.
[27] Guthrie, *Hebrews*, p. 48.

various stages in this volume we have had cause to think about the nature of God's glory. Right from the first chapter, in which we noted Isaiah 40:5, we have adopted a working proposition that the glory of God is primarily seen in the fact that God speaks and, in speaking, acts. And so it is here. God has spoken through his Son 'at the end of these days', or in some ultimate way. At the same time the Son continues to *[sustain] all things by his powerful word* (3). Therein is the glory of God seen, that the Alpha and Omega, the heir and creator, continues to speak with humankind, and in speaking, acts and sustains.

4. The redeeming Word

If all we talk about is God as creator, though, we have not said enough. The work of the Son as redeemer is a profoundly important part of the dynamics. The writer of Hebrews does not say much on that front in these few verses, but the brief allusion to the Son's provision of the *purification for sins* (3) should not be ignored. One of the ways that this work of purification is expressed in Hebrews is by reference to Jesus as the one who 'suffered outside the city gate'.[28] By so doing he identified with the exclusion that is part of the fallen condition. Paradoxically, by means of this type of suffering he became the one entitled to '[enter] the inner sanctuary behind the curtain',[29] and perform the priestly act of sacrifice for the purification of the people.

This recalls the encounter that we examined at Mount Sinai described in Exodus 19.[30] There we noted the problem of God in his holiness being set apart from the people, and the challenge to establish a covenant by means of which God and humanity may meet across the boundaries created by the otherness of each party. In the book of Hebrews we find Jesus as the one uniquely equipped to step across that boundary and to operate safely in both spheres, or, in another picture from the life of Moses, to encounter God face to face.[31] He was entitled as high priest to enter the inner sanctuary because he suffered 'outside the city gate' as the sacrificial offering. He became the boundary crosser by means of his redemptive work. This is an important part of our understanding of God's speaking in Christ. For now, we simply note it but we explore it more once we

[28] Heb. 13:12.
[29] Heb. 6:19–20.
[30] See ch. 6.
[31] Exod. 33:11.

come to Revelation 5 and the character of the slain Lamb who is also the Lion of Judah.[32]

5. Superior to the angels

Finally, we are told, the son is *superior to the angels* (4). The syntax of this section makes a causal link between verses 3 and 4, hence *so* at the start of verse 4. In light of the fact that Jesus has done his redemptive work (alluded to by the writer of Hebrews as *purification for sins*, 3) and is seated at the right of God, and in light also of his status as heir and creator, the Son is demonstrably superior in rank to angelic beings. To reinforce the point, the writer reverts to the image of inheritance used in verse 2, and in so doing implies that the angels are of a different order entirely from the one who is the heir of God (4).

Given that the idea of angels does not bear much currency in Western culture, it is worth asking what the earliest readers or hearers of this epistle may have thought when told that Jesus was *superior to the angels*. The primary sense of 'angel' (*angelos*) during the period of the Second Temple was 'messenger'. It was mostly used by the Septuagint to translate the Hebrew word *mal'āk*, which means 'messenger'. The term could refer explicitly to heavenly messengers,[33] or have a quite 'secular' sense of messenger in the way that we would most naturally use the word.[34] Occasionally there is an ambivalence in the term, such as when the two 'messengers' arrive in Sodom and Gomorrah.[35] And sometimes it refers to those who are identified as prophets, particularly in the post-exilic period. Haggai is at one point described as a 'messenger' (*mal'āk*),[36] and this is translated as 'angel' by the Septuagint. And there is an argument for understanding Malachi, not as the name of an individual prophet, but as the Hebrew title, 'my messenger'.[37]

The variability in usage of the Hebrew term illustrates the vagueness of the Old Testament around these categories.[38] By the time of the New Testament, the term 'angel' probably bore a more explicitly other-worldly connotation, but had not lost the sense of an angel as

---

[32] See ch. 15.
[33] Gen. 16:6–11; 19:1, for example.
[34] 1 Sam. 11:3 for example.
[35] Gen. 19:1.
[36] Hag. 1:13.
[37] R. J. Coggins, *Haggai, Zechariah, Malachi*, OTG (Sheffield: JSOT, 1987), p. 73.
[38] *DDD*, pp. 89–96.

a messenger of God.[39] The writer of Hebrews quotes Psalm 104:4 to refer to angels as '[God's] servants'.[40] And their messenger function echoes strongly in Hebrews 2:2, in which the 'message [was] spoken through angels'.[41] In fact, the 'message' is the *logos*, or word of God. And yet it is clear that angels, even faithful angels delivering God's message, are not at the *right hand of the Majesty*,[42] and in some respects are rivalled by God's aspirations for humanity.[43] As with humanity, there are limitations to what they can achieve. In contrast, Jesus, the heir of God, is of an entirely different order of being. Only he has inherited a name (4) that places him in the centre of *the radiance of God's glory* (3). As we have seen, this glory is the effective word of God.

That is why all Scripture, which has come to us through the agency of various messengers or *prophets* (1), is read in the light cast by the radiance of God, that is, in the light of Christ. God has spoken fully and finally in Jesus, but in a way that does not in any sense negate the speaking *at many times and in various ways* (1) that has come down to us in the text of Scripture. The mystery with which we struggle is that we know enough of the Word of God in Christ to know that there are points at which the ancient records of God's speech and act, the word of God in the text of Scripture, may only be fully appreciated when subjected to the scrutiny of the story of Jesus. In that respect, our interpretation is unavoidably Christological. And, since Christ *is the exact representation of [God's] being* (3), it is unavoidably theological. Marcion was right to place Christ at the centre of his reading, but wrong to separate Christ the Word from the word of God in all of Scripture, including the Old Testament. For, as the writer of Hebrews has shown, the fullness of Scripture is a necessary part of encountering the redeeming purifying work of Christ the Word.

---

[39] *DBI*, pp. 23–24.

[40] Heb. 1:7.

[41] According to W. L. Lane, *Hebrews 1–8*, WBC 47A (Dallas: Word, 1991), p. 17, 'The angels in v 4 are the counterpart to the prophets in v 1'.

[42] See also Heb. 1:13.

[43] See the use of Ps. 8 in Heb. 2:6–9.

Matthew 5:17–48
13. Christ fulfills the Scriptures

'Be holy because I am holy,'[1] says the writer of the book of
Leviticus. Just in case you blinked and missed the phrase the first
time, the writer says it again just one verse later. This is arguably
one of the hardest sayings in the Bible, and one which attracts a
great deal of effort to soften it. Without wishing to add further
to the effect, I note that the context of the saying in Leviticus is
instructions about purity and impurity, and particularly clean and
unclean food. In that setting, holiness has the sense of remaining
separate from food that has been determined to be unclean. On the
face of it this kind of holiness seems relatively accessible, unless you
have developed a taste for storks, cormorants, owls and such like,
or insects with unjointed legs.[2] It is a little harder perhaps for those
with fairly catholic tastes in meat,[3] but still achievable.[4] On a more
serious note, the lawgivers were always clear that the laws of purity
were never an end in themselves, but always in the complex service
of a relationship with the divine.[5]

The instruction becomes somewhat harder to wriggle out of,
though, when the apostle Peter quotes it in his first letter. There the
instruction to be holy as God is holy is detached from its original
Holiness Code context, and applied to the appropriation of first-
century faith in Jesus. In that context, holiness has to do with

---

[1] Lev. 11:44–45.
[2] Lev. 11:13–20.
[3] Lev. 11:26–27.
[4] Fathoms of ink have been expended on the reason for regulations such as
these, and I do not plan to add to them. But see M. Douglas, 'Sacred Contagion',
in J. F. A. Sawyer (ed.), *Reading Leviticus: A Conversation with Mary Douglas*,
JSOTSup 227 (Sheffield: Sheffield Academic, 1996), pp. 86–106.
[5] G. J. Wenham, *The Book of Leviticus*, NICOT (Grand Rapids; Eerdmans,
1979), pp. 15–29.

separation, not from cormorants and rigid-legged insects and dead bodies, but from the 'evil desires' of our 'ignorance'.[6] The wider context is the appropriation of the wonderful inheritance of our salvation 'through the resurrection of Jesus Christ'.[7] This appropriation has an ethical aspect which is summarized in the awesome instruction to 'be holy because I [God] am holy'.[8] Now that holiness is attached to the ethics of salvation living, the command to be holy really is a frightening instruction.

But Peter has good grounds for the way he has appropriated the notion of holiness. He has taken his lead from Jesus, who in some of his discourses set extraordinarily, if not impossibly, high standards of human behaviour and motivation. There is a string of such instructions in the Sermon on the Mount, especially in Matthew 5. There Jesus raises the bar on murder and adultery, redefines divorce and oath-taking, and asks his hearers to go the second mile and love their enemies. The culminating instruction is to *be perfect . . . as your heavenly Father is perfect* (48). Cumulatively the effect is daunting indeed; in fact, it feels more like impossible.

One response is to exegete one's way towards more possible positions. This effect is well illustrated by treatments of Jesus' saying, 'it is easier for a camel to go through the eye of a needle than for the rich to enter the kingdom of God'.[9] One classic response to this hard saying is the assertion that 'the needle' was a narrow gate into the city, the passage of which required camels to be unloaded first. This idea is convenient but without support.[10] It is best to allow the hyperbole to have the effect that it has, namely that those who have possessions do find it next to impossible to enter the kingdom of God; possessions are a major encumbrance to the spiritual life. Still on the matter of wealth, Jesus' remark was occasioned by his encounter with the so-called rich young man, to whom he had given the unvarnished instruction to 'sell [his] possessions'.[11] At this point expositors often take refuge in the fact that Jesus did not ask that of everyone. After all, he only asked Zaccheus to make the most of his wealth, not to dispense with it entirely,[12] and so he is probably saying the same to us. Ironically, by taking this route we apply the word of God by declaring that it does not really apply. The thought is seldom entertained that the requirement of Jesus to

[6] 1 Pet. 1:14.
[7] 1 Pet. 1:3–9.
[8] 1 Pet. 1:15.
[9] Matt. 19:24.
[10] M. Green, *The Message of Matthew*, BST (Leicester: IVP, 2000), p. 209.
[11] Matt. 19:21.
[12] Luke 19:8–10.

sell possessions may be exactly what God is saying to some readers. After all, according to Jesus that is the path to the very 'perfection'[13] of which he spoke in verse 48. At the same time, Christian experience suggests that the rich do sometimes achieve the impossible and enter the kingdom, and that there are Christians who do not in fact sell all their possessions, but, like the reformed Zacchaeus, use them faithfully. For these reasons, ingenious exegesis is not the only answer.

A fuller response must be theological as well as exegetical. As we concluded in the previous chapter, this entails reading the Scriptures by the light of the 'radiance' of God's glory seen in Christ.[14] There we named that as Christological, and hence theological, reading. When we turn the lamp of that 'radiance' onto some of these hard sayings of Jesus we find ourselves in the place where the word of God in Scripture meets the Word of God embodied in Jesus. In that place, the hard sayings of Jesus do not become easy, but they do become a living encounter with the God who speaks and who has spoken in Christ. Reading some of them in part of the discourse of the Sermon on the Mount (Matt. 5:17–48) also tells us more about how the word of God in Scripture and the Word of God in Christ relate to one another. An examination of those verses is the task of this chapter.

1. Continuity and discontinuity

A refrain echoes through Matthew 5:21–48, each occurrence serving to introduce teaching on a major topic. On five occasions Jesus says: *You have heard that it was said . . . but I tell you* (21–22, 27–28, 33–34, 38–39, 43–44). On a sixth occasion, for some reason the formula is varied to: *It has been said . . . but I tell you* (31–32), but the effect is the same. In any case the words *but I tell you* are identical each time. Each time, Jesus uses the technically redundant personal pronoun *I* (*egō*) for emphasis. There are only six other times in the New Testament when this emphatic pronoun is used with the extremely common 'I tell you'. The three other occasions in the Synoptic Gospels all relate to the same incident.[15] That this infrequently used phrase occurs so often in this section of the Sermon

[13] Matt. 19:21.
[14] Heb. 1:3.
[15] Matt. 21:27; Mark 11:33; Luke 20:8. Of other occurrences, John 14:10 is also about authority although this is less the case at John 16:7. And in Gal. 5:2 Paul is speaking emphatically of himself, thus illustrating the emphatic usage.

on the Mount is a signal that an important contrast is being drawn between the words of Jesus and those that the disciples have previously heard and/or read. It is hard to escape an emphatic discontinuity between Jesus and the written and spoken religious tradition from which he emerged. Something new is happening.

At the same time, the rarity of the phrase brings into play the several other occasions on which it is used in the Synoptics. It is of interest that each usage, as already indicated, is in the incident recorded in all three Synoptic Gospels in which Jesus' opponents question his authority to teach. In an oblique way, the Gospel writer, by employing this particular emphatic expression, is affirming the entitlement of Jesus as the Word of God to stamp his own mark on the word of God. Although it does not emerge in the present context, we have seen elsewhere that this entitlement is both inherent in Jesus' own speech-acts and in the defining nature of his interpretation.[16]

The discontinuity between Jesus and what has gone before, while defining, should not be over-stated. This is all the more the case in that the section immediately preceding the string of contrastive expressions says: *I have not come to abolish [the Law or the Prophets] but to fulfil them* (17). Arguably, this section (17–20) sets the reading agenda for what is to follow. Indeed, Jesus labours the point: *not the least stroke of a pen will . . . disappear* (18). So important is the written word that, as the Authorized Version famously expressed it, not one jot or tittle is negotiable. Jesus then alludes to the whole process that we examined in Deuteronomy 4:1–20 whereby this law is taught and transmitted.[17] It is essential that those who teach respect the entire written word. Not even *the least of these commands* should be *set aside* (19) in the course of their transmission. By implication, what Jesus is about to do in the string of commentary on various behavioural issues, while breaking new ground, does not set aside what has gone before.[18] For those of us who read and teach Scripture in the light of and in the name of Christ, there is nothing about doing so that gives permission to shelve parts of what has been written, or to interpret in such a way that their meaning is somehow denied them.[19]

[16] Compare ch. 10 on Matt. 12:1–21 and ch. 12 on Heb. 1:1–4.

[17] See ch. 7.

[18] F. P. Viljoen, 'Jesus' Teaching on the *Torah* in the Sermon on the Mount', *Neotestamentica* 40 (2006), p. 141.

[19] Much more could be said on the location of meaning, and we have discussed at various points the freedom of and obligation on the reader to interpret out of his or her own context. The meaning of some parts of Scripture can be many-voiced. Nevertheless, interpreters are neither free simply to ignore particular parts of the

2. The law and the prophets and those who teach

So far I have begged an important question by my equation of 'Scripture' with what Jesus describes as *the Law or the Prophets* (17). The New Testament employs various shorthand expressions to refer to the Hebrew Scriptures. For instance, the apostle Peter speaks of the 'prophetic message' and the 'prophecy of Scripture',[20] which, as we have argued,[21] almost certainly means the entire corpus of Scripture, not just the parts that we now label as prophetic, nor what the Hebrew canon named as 'the prophets'.[22] The book of Acts illustrates the various expressions well. 'The law and the prophets' or variations thereof[23] reflects the most common usage.[24] Sometimes it is 'the law of Moses'[25] or the abbreviated 'Moses' as shorthand for the law.[26] Uniquely, Luke 24:44 refers to the 'the Law of Moses, the Prophets and the Psalms', thus encompassing all three divisions in the ordering of the Hebrew Bible: the law, the prophets and the writing.[27] It is striking that the New Testament documents are quite uninterested in defining the boundaries of these authoritative writings, but deeply concerned with their appropriation.

On that basis it is a reasonable assumption that when Jesus speaks of *the Law or the Prophets* (17) he is referring approximately to what we today recognize as the Scriptures of the Old Testament. Therefore the instructions from the mouth of Jesus are that these should in no way be set aside. I have also argued that it is a legitimate interpretive move to apply this same attitude to the eventual body of New Testament Scripture, which was probably in embryonic form at the time these words were written down.[28] That does not mean, though, that every time Jesus says *you have heard that it was said* in Matthew 5 he is referring to what we now name as the Scriptures. As

Bible, nor to read capriciously such that meaning is derived without respect for the intention of the text. See J. E. Goldingay, *Models for Scripture* (Grand Rapids: Eerdmans, 1994), p. 239.

[20] 2 Pet. 1:19–20.

[21] See ch. 5.

[22] Joshua – 2 Kings (excluding Ruth) and the writing prophets.

[23] Acts 13:15; 24:14.

[24] For example Matt. 7:12; 22:40; Luke 16:16.

[25] Acts 28:23.

[26] Acts 26:22.

[27] The existence or otherwise of a formal corpus of Scripture along those lines prior to the destruction of the temple in 70 AD is hotly debated. See R. T. Beckwith, *The Old Testament Canon of the New Testament Church and Its Background in Early Judaism* (London: SPCK, 1985), pp. 110–165.

[28] Again, see ch. 5.

we will see below, he may also be referring to some of the additional provisions that had grown up around the law.

In the Gospels, these accretions are particularly associated by Jesus with the Pharisees, and the technical hedge that they placed around the law.[29] Remember that the Pharisees are not a uniformly unsatisfactory group, even in the pages of the New Testament, and should not be thought of in that way. Their intent was good, in that they sought to enable the keeping of the law, but so often the effect could become a denial of the law's essence. That is why Jesus particularly notes the responsibility on those who teach to teach and interpret in a way that allows the law to speak as the voice of God and not in a way that dulls the sound of that voice. To put it another way: to commend the word of God in a way that leads to righteousness (19–20).

3. But I say to you

Jesus refers to these ancient yet ever contemporary documents when he says, *you have heard that it was said to the people long ago* (21). In contrasting his words with that which was said long ago, Jesus is not dealing so much with Scripture itself as with what has been made of those Scriptures.

a. Oaths

This is most obvious in the fourth of the six segments of teaching, that on the taking of oaths. There is no cross reference in verses 33–36 to an Old Testament Scripture, and it seems that the primary reference is to some contemporary practice that has no warrant in the *torah*.[30] The problem appears to be the habit of swearing by important things, like Jerusalem or earth and heaven or one's own person (34–36). It is patently ridiculous to do so given that we have no control over any of these things. We do not even have a say in our hair colour (36).[31] Even in this instance, though, the point is that Jesus' audience needs to hear the words of Scripture unadorned. In this case, they need to do less than they normally do; they are to settle for a simple *'Yes'* or *'No'* (37). Any other form of oath, by claiming more than any human is entitled to claim, is effectively a

---

[29] See ch. 10 on the Pharisees.
[30] C. S. Keener, *A Commentary on the Gospel of Matthew* (Grand Rapids: Eerdmans, 1999), p. 194.
[31] Technically anyway, although try telling that to my daughters.

type of blasphemy. That is why Jesus so vigorously condemns the practice as *from the evil one* (37). In this case, true keeping of the law entails the right attitude towards God as supreme over all that he has created.

b. Murder

The other segments of teaching each begin with the command of Scripture itself. Then they turn to the way that Scripture has been abused or misunderstood or simply found to be too hard when human frailty meets life's challenges. This happens in various ways. Jesus notes this effect in the case of the command against murder. While it is definitely the case that people should not kill other people, it is also the case that this prohibition is based on a fundamental respect for the dignity, or what Maori would call the *mana*, of all people before God. The command not to murder therefore indicates an attitude of respect for all people. It is possible to deny people that respect while still keeping the letter of the law by not murdering them. When that happens the commandment might as well have been broken, and the judgment is as severe as if it were.[32]

It happens when we insult somebody, in this case by calling him or her '*Raca*', a term of contempt. I am reminded by this of the Aramaic phrase used to describe the denunciation of the three young men who refused to bow to Nebuchadnezzar's statue, and translated by TNIV as 'denounced'.[33] Literally, it means 'they ate pieces of them'. This is a wonderful evocation of the destructive effects of actions that only technically fall short of murder. Murder is not the only way to destroy a person.[34] Jesus raises the bar even further when he comments that whenever we do not do all in our power to repair a ruptured relationship, we are similarly in breach of this law (23–26).

c. Adultery

There is a similar dynamic at work in the case of adultery (27–30). Again, Jesus moves beyond the technicality of the command, which is relatively easy to keep for many people, especially those who are in successful committed relationships. But the heart of the matter is something more, and may best be understood in the context

[32] R. T. France, *Matthew*, TNTC (Leicester: IVP, 1985), p. 120.
[33] Dan. 3:8.
[34] M. J. Wilkins, *Matthew*, NIVAC (Grand Rapids: Zondervan, 2004), p. 242, speaks of identity theft.

of first-century Jewish society. The command is to some extent androcentric in that it concerns behaviour towards women who are married to other men. Such women were regarded in law as chattels and hence the property of their husbands.[35] The crime of adultery, as well as being relational infidelity, was also a property offense against the cuckolded husband and his honour. In certain respects, the command itself has already objectified women in the context of a patriarchal society. Jesus picks up on this in his comments on lust (28), which is the objectification of another person for sexual gratification. It is a male problem, although not exclusively so, but in any case the manner in which the law has been couched enshrines the male perspective. When a man *looks at a woman lustfully* (28) he has reduced her to a thing to the extent that he may as well have committed adultery with her, with all the breach of honour entailed by that in the society of his day. If it is relatively easy to avoid technical adultery, and certainly not impossible (though hard) to avoid trampling on people's dignity, avoiding a lustful look is another matter entirely.[36] It is made all the harder by the preventive measures proposed (29–30). There would be few sighted men (I cannot speak for women) left in the world if this were taken literally.

Note that Jesus has not amended the requirements of Scripture in any way in his responses to adultery and murder. Rather, he has shone the light of Christ on them, and called for a yet deeper response to God's word in the light of Christ. It is incidental that the bar has been lifted as far as keeping the law goes. In each instance, the essence has been a focus on the point of the law in the light of the person of Jesus.

d. Divorce

This focus on the essence has a somewhat different outcome in the case of divorce. On murder and adultery, Jesus expanded the scope of the command; with respect to divorce, he reduces the scope. Moses permitted divorce under a range of circumstances, but essentially at the will of the aggrieved husband (31).[37] Still responding within this essentially patriarchal paradigm, Jesus notes the permissive nature of this approach by stating that it effectively condemns the woman, along with any future husbands, to a life of adultery

[35] E. Schweizer, *Matthew*, tr. D. E. Green (London: SPCK, 1976), p. 121.

[36] With little basis, and by no means alone amongst male commentators, Keener, *Matthew*, p. 189, reassures his readers that 'Jesus does not, of course, refer here to passing attraction'. Surely this is a case of wishful exegesis on his part.

[37] Deut. 24:1–4.

(32).[38] By so doing, he has named the essence of divorce as unfaithfulness. Therefore the cause of divorce can only be unfaithfulness, expressed in the terms of the day as adultery.[39] When divorce does not arise from unfaithfulness, then the divorce itself constitutes unfaithfulness and so is effectively a form of adultery. This time Jesus' approach has narrowed the scope of the law to the ideal, but still he is driving his hearers back to the attitudinal essence, once again an essence that is found in the person of Jesus himself. And once again it results in a very hard law.

e. Revenge

On the matter of revenge, Jesus' approach is different again. With murder, adultery and divorce, Jesus is concerned that the law should be kept more strictly than required in order truly to capture its essence. Now, on the matter of *'Eye for eye, and tooth for tooth'* (38), Jesus suggests that, in order to capture its essence, the law should not be kept at all. Or so it seems at first glance. The so-called *lex talionis* was probably intended as a limiting law, to prevent disproportionate actions being taken against somebody who had wronged another. Arguably, also, it was in recognition of the need to restore *šālôm* when some imbalance has been created in the community through wrongful action. [40] Accordingly, Jesus goes to the heart of the matter, the restoration of *šālôm* or right relationship, and by implication questions whether a system of arithmetically calculated retaliation is capable of effecting restoration. In fact, the very opposite of retaliation is likely to be more effective. When somebody wrongs you, give him or her the opportunity to compound the wrong: offer the *other cheek* (39) or walk the extra mile (41) or lend to the one who asks (42). By such actions are wrongs truly countered.

This is not a quietist resignation so much as an active response to wrongdoing and evil. A slap on the right cheek (39) is an insulting backhander that assumes an imbalance of power, while asking for the necessarily forearm slap on the other cheek forces the perpetrator to treat his victim as a fellow combatant.[41] The difference is

---

[38] Schweizer, *Matthew*, p. 126.

[39] How we read this in a world of no-fault divorce is another, and important, discussion, but is not germane to the present argument, which is about Jesus and the word/Word of God.

[40] C. D. Marshall, *Beyond Retribution: A New Testament Vision for Justice, Crime, and Punishment* (Grand Rapids: Eerdmans, 2001), pp. 78–84.

[41] M. C. Brett, *Decolonising God: The Bible in the Tides of Empire*, BMW 16 (Sheffield: Sheffield Phoenix, 2008), pp. 141–142, characterizes this response as 'resistance'.

subtle, but important. By the same token, the one forcing the hearer *to go one mile* (41) was likely to have been a Roman soldier.[42] By doing more than is required the victim of injustice assumes the role of one bestowing a favour. The power relation is reversed, often to the discomfort of the perpetrator of the original injustice.[43] The wisdom of Proverbs understands this dynamic well in saying that the doer of undeserved good deeds 'will heap burning coals' on the head of his or her enemy.[44] By the example of his own life, Jesus commends a better way to realize the intent of *'eye for eye, and tooth for tooth'*.

f. Love

But it is not enough merely to 'heap coals of fire'. If that is the intent of the actions, then they are ultimately no better than observation of the *lex talionis*. Love needs to be in the mix somewhere (43–47). This time, the law is not kept by expanding it or by suspending it, but by turning it on its head: *love your enemies and pray for those who persecute you* (44). The Jewish hearers of this discourse knew about love, for they had been directed to *love [their] neighbour* (43), a commandment that was based on respect for all members of the covenant people of God. Within the covenant, each one has a God-given inheritance. To fail to love anybody within that covenant is in one sense to deny them their heritage.[45]

But the life and work of Jesus redefined the covenant and pointed towards the fulfilment of the promise to Abraham that many nations would be blessed as a result of the blessing of Abraham.[46] A further outcome of that was the realization that the body of believers functions as 'a kind of firstfruits of all [God] created'.[47] That being the case, all that applies to relationships within the covenant must now apply to all people that God has made.[48] And so it is inescapable that the command to love can no longer stop at neighbours; it must apply to everybody – including our enemies. In

[42] Schweizer, *Matthew*, p. 130.

[43] An understanding of these dynamics is still an important part of non-violent resistance to unjust and exploitative situations. In the Palestinian context, I have been privileged to observe how insisting on being treated as an equal can destabilize a power imbalance.

[44] Prov. 25:22.

[45] B. C. Birch, *Let Justice Roll Down: The Old Testament, Ethics, and Christian Life* (Louisville: Westminster John Knox, 1991), pp. 179–180.

[46] Gen. 12:3.

[47] Jas 1:18.

[48] D. L. Turner, *Matthew*, BECNT (Grand Rapids: Baker Academic, 2008), p. 25.

that respect, the parable of the Good Samaritan,[49] with its redefinition of 'neighbour', is a companionpiece with the command to *love your enemies* (44). A failure to love them is effectively a denial of the place that God has for them. For we are the firstfruits of *all* that God has made.[50] The *sun* and the *rain* do not distinguish (45–46); no more should we. Once again, Jesus' instruction has penetrated to the essence of a particular word. The Word has illumined the word.

4. The call to perfection

In the light of all that, Jesus says: *Be perfect, therefore, as your heavenly Father is perfect* (48). The Greek word here translated as 'perfect' has a primary sense of having arrived at a particular goal or state at the end of a journey or process. If there is perfection, it is the perfection of having matured or been completed in some way. It does not so much imply a flawless nature in the way the English 'perfect' does, although it may have that meaning. The word is often translated as 'mature' or 'complete' elsewhere in the TNIV and other versions. For example, Paul refers to the mature who are still straining towards completeness.[51] In 1 Corinthians 13:10 the word speaks of completeness in contrast to the partial, while in the next chapter it speaks of adults as against children.[52] Particularly illuminating is Ephesians 4:13, wherein Paul looks to the day when 'we all . . . become mature, attaining to the whole measure of the fullness of Christ'.

Jesus' instruction to *be perfect* (48) is therefore a call to a process, which culminates in our becoming like God, or, in the words heard by the Ephesian Christians, 'attaining to the whole measure of the fullness of Christ'. The journey to that goal entails a continuous encounter with the word of God in Scripture read in such a way that Christ as the Word of God allows us to hear and see more clearly the words and acts of God in the text. In the passage that we have been examining, this has particular ethical outcomes, but it is exemplary of the wider process of reading in the light of Christ.[53] Sometimes Christ turns the text upside down; sometimes he lightens the load of the text; sometimes he poses a bigger challenge than we have heretofore perceived; sometimes he undermines traditional

---

[49] Luke 10:25–37.
[50] Jas 1:18.
[51] Phil. 3:15.
[52] 1 Cor. 14:20.
[53] Turner, *Matthew*, p. 167.

interpretations.[54] Always Jesus as the Word draws the reader to a clearer and deeper appreciation of the word of God as preserved in Scripture, and always he calls the reader on to live the word/ Word as well as read it. For those who teach, there is a particular responsibility to get this right. Not only do we pass on the word of God as it comes down to us in the text, a responsibility enjoined by Deuteronomy 4:9–10, but we also now do so in the light of the life and words of Christ the Word. And thus we become holy because God is holy.

[54] For further see D. Tidball, *The Message of Holiness: Restoring God's Masterpiece*, BSTBT (Leicester and Downers Grove: IVP, 2010), pp. 122–124: 'Jesus is not intensifying the law so much as radicalizing it.'

Romans 10:5–13
14. God's word and righteousness

At the risk of offending the theological purist, it is possible to think of Genesis 1 – 11 as a series of accounts of various 'original sins'. Of course the theological phrase, 'original sin', is normally used to describe the state of the heart rather than particular actions.[1] Nevertheless, the fallenness of humankind expresses itself in some key archetypal ways in those first few chapters of Scripture, culminating in the sin perpetrated by the builders of the tower of Babel. They aspired to '[reach] to the heavens' and thus to 'make a name for [themselves]'.[2]

From earliest times humanity has displayed this impulse to become well known. An overweening pride, well expressed in the Greek concept of hubris, often comes hard on the heels of fame. It is less common for that further to result in a direct challenge to the divine, but there are all sorts of other ways in which human beings factor out God by virtue of their success. Still today, we see the sin of the Tower of Babel all around us. It is evident in the celebrity culture of our times, wherein personalities assume a significance for themselves well beyond the scope of their actual achievements or contribution towards human flourishing. Writing this at the time of Michael Jackson's death, I note also the willingness of ordinary folk to collude in that process. We see it in a corporate culture that has convinced itself that some individuals are worth so much remuneration that the amount is effectively meaningless. This culture is often accompanied by a sense of entitlement that is out of all proportion to reality. And we see the effects of the Tower of Babel perhaps

---

[1] It is not part of my purpose to define exactly how this concept should be understood, other than as an expression of the rebellion and sin that is found at the heart of human nature.
[2] Gen. 11:3–9.

most brutally in contexts where a particular state leader enforces an almost absolute devotion to (usually) himself. The North Korean regime is the most obvious example at time of writing, but 'The Dear Leader' is not alone.

One of the goals of the builders of the Tower of Babel was that they 'not be scattered over the face of the whole earth'.[3] That impulse translates into a drive for uniformity. Totalitarian regimes are marked by intolerance, and are the best illustration of a contemporary expression of that particular Tower of Babel effect. But all hubris contains at some level unhappiness with dissent and a tendency to repress diversity. The church, as we will mention, is unfortunately not immune from this phenomenon.

In Scripture, God's answer to the Tower of Babel is the gift of the Spirit at Pentecost with all its freedom and exuberance and diversity of expression.[4] As a result of that gift, the breach brought about by the pride of Babel was healed by an affirmation of diversity harnessed together into a common object of worship. The signature mark of that effect was the gift of tongues.[5] Just as the disruption of language was the punishment of pride at Babel, so now the restoration of understanding alongside diversity of language brings healing. Given that God is made manifest amongst humankind as the Word, it ought not to surprise us that the Spirit of Jesus demonstrates the possibility of Jesus the Word in the manner seen at Pentecost.

Paul alludes to that event as he reflects on faith and the location of the word of God in the light of Jesus in Romans 10:5–13.

1. The link with Pentecost

The culmination of Paul's train of thought in these few verses is in verse 13: *'Everyone who calls on the name of the Lord will be saved.'* This is a direct quote from the Septuagint of Joel 2:32, and echoes Peter's earlier use of the same words during his sermon in Jerusalem on the occasion of Pentecost.[6] In the book of Joel these words are the culminating response to a series of events that will signify the

---

[3] Gen. 11:4.

[4] The link between Babel and Pentecost has been discussed since early in the history of the church. For a summary, see J. Davis, 'Acts 2 and the Old Testament: The Pentecost Event in Light of Sinai, Babel and the Table of Nations', *CTR* 7 (2009), pp. 29–48.

[5] Acts 2:1–12.

[6] Acts 2:21.

'great and dreadful day of the Lord',[7] including the pouring out of the Spirit of prophecy on all people. Peter saw one fulfilment of those prophecies in the gift of many tongues at Pentecost.

Paul here uses those same words of Joel somewhat differently. His interest is more on the word *everyone*, to reinforce his point that the Lord responds to *all who call on him* and that *there is no difference between Jew and Gentile* in this matter (12). Nevertheless, the echo of the longer passage and its significance to the early church is unmistakeable. Among other things, it reminds Paul's readers of the coming of the Spirit and the significance of the Word of God still present among them. In that respect, it draws together several themes that we have already encountered in this study of the message of Scripture: the role of the Spirit, the witness of the written Scriptures and the presence of Christ the Word.[8]

2. The pride of Babel

These verses are part of Romans 9 – 11, in which Paul is grappling with God's ongoing involvement with the people of Israel in the light of new Gentile possibilities opened up by the life and work of Christ. In the verses under consideration, Paul draws one of a number of contrasts between righteousness that is of the law and righteousness that is of faith. Of the former, he says that it is realized in doing the requirements of the law (5). Of the latter, righteousness by faith, there are a number of points made. The one that immediately concerns us is that such righteousness does not presume to domesticate the Word of God in Christ; it does not say that Christ can be brought down from heaven or brought up from the deep (6–7).[9] This seems to be a reflection of the presumption that was present at the Tower of Babel, to go up to heaven and to make a name for themselves.

For all the wonder of God's having spoken with his people in the law, and indeed in creation, there remained something missing. The longing to know God and to travel with God that permeated events at Mount Sinai has somehow not been fully satisfied. At its best, this longing gave rise to the sort of holy unrest seen as Moses struck a deal for God to travel with the people,[10] as Abraham pleaded for

---

[7] Joel 2:31.
[8] J. R. W. Stott, *The Message of Romans: God's Good News for the World*, BST (Leicester: IVP, 1994), p. 285.
[9] A. Schlatter, *Romans: The Righteousness of God*, tr. S. S. Schatzmann (Peabody: Hendrickson, 1995), pp. 212–214.
[10] Exod. 33:15–18.

Sodom to be spared,[11] or as Jacob wrestled with the angel of the Lord at the Brook of Jabbok.[12] At its worst it differed little in kind from the presumptive pride of the people of Babel.[13] Whatever the case, Paul argues, still there is a desire to capture the word of God, even as it is expressed in Christ, and somehow lasso it to human purposes (6–7). Sadly the church, like the Zealots of Jesus' day, is not immune from this impulse to totalitarian behaviour that has dogged humanity. Still today, there is a tendency in each of us to claim a more complete knowledge of Christ and of the word of God in Scripture than what we see in those who differ from us. Still today, there is a tendency to domesticate Jesus to our own ends rather than to trust the dangerous winds of the Spirit.

3. Righteousness that is by faith

It is important at this point to be clear what Paul means by righteousness. For Paul, righteousness is 'essentially [God's] covenant dealings with his people, who are thereby constituted a new humanity'.[14] This righteousness may not be foiled by human sin, but instead God has brought into being a new humanity comprising both Jew and Gentile.[15] This new humanity is drawn into the righteousness of God as a result of the work of Christ. It cannot therefore be characterized by the pride of Babel.

There is a double focus to the slightly obscure way that Paul has chosen to make his point. On the one hand, such righteousness cannot be at the beck and call of human beings. As we have just noted, it is not for one living the life of faith to presume to make Christ somehow accessible by bringing him down from heaven or forcing him up from Sheol (6–7). That is simply not within the prerogative of humankind. On the other hand, the life of faith no longer has to achieve particular acts of righteousness as defined in the law. These acts are impossible, anyway, within the limits of our human nature, as Jesus demonstrated so vividly in the Sermon

---

[11] Gen. 18:22–33.

[12] Gen. 32:22–32.

[13] J. D. G. Dunn, '"Righteousness from the Law" and "Righteousness from Faith": Paul's Interpretation of Scripture in Romans 10:1–10', in G. F. Hawthorne (ed.), *Tradition and Interpretation in the New Testament* (Grand Rapids: Eerdmans, 1987), pp. 221–222, links the quote from Lev. 18:5 in v. 5 with the nationalist piety of the Zealots in first-century Palestine.

[14] *NIDNTT* 3, p. 363.

[15] D. J. Moo, *Romans*, NIVAC (Grand Rapids: Zondervan, 2000), p. 331.

on the Mount and at other times.[16] The notion that God may be attained through human effort leads eventually to the sin of Babel. Rather, the word of God is never far away; for sons and daughters of God, it is as close as breathing. For Paul, this is something that comes about through knowing the incarnate Word, Jesus (8).[17] In that respect Christ becomes the fulfilment of a much older insight that potentially the fullness of God's word is known in the intimacy of relationship with God.[18]

4. Righteousness and the declaration of the w/Word of God

We see in this passage three elements of the word of God, all of which we have already encountered, working together in the dynamic of righteousness: the Scriptures, the Word of God in Christ and the spoken word of faith (8). Paul demonstrates the importance of the first by his constant reference to Old Testament material, some of which we have already referred to above. This is most explicitly expressed in reference to *Moses* (5) and *Scripture* (11). For Paul, the written word of God continues to be a live witness to the ongoing work of God in implementing the righteousness of God. Although Paul is selective in the Scriptures that he refers to, there is no sense of any others being set aside.[19] However unorthodox to our minds Paul may have been in some of his handling of the Old Testament, he never calls into doubt their usefulness or authority.[20]

At the same time, though, he does convey a sense of a new thing being done. *Righteousness that is by faith* (6) is not the same thing as what has so far applied, namely, *righteousness that is by the law* (5). The speech of God in the words known as the *torah* or law has not been rejected, but now those words meet Christ the Word. The intent in giving the law had always been that the written words of God's acts should become internalized in following genera-tions.[21] Now Paul indicates that this is made possible in the life of Christ in the believer. The believer's declaration that *'Jesus is Lord'*

[16] See ch. 13 on Matt. 5:17–48.
[17] Stott, *Romans*, p. 284.
[18] Deut. 30:11–14.
[19] See Dunn, 'Paul's Interpretation of Scripture', pp. 225–226, on the *'continuity* [Paul] saw between the OT and the gospel of Christ' (emphasis original).
[20] Of much that could be cited see the collection of essays in S. L. Porter and C. D. Stanley (eds.), *As It Is Written: Studying Paul's Use of Scripture* (Atlanta: SBL, 2008).
[21] Deut. 4:9.

arising from a knowledge of the living Christ (9) illustrates the point.

Thirdly, this word is also, according to Paul, *the message concerning faith that we proclaim* (8). In the Greek this phrase is quite succinct, and may be rendered more literally in English thus: 'the word of faith which we preach.' The word of God continues as the living word preached through the generations, and this preaching arises out of the fact that God's word indwells all those who have set their faith in Christ.

The result of this indwelling is succinctly conveyed in the Greek of verse 10. Once again, this is not easily portrayed in English but a more literal translation is thus: 'by the heart it is believed into righteousness and by the mouth it is spoken into salvation.' The Greek bears a sense that the heart's belief and the mouth's declaration together play a part in bringing about the righteousness and salvation of God in the believer. This possibility must be treated with care; no human carrier of the gospel is ever sufficient on its own for salvation. Grammatically also, the form of the Greek further de-emphasizes the agency of the action. Nevertheless, it seems that the spoken word of the believer is one element, along with Scripture and Christ, in the ongoing speech-act of God amongst all those whom he has made. This is a natural outworking of the fact that Christ the Word indwells the believer, and is further emphasized in verses 14–15.

5. The effective word of God

Three aspects of the word of God are emerging as we read the Scriptures around the theme of the message of Scripture: the word of God in Scripture itself, the Word of God in Christ, and the word/Word of God declared through the preaching of the believer in the present. At this point the temptation to systematize should be resisted. To rank the three in order of importance or to prescribe the manner in which they interact is simply to read more into the text of Scripture than has been made available to us. One might even say that to attempt to do so, in the manner of many expositions on Scripture and authority, is to fall prey to the temptation of verse 6, the domestication of Christ after the manner of the people of Babel. The ironic effect is a reversion to a *righteousness that is by the law* (5), the very thing that Paul has set out to counter in this passage. We must remain content that God continues to speak in the Scriptures, through Christ and in the ongoing miracle of God's indwelling the believer and the church as the body of believers. God's voice is muted when any of these elements are discounted. If that feels like a risky position to take, we can be assured by the words of Peter on the pervasive influence of the Spirit of God.[22] We can also be challenged in our own practice to set our sails to catch the wind of that Spirit.[23]

It should not be forgotten, either, that the whole point of God's speaking is not primarily to provide the raw material for a correct doctrine of Scripture and of scriptural authority.[24] Rather, God speaks, on the evidence of this passage, for the sake of righteousness. The righteousness of God, and the connection of humanity with that righteousness, is an inexhaustible concept. Suffice to note that, as we have already mentioned, it includes the emergence of a covenant people of God whose salvation is made possible by the work of Jesus (9) and the outworking of whose lives is the result of faith (6). In the righteousness of God we find deliverance and freedom from the pride, tyranny, confusion, misunderstanding and fragmentation that lay at the heart of the Tower of Babel experience. This righteousness that comes by God's word brings rich blessing (12), and is there for *all who call on him* (12). It is a righteousness that answers the evidence around us that Babel is alive and well. There is a great responsibility on all those who handle and live the word/Word of God not to do so in a way that reinforces the tyranny of Babel.

Jesus is at the centre of God's speaking this righteousness into being. Because, as we will see in the next chapter on Revelation 5, he is the one found worthy to open the scroll.

---

[22] See ch. 5 on 2 Pet. 1:19–21.

[23] 2 Pet. 1:21.

[24] Although see ch. 3 on the infallibility and sufficiency of Scripture in the context of a discussion on Prov. 30:5–6.

Revelation 5
15. Worthy to open the scroll

So far in this section on God's speaking in Christ, we have seen the revelation of God in Christ the Word, and linked that to the speech-act of God. We have discovered in the book of Hebrews that God has spoken fully and finally in Jesus but not in a way that negates the speech of God in the Scriptures. Indeed, from the Sermon on the Mount, we saw that those Scriptures are illumined by God in Christ. And Paul, in Romans 10, discerned that the speaking of God in Christ and in the Scriptures that formed him and are fulfilled by him has the effect of bringing about the rich blessing of righteousness.

If we are honest, there are times when the theory of all this is out of synch with our experience. Sometimes we find the interpretation of Scripture difficult. We hear Jesus as more cryptic than revelatory. Like the Psalmist, we occasionally find God silent and deaf to our appeals.[1] As we look around us we see a world not so much 'charged with the grandeur of God' as 'seared with trade; bleared, smeared with toil'.[2] For all of our Christian assertions about the word of God, there is little sign in a broken world of the divine glory that is the expression of God's word amongst humanity. At a personal level, our encounter of the word of God in Scripture is occasionally a lifeless and duty-bound thing.

At such moments, doubt crouches at our door. We find ourselves in perhaps the most difficult place in the landscape of faith: the valley between promise and fulfilment. At its worst that doubt can turn us into Vladimir and Estragon, who are 'waiting for Godot',

---

[1] Ps. 88:13–14.
[2] G. M. Hopkins, 'God's Grandeur', in *Poems of Gerard Manley Hopkins*, ed. R. Bridges (London: Humphrey Milford, 1918), p. 20.

the subject of Samuel Beckett's play of that name.[3] Because Godot never comes, history dissolves for the characters into a series of repeated and unremembered events. There is no hope for Vladimir and Estragon because nothing happens and they are thereby denied both an anticipation of the future and a coherent memory of the past; they are enslaved by a perpetual present.

In the world of Scripture, however, the valley between promise and fulfilment is the place to which God calls his people. He did so, for example, through Jeremiah when the prophet called on the people of Judah to go to Babylon and experience for themselves the šālôm of God as they worked for the šālôm of that strange and distant place.[4] At the same time, however, it is a place out of which we constantly seek route maps to fulfilment. We live in hope, not merely in the sense of waiting for an unscheduled bus to arrive, but in the sense that our valley is part of a larger and richer environment which one day we will have the opportunity to explore more fully. Because God 'has set eternity in the human heart',[5] we are shaped by memory and anticipate a future. We are thereby equipped both to live well in the present in which God has placed us and to share a reasonable hope that our present is part of a larger and longer story to which we can contribute. At the same time, within the limitations of our humanity we cannot 'fathom what God has done from beginning to end'.[6] We are creatures who, at least for the moment, can only experience time from the inside, as it were. In that respect, the 'eternity' within us is more often a yearning than an experience. Like John, the visionary responsible for the book of Revelation, we weep that the scroll remains unopened (4).

And we wait and hope. But, in contrast to Vladimir and Estragon, we wait and hope not for Godot but for God. We have the memory of the words of God in relation to humanity and the cosmos in Scripture, and the lived experience of God by means of those texts. We have seen them interpreted and fulfilled in the person of Jesus, God with us. The 'eternity' in our hearts then asks the question: as the Scriptures and the Christ to whom they bear witness bring God's story into our remembered past and our lived experience, is it possible that they also take us into an anticipated future? In more technical terms, might Scripture have an eschatological function? On the evidence of Revelation 5, the answer to those questions is

---

[3] S. Beckett, *Waiting for Godot: A Tragicomedy in Two Acts* (London: Faber & Faber, 1965).
[4] Jer. 29:7.
[5] Eccl. 3:11.
[6] Ibid.

that they do and it does. The words and deeds of God enable the people of God to live in anticipation of and within sight of the reign of Christ over all things and for all time. These words and deeds are encapsulated in the Scriptures, and come alive through the living Word, Christ. The people of God are thereby enabled to live with a sense of hope for what is yet to be. But there is more. If we have been right that the text of Scripture itself becomes the speech-act of God, then we could also say that those Scriptures help to bring about the fulfilment for which we wait and hope. Ultimately they do so because Jesus is *worthy* (4) and *able* (5) to open the scroll. And so we turn to Revelation 5.

1. An eschatological view

But first a slight diversion is in order concerning the phrase *for ever and ever* (13). The Greek word being translated is *aiōn*, which is usually translated as in verse 13, by 'forever' or a word of similar meaning. It is also the term that the Septuagint usually uses to translate the Hebrew word *'ôlām* in the Old Testament, a word also normally translated into English as 'forever'.[7] As we have seen, the word in post-biblical usage came increasingly to apply to space as well as time,[8] a usage that would have been known, although probably not particularly common, in the first century AD. It conjures up a picture of the God who reigns through all of space and time. The history of humanity and the much longer history of the cosmos are all overseen by him. So, when *every creature in heaven and on earth and under the earth and on the sea, and all that is in them* (13) declares praise and power to the Lamb *for ever and ever* (13), they reflect this understanding. They are saying much more than that the Lamb will rule for an extremely long time; they are declaring that the influence of the Lamb is cosmic in scope. The worth of Christ is not merely in his longevity; it is in the breadth and depth of his reign.

That this vision is spatial as well as temporal does not in any way limit its eschatological impact. It is part of a book (Revelation) which declares itself right at the start as concerning things that 'must soon take place'.[9] Within that overview statement the vision of Revelation 5 is nested in a division of the book that begins at 4:1.[10]

---

[7] Gen. 3:22 for example.
[8] See ch. 12.
[9] Rev. 1:1.
[10] S. W. Pattemore, *The People of God in the Apocalypse: Discourse, Structure*

Therein the visionary reiterates that we are reading of things that will come to pass 'after this'.[11] How to read this phrase is somewhat debated, but it is widely agreed that it is 'generally eschatological in scope',[12] and close in concept to a range of similar notions expressed elsewhere in the New Testament.[13] It means that what is in store in the subsequent visions are events that have begun but have not yet been consummated.[14] Revelation 5, which describes the one who is worthy to open the scroll, therefore indicates that the scroll bears an eschatological significance. To put it another way, its opening has something to do with the hope of the Christian. And this opening is made possible by the *Lamb* who has *been slain* (6), *the Lion of the tribe of Judah, the Root of David* (5).

The spreading circle of praise seen by John the visionary is in response to this anticipated opening of the scroll. It begins with the *four living creatures and the twenty-four elders* (8) and spreads to the *thousands upon thousands, and ten thousand times ten thousand* (11), and then eventually *every creature in heaven and on earth and under the earth and on the sea, and all that is in them* (13) pick up the tune. Whatever the technicalities of interpretation of those groups may be, it is a comprehensive recognition of the Lamb of God. The circle of praise expands numerically as well as conceptually. The movement from twenty-four to thousands to 'every' parallels the expanding focus from elders to angels to 'every creature'. The entire universe gradually comes into view in consideration of the one who is worthy to open the scroll.

2. The scroll

It seems important then to appreciate just what might be intended by the scroll. Unfortunately there is little agreement amongst commentators on its contents, and each proposal brings with it some problems.[15] For example, those who argue that it contains the names of believers do not take account of the fact that subsequent opening

---

and Exegesis, NSTSMS 128 (Cambridge: Cambridge University Press, 2004), pp. 220–225.

[11] Rev. 4:1. See M. E. Boring, *Revelation*, Interpretation (Louisville: John Knox, 1989), p. 101, on the structural links between Rev. 4 and 5.

[12] G. K. Beale, *The Book of Revelation: A Commentary on the Greek Text*, NIGTC (Grand Rapids: Eerdmans, 1999), p. 317.

[13] Mark 1:15; Acts 2:17; Gal. 4:4; 1 Cor. 10:11; 2 Cor. 6:2; 1 Tim. 4:1; 2 Tim. 3:1; 1 Pet. 1:20; 2 Pet. 3:3; Heb. 1:2; 9:26; Jas 5:3; 1 John 2:18; Jude 18.

[14] Beale, *Revelation*, p. 318.

[15] Ibid., pp. 339–340.

of the scroll's seals entails events that affect the whole cosmos.[16] That it may be the contents of the Old Testament is somewhat at odds with the strong echoes of Daniel 7 and 12 and Ezekiel 2 – 3, which are primarily decrees of future judgment and are not representative of the Old Testament as a whole. The argument that it is a book containing the great events of the future anticipated by the Apocalypse, does not seem quite to take account of the engagement with the past and present that is also part of the revelation received by John. That the scroll may be the particular contents of the rest of the book of Revelation receives no warrant from the text itself.

The physical detail that the scroll is two-sided seems to be important somehow. Yet attempts to say how add little to our appreciation of the meaning of this complex little chapter. It is commonly noted that the description of the scroll matches ancient contract documents, written as they are on the outer side and sealed by several witnesses (1).[17] It is further noted that this was typical of divorce notices. Yet none of this adds particularly to an understanding of what the scroll may have been about.

Given the failure of interpreters to come up with an agreed sense of the contents of the scroll or its essential nature, it is probably best to think of it, like much else in the book of Revelation, as 'an evocative symbol'.[18] This means that a range of thoughts and ideas are evoked by the image of a scroll that is sealed. Furthermore, it is important to remember that visions and dreams bear multiple meanings, and can sometimes defy literal explanation. In this context, the scroll evokes a range of notions that are already in the hearer's/ reader's mind. That the scroll is written on both sides is a clear allusion to Ezekiel 2:10. The prophet was told to eat that scroll, with the implication that his being filled by it would bring the fullness of God's message to Ezekiel's people. Similarly, John himself echoed Ezekiel's prophetic ministry in obeying a divine command to eat a scroll, as a result of which he prophesied 'about many peoples, nations, languages and kings'.[19] In this way the presence of a scroll implies a prophetic message to the nations that the visionary weeps to hear (4). Perhaps he weeps as we do also with longing to see God act in a world where pain and injustice seem usually to prevail and hope recedes.

---

[16] Rev. 6.

[17] G. R. Osborne, *Revelation*, BECNT (Grand Rapids: Baker Academic, 2002), p. 249.

[18] I am grateful to Stephen Pattemore for his use of this phrase in a private conversation.

[19] Rev. 10:9–11.

There are also two other books in the Apocalypse which are evoked by the appearance of the two-sided scroll, although not quite as directly.[20] Both books are implied in the judgment scene of Revelation 20:11–15. One is the book that records the deeds of all people and the other is the 'book of life', which is a kind of register of heavenly citizenship.[21] Both of these ideas have an ancient pedigree, as witness Moses' reference to being blotted out of the book of life,[22] and the Psalmist's allusion to events that have been preordained.[23] The scroll of Revelation 5 brings to mind these books also, and so speaks of judgment and of hope and of the future. All of these are evoked by the appearance of a sealed scroll. No single description of the contents of this range of ideas behind the scroll fully suffices. 'God's plan for human history' is not a bad attempt,[24] although I would want to expand that to include the entire history of the cosmos.

On a yet broader canvas, this picture of a sealed scroll, with its accompanying emphasis on the power of what has been written, occurs in the context of a collection of writings that are believed to express the words and actions of God towards his people and the world in which he has placed them. As we think about this particular scroll and its writing, we are led to think more widely of the word of God written, of what we have come to call Scripture. The nature of the scroll as the written word of God can tell us something more of the nature of God's word written more generally. It suggests the mystery of Scripture and the contingent nature of its interpretation. Like Daniel and John, when we look at Scripture we see a collection the full understanding of which we still await. Now we see the counsel of God only partially revealed; but we glimpse the possibility of a fuller revelation as Scripture points us to the words and activity of God that bring hope both for our individual futures and for the future of the world that God has spoken into being. In that respect, the written words of God in Scripture act with an eschatological impact. And the key to that impact is the work of the one described in John's vision as the *Lamb looking as if it had been slain* (6) and *the Lion of the tribe of Judah* (5), the one whom Scripture elsewhere names as Jesus the Christ.

---

[20] J. P. M. Sweet, *Revelation* (Philadelphia: Westminster, 1979), p. 123, implicitly identifies scroll with book.
[21] See also Rev. 3:5; 17:8; 21:27.
[22] Exod. 32:32.
[23] Ps. 139:16.
[24] *DBI*, pp. 764–765, 114.

3. The one who is completely worthy

The seven seals on the scroll are also an important part of this effect. Rather than concerning ourselves over the exact type of Ancient Near Eastern document that may be intended, it is helpful to focus on the symbolic effect of the seals. The sealing of a document suggests two things. First, it is a sign of authenticity and authority. Only the one qualified to do so may seal a document and subsequently break the seal.[25] At the same time, the seals bring an air of mystery and anticipation in that they are not to be broken open before their time. We might suppose that the minds of John's hearers at this point went to the ancient words of the angel to Daniel, who was told that the things he had heard would be 'sealed until the end of time'.[26] That comment was in reply to Daniel's yearning to understand the mysteries of his visions.[27] The same yearning was felt by John as he observed the seven seals continuing to shut up the mysteries. The seals may have been indications of the authenticity of the contents, but that only made the anticipation of their inaccessible contents harder. Must he wait interminably, as Beckett's characters had to wait, to know what the seals concealed? The question is all the more urgent in that the number of seals, seven, is another sign of the 'completeness' of God's plan hidden therein.[28]

But the answer comes quickly. The path from promise to fulfilment is not blocked; it is accessible through the one who is worthy to break the seals and open the scroll. And the worth of that one is as full as the message that he is entitled to unveil. In counterpoint to the seven seals, he has *seven horns and seven eyes* (6). These point to the powerful and all-seeing nature of the Lamb who opens the scroll.[29] It is further reinforced in the sevenfold declaration by the myriads of angels that he is worthy *to receive power and wealth and wisdom and strength and honour and glory and praise* (12). While we can debate the distinctions between and significance of each element in this expression, the overall effect is unmistakable. In this context of repeated sevens, it is almost certainly deliberate that there are seven qualities ascribed to the Lamb. He is as comprehensive as it is possible to be and knows as comprehensively as it is possible to know. Accordingly, whatever else we might say about the nature of our knowing and of our interpretation of Scripture, it is informed

[25] *NIDB* 5, p. 137.
[26] Dan. 12:9.
[27] Dan. 12:8.
[28] *DBI*, p. 765.
[29] D. E. Aune, *Revelation 1–5*, WBC 52A (Dallas: Word, 1997), p. 353–354.

by the Lamb who opens the scroll, by the one who alone is worthy by virtue of his own completeness to unseal the mind of God. To put it in more technical terms, both our epistemology and our hermeneutics are incomplete without Christ.

The seven eyes of the Lamb echo Zechariah 4:10, in which the seven eyes of the Lord 'range throughout the earth'. In an innovative move, John interprets the eyes as *the seven spirits of God sent out into all the earth* (6).[30] The manuscript evidence for the inclusion or not of 'seven' as a modifier of 'spirits' is conflicting and finely balanced.[31] In light of the references to 'seven spirits' in Revelation 1:4, 3:1 and 4:5, and of the proximity to the seven horns and seven eyes, it is a reasonable assumption on the part of the TNIV translation that *seven spirits* is intended here also.[32] Given the proximity of the spirit of the Lord in Zechariah 4:6 to the seven eyes of the Lord in Zechariah 4:10, it is likely also that the seven spirits that are the seven eyes also signify the presence of the Spirit of the Lord. With Beale and others I read the *seven spirits* (6) as an expression of the Spirit of Yahweh, which is inherent in the Lamb.[33] Although the book of Revelation does not have a particularly developed understanding of the Holy Spirit as a distinct person of the Godhead, we can read here a hint that the breaking of the seals and the release of the scroll to bring about God's future in the world is an ongoing presence of the Spirit of God as much as an outcome of the work of Christ.[34] The ranging of the Spirit *into all the earth* (6) translates this heavenly vision of Christ into an earthly reality. Just as our knowing and our interpreting is only complete in Christ, the all-seeing one, so the realization of this vision in the daily stuff of life is powered by the Holy Spirit informing the contexts in which we seek to know and interpret more truly and fully.

4. The Lion and the Lamb

All of this is made possible because the one who is worthy to open the seals on the scroll is the Lion and the Lamb. As the *Lion of the tribe of Judah* and the *Root of David* no less (5), he fulfils all the hopes for the reign of God that were invested in the line of David in

[30] Ibid., p. 354.
[31] See ibid., p. 324, on the text-critical details.
[32] Beale, *Revelation*, p. 356.
[33] Ibid., p. 355.
[34] See ch. 5 on the role of the Spirit in Scripture and its interpretation. For a theological account, see M. Habets, *The Anointed Son: A Trinitarian Spirit Christology* (Eugene: Pickwick, 2010), p. 197.

the post-exilic period. And yet, in a startling reversal of expectation, he is also compared to a slaughtered lamb. The writer has used the Greek word, *arnion*, also used in the Septuagint of Jeremiah 11:19 of the sacrificial lamb. Isaiah 53:7–12 also conveys the idea of the Servant as a sacrificial lamb. To the extent that Jesus is the fulfilment of the hopes invested in a servant figure in the book of Isaiah, he is an offering for sin. This then leads to his identification with the Passover lamb, an identification that is evident in John's Gospel and elsewhere.[35] The victory that is made possible by the Lamb is not of the sort conveyed in the apocalyptic book of 1 Enoch, chapters 89–90, wherein a lamb grows into a great horned ram and engages those who harass the sheep of God's people until he is victorious in battle.[36] On the contrary, the contrasting images of Lion and Lamb together convey that the victory of Christ the Lion is somehow inherent in Christ the slain Lamb.

Jesus is worthy to break the seals and read the scroll by virtue of his sacrificial yet victorious death. He has access where nobody else has. This reflects something of the dynamic that we saw in chapter 12 in our examination of the book of Hebrews. There we noted another paradox, that the one who is now entitled to '[enter] the inner sanctuary behind the curtain'[37] is also the one who 'suffered outside the city gate'.[38] By so doing he was worthy to step across the boundaries that have grown up between God and humanity as a consequence of God's holiness.[39] He became the boundary-crosser by means of his redemptive death.

In Revelation 5 this same paradoxical redemptive suffering enables the crossing of another boundary, that represented by the sealed scroll. The one who has been slain and is victorious not only breaks the seals but also, as the next few chapters unfold, draws those who witness their breaking into a knowledge of what has previously been hidden. In talking about these matters, distinctions between past, present and future tend to blur a little. Nevertheless, in broad terms we might say that, if the boundary-crossing Saviour of the book of Hebrews points to the historic aspect of salvation, the one who breaks the seals ushers his audience into the future. The

---

[35] John 1:29; 19:11; 1 Cor. 5:7; 1 Pet. 1:18–19; 2:21–25. See Sweet, *Revelation*, p. 124, for a summary of these echoes.

[36] 1 Enoch is a composite book, so dating is difficult, but the material in question is probably either first century BC or first century AD. It is likely to have been well known to John's hearers, or at least roughly contemporary with them and part of a shared world of thought.

[37] Heb. 6:19–20.

[38] Heb. 13:12.

[39] See ch. 6 on Exod. 19.

eschatological aspects of salvation begin to be revealed, and in the process also effected.

To place this dynamic on the broader canvas of our consideration of the nature of the word of God, it is Christ ultimately who enables the understanding of the written words of God on the scroll. Given the allusive nature of the scroll and its contents, we might then also say that this can entail the broad sweep of the purposes of God expressed in the written form of the Scriptures delivered to the church. In the context of the book of Revelation, we find that the written words of God concerning humanity are most fully unveiled in the life and death of the Lion and the Lamb. This means that the future is ultimately understood in the light of Christ. Again, in terms of the symbolism present in the book of Revelation, this is worked out by the pervasive presence of the spirit of Christ, the *seven spirits* of the Lamb (6).

5. Responding to the unsealed scroll

To a people who wait for the implementation of the contents of the two-sided scroll, there is a twofold effect. We have noted the link between the worthiness of the Lamb to unseal the scroll and the fact of his sacrificial death. The twenty-four elders also recognize this link, but then add an element: the formation of a people, *a kingdom and priests* in fact, who will *reign on the earth* (10). This is the first effect of the scroll unsealed. There is much that could be said on what this reigning as priests might entail, but we consider it here in light of our focus on the written word of God and the one who ultimately unveils what is written. In those terms, this appears to invite the people of God to join with Christ in knowing and interpreting the words of God for the world in which they/we have been placed. The epistemological and hermeneutical implications are profound. When we say that Scripture is read in the light of Christ, we do not speak of a mysterious and unattainable proposition. It is an attainable reality to be carefully worked out by the people called to *serve our God* (10). And it has to do with *[reigning] on the earth* (10). This entails much more than the exegesis of the words of Scripture; it involves working out the purposes and mind of God for every aspect of life on God's earth in the light of Scripture and the one whose death and victory enable Scripture's interpretation. This reading and interpretation is undertaken under the guidance of the Spirit of Christ whom *God sent out into all the earth* (6), the very place in which the people of God are working out the reign of Christ.

And it is a signal of hope to the people of God who live in the landscape between hope and fulfilment referred to at the start of this chapter. It means that, in the light of God's word written and God's Word lived, we have a sense of where we have been, who we are and where we are going. We are not enslaved by the present. This enables us to make a meaningful home in that place, just as the Hebrew residents of Babylon were urged by Jeremiah to do, and to begin with God to build the road to the fulfilment envisaged by John of the Apocalypse.

The second effect of the unsealed scroll is an outpouring of praise. Accordingly, we join with the *four living creatures* (6), the *elders* (6), the myriads of angels and *every creature in heaven and on earth and under the earth and on the sea* (13) in worship of Christ the Word, in whom the words of God are spoken.

Part 4
God speaks today

Acts 8:26–39
16. Individual encounter with the word of God

St Francis of Assisi is famously reputed to have said to his fellow friars, 'Preach the gospel at all times. Use words if necessary.' There is no evidence of Francis having said this, although it has been observed that it is a Franciscan sort of thing to say.[1] And if he didn't say it, somebody should have. If there is a basis to the quote, it may be from his instruction about preaching in the Earlier Rule of 1221, in which he observes that, whether one has permission to preach or not, 'Let all the brothers . . . preach by their deeds.'[2] Ironically, the popular misquotation of Francis entirely shifts the emphasis of the probable source of the original. Instead of affirming the importance of verbal proclamation for approved members of the brotherhood, as the Earlier Rule sought to do, the popular saying relegates proclamation to the second tier. In any case, the history (or non-history) of the quote illustrates the important question of how the voice of God is promulgated, heard and experienced.

The final major section of this volume gathers around the proposition that 'God speaks today'. Or, to put it another way, the voice of God that we hear in the written word of Scripture and see and hear in the Word, Christ, still comes to us in both word and Word today. In that respect, whatever Francis of Assisi may or may not have said and written, the popular quote and what he probably actually said together remind us of several important aspects of that process. First, and as a general observation, the concept that God

---

[1] See <http://www.americancatholic.org/messenger/oct2001/Wiseman.asp>, accessed 23 December 2010.
[2] Earlier Rule, XVII, in R. J. Armstrong and I. C. Brady (tr. and eds.), *Francis and Clare – The Complete Works*, Classics of Western Spirituality (Mahwah: Paulist, 1982), pp. 107–135.

speaks today in Scripture is meaningless apart from some notion of the conveying and reception of the word of God. Inherent in any commentary on the nature of Scripture is some appreciation of the dynamics of this process.

Secondly, the ironic nature of the misquotation of Francis points up that the process of hearing God's word entails proclamation and hearing. While it is true enough that words on their own are not enough, it is also the case that the utterance of words and their reception are inescapably part of the means by which God speaks, even when the words are only implicit in some kind of action. There is inescapably a verbal aspect to God's speaking today.

At the same time, and thirdly, the reason why the words that Francis did not utter have gained so much currency is that they express an important truth. In them Francis reminded his brothers that, whether they were speaking or not, their actions also conveyed the word of God. This is in tune with the dynamic that we have seen emerging, that the word and act of God are inseparable. As a consequence, we might expect that in the experience of the word of God today we find both word and deed, speech and act, working together. If either word or act deny or contradict the other, the word of God is dulled.

These final chapters will look further at this process of proclaiming and hearing, conveying and receiving, the word of God today and the place and nature of Scripture in that discourse. This entails a look at an individual exchange between a seeker and an apostle (Philip and the Ethiopian eunuch, the subject of this chapter), and a communal interchange around the reading of Scripture (Neh. 8). Each of these episodes illustrates the interaction between the words of Scripture, the Word Jesus, and those who convey and receive those words. They also hint at the importance of the community to which the words of Scripture have been entrusted and so provide a glimpse into the significance of the church to the ongoing presence of God's word today. A chapter on the usefulness of Scripture (2 Tim. 3:10–17) and a return to the theme of the Spirit (John 14:15–26) fills this out further. Finally, and in conclusion, we return more explicitly to the church and the word of God in a consideration of 2 Thessalonians 2:13–17.

But let us turn now to the well known story of the Ethiopian eunuch on the Gaza road.

1. The Ethiopian eunuch and Philip

A key figure in this story is the *Ethiopian eunuch* (27). The Ethiopia of the ancient world probably covered roughly the area of modern day Ethiopia, Sudan and parts of upper Egypt, and was an ancient civilization of some significance.[3] The empire seems routinely to have been ruled over by a queen; *Kandake* (27) is a royal title rather than a personal name, analogous to Pharaoh or Herod or Caesar.[4] In the manner of the ancient world the queen's treasury would have been a central institution in the running of a large empire, and the unnamed eunuch of the story *in charge of all the treasury* (27) must have been one of the key figures in the realm. And he was a man used to authority. While the TNIV tells us that he *invited Philip* (31) up into the chariot, the meaning of the verb so translated ranges from polite invitation to direct summons. The TNIV translation 'invited' is possibly generous. Later on the eunuch initiated the baptism, and seemed in a mood to brook no hesitation from Philip (37). The detail, *He gave orders to stop the chariot* (38), is not essential to the progress of the story, but adds to our sense of the Ethiopian as a man used to being in charge. The term 'eunuch' used to describe him had its origins as a term for one in charge of the harem. This would have been a man who had been castrated or rendered sexually incapable by some naturally occurring physical disability. Over time eunuchs came to hold a number of roles in the courts, to the point where the term was sometimes used generically for a court official. So we cannot be certain whether the man riding in the chariot is physically a eunuch or simply a high official.[5] In any case, he was a man used to exercising power.

He is a man of mystery in other ways also. He was evidently a seeker after truth, having just been up to Jerusalem, we are told, *to worship* (27). And he was interested enough to be reading from the Isaiah scroll on his way home. But what was leading him to Jerusalem? And what was he doing with the scroll of the prophet Isaiah? There would have been few copies of it around, and he presumably was one of a very small number of private individuals who could afford one. Or perhaps he was delivering it to a repository back in the Ethiopian treasury, and was whiling away the hours by reading it. Behind all the unanswered questions, though, we sense a

---

[3] *NIDB* 2, pp. 348–349.

[4] I. H. Marshall, *The Acts of the Apostles: An Introduction and Commentary*, TNTC (Leicester: IVP, 1980), p. 163.

[5] See the discussion of his possible status by L. T. Johnson, *The Acts of the Apostles*, SP 5 (Collegeville: Liturgical Press, 1992), p. 155.

man on a quest for truth. He is used to getting what he wants and is determined to find what he is looking for. The search has apparently led him to Jerusalem and now into the Hebrew Scriptures, but the light has not yet quite dawned.

And then there is Philip. He is directed onto the road south to Gaza from Jerusalem, and is overtaken by a chariot going in the same direction. By some prompting he is led to run up to the chariot, which presumably was moving sedately enough for him to do so, and he heard the eunuch reading out loud, as was the custom of the day. Philip must have been dumbfounded at the words he was hearing. And probably relieved to be invited up into the chariot so that he could catch his breath and begin his explanation.

What is striking about this encounter of the word of God through the prophet Isaiah is its material nature. The physical detail of the setting and action are vivid, albeit allusive: the road south to Gaza; Philip's running to get close enough to the chariot to eavesdrop; the (almost) peremptory indication for Philip to get in the chariot; the manner of the eunuch's suggestion of baptism. Even at the defining moment of his baptism, we sense the individual character of the high official. And this is made possible by Philip's action of obedience in being on the road, obeying that nudge to get closer, initiating the dialogue and acceding to the request for baptism. God speaks into and within the physical experience of our lives.

2. The Spirit of God

A third 'character' in this story is the Spirit of God. We can only surmise what the Holy Spirit has been doing in the heart of this wealthy powerful man who has been drawn to Jerusalem to worship and is actually interested enough to be reading from Isaiah.[6] In an age when we buy books to read on airplanes and then dispose of them, and where most people need to read (and some enjoy it), it is hard to imagine how unusual it was for the eunuch to be reading, let alone reading from the prophet Isaiah. Philip could hardly have expected him to be literate, although on learning of his role as the man in charge of royal treasury, he would have understood. In any case, the voice of God in Scripture is about to be heard because there is a man who wants to hear that voice and whose heart is being prepared to do so. Scripture is not a book of incantations, but a story that comes alive in the encounter with the reader and the Spirit who prompts the reading.

[6] Was he Gentile or diaspora Jew? Or a full proselyte? We cannot know, but see the discussion in D. L. Bock, *Acts*, BECNT (Grand Rapids: Baker, 2007), p. 338.

This Spirit is more in the foreground when it comes to Philip.[7] Having been directed by an *angel of the Lord* (26), he is further prompted to run close enough to the chariot to hear the eunuch reading out loud (29). Then, after the baptism, *the Spirit of the Lord suddenly took Philip away* (39). In this encounter with Scripture, the Spirit pervades the whole event. Previously we considered the role of the Holy Spirit in the production of Scripture and subsequently its interpretation.[8] Now we find that the word of God in Scripture becomes the active word of God also because it is read and interpreted in a world that owes its being to the Creator Spirit, and in partnership with the explicit work of the Spirit in the lives of those whom God is calling to himself.

3. The eunuch's guide

For all that, however, the eunuch was struggling to make sense of what he was reading. He would not have been alone in this as Isaiah 53 generally presented a puzzle to first-century readers.[9] In response to Philip's question, his blunt appraisal is that he cannot understand without a guide (31). As a person of some responsibility in that part of the world, the eunuch would have been able to function well in Greek, the *lingua franca* of the day. It is likely that he was reading this passage in the Greek of the Septuagint.[10] His later questioning of Philip (34) clarifies that he understands the words but not their significance. All the same, his reading suggests a man of considerable intelligence, along with the power and wealth we have already noted. It also bespeaks a longstanding interest on his part in the God of the Jews and the worship of him in Jerusalem. The trip to worship in Jerusalem on which he encountered Philip was almost certainly not his first.

But he needed help. The phrase *unless someone explains it to me* (31) translates a verb that carries the sense of showing somebody the way or the path. The NRSV represents this well with 'unless someone guides me'. The eunuch found in his reading that he needed a guide. To remain with that metaphor for a moment, the way and the means existed for him in the Scriptures; he was not asking for any new information. Finding the way was required, and Philip, by

---

[7] J. R. W. Stott, *The Message of Acts: To the Ends of the Earth*, BST (Leicester: IVP, 1990), p. 161.

[8] See ch. 5.

[9] Marshall, *Acts*, p. 163.

[10] Bock, *Acts*, p. 343.

means of his exposition, was able to signpost that for the Ethiopian official.

And so we see that inherent in the reception of the word of God in Scripture is the work of one who is the guide. The tasks of exposition and interpretation are an essential part of our reading. But care must be taken in what is done with this idea. Before exploring it a little more fully, there are two things that do not follow from this affirmation of interpretation.

The first concerns what is sometimes presented as the three-legged stool of authority: Scripture, tradition and reason.[11] This is often taken to mean that each of these aspects is as significant as the other in the matter of hearing the word of God. In a sense that is true, in that we never read the Bible in a vacuum. We bring a set of assumptions about the Bible and how to read it, and it would be impossible to begin to read without them. This is what is meant by tradition. We also cannot read, even as individuals, without interpreting, applying and questioning the text. We use our God-given reason in our reading. To pretend that we read in a pure way with no reference to these external influences is to be blind to their impact on us, and so prone to the distortions of our own humanity in our reading. In that respect, the reading of Scripture is inseparable from tradition and reason. This is a corollary of the incarnation. As God meets us in Christ as one who dwells with us as one of us, so his word in Scripture constantly engages with the particular contexts and lives of those who hear the voice of God in the reading of Scripture.

However, there is a primacy about Scripture. Tradition and reason must be in constant submission to Scripture and open to change in the light of the words of Scripture, while the opposite cannot be said. While a guide was essential to the Ethiopian eunuch and to any reader of Scripture, the guide is never as important as Scripture and does not have a final mandate to define the meaning of Scripture over against the text. The signpost should not be confused with the way itself.

In affirming the importance of interpretation and interpreters, neither are we saying that the individual Christian cannot read the Bible on his or her own and hear the voice of God in so doing. William Tyndale, translator of the first New Testament in English (1525–6) was supposed to have said to a visiting priest, 'If God spare my life, before very long I shall cause a ploughboy to know

---

[11] For a classic twentieth-century expression of this see J. MacQuarrie, *Principles of Christian Theology* (London: SCM, 1966), pp. 340–342.

the scriptures better than you do!'[12] This sentiment represents one of the hard-won principles of the Reformation. There will always be a need for expertise in the branches of knowledge that enhance the reading of the Bible – linguistics, literary criticism, ancient history, archaeology, anthropology and so forth – but the holders of this expertise do not own the Bible; it belongs to the whole church and to every member of it. Philip was indispensible to the Ethiopian eunuch's understanding, but as a guide, as one who showed the way, not as a gatekeeper. The task of the interpreter is to point people into Scripture, never to keep it from them, and in so doing to point them to the one of whom Scripture bears witness.

4. Jesus

The passage that the Ethiopian was stuck on when he met Philip was Isaiah 53:7–8. These words lie at the heart of the most famous of the songs of the servant in the second part of the book of Isaiah. They are part of a gradual working out on the part of the Isaiah scroll of what it means for Israel to be God's servant. This servant is on the one hand blind and deaf to God's word and profoundly disobedient.[13] This extends to Israel's idolatry, a regular theme in these chapters of Isaiah. Along those lines Isaiah 44:12–20 is one such sustained parody of the idolater, explicitly directed to 'Jacob ... Israel, my servant'.[14] The servant Israel has become an all-too-successful realization of Isaiah's prophetic commission concerning a people 'ever hearing, but never understanding; ... ever seeing, but never perceiving'.[15] Yet despite this, God has not allowed the servant people collectively to shrug off the call that has been with them since the promise to Abraham, that they are blessed for the blessing of all the nations of the earth.[16] In the work of Isaiah, the retrieval of this calling gradually emerges in the form of an idealized picture of the servant of God: one who brings forth justice,[17] whose proclamation is patiently formed by God,[18] whose face is set like

[12] W. Tyndale, *The Obedience of a Christian Man*, ed. D. Daniell (New York: Penguin, 2000), p. xvii.
[13] Isa. 42:18–25.
[14] Isa. 44:21.
[15] Isa. 6:9.
[16] Gen. 12:3.
[17] Isa. 42:1.
[18] Isa. 49:2.

flint on the mission of God,[19] and who finally is drawn to a suffering that is somehow effective on behalf of others.[20]

In the process Israel is increasingly personified, until by the time we get to Isaiah 53 the Isaianic hopes for a faithful and effectual Israel are expressed almost entirely in terms of a particular person.[21] This impulse towards personification would gain momentum during the Second Temple period in the centuries leading to the time of Christ. The best examples we have come from the Dead Sea Scrolls, wherein we read of a community who believed that true Israel, as God intended her to be, was no longer to be found in the great institutions of faith: temple and sacrifice and priesthood. Rather she was to be found in the temple of a faithful community.[22] In such an environment of thought, Jesus takes the idea a step forward in declaring that the true temple is realized in his person, as the place of meeting for God and humanity.[23] Jesus thereby becomes the expression of all that Israel was called to be, and so he is the embodiment of all that Isaiah envisaged those many years ago for servant Israel.[24] The New Testament writers were in no doubt that Isaiah's servant was realized in Jesus whom they now worshipped.[25] Indeed, they saw that the whole of their Scriptures, roughly what the church now calls the Old Testament, pointed the way to Christ.[26]

But arguably this is nowhere more clearly the case than in Isaiah 40 – 55 and nowhere more evident to the earliest post-resurrection followers of Jesus in those chapters than in chapter 53.[27] The eunuch was reading that section when Philip encountered him, but Philip merely *began with* (35) those verses in his declaration of the good news of Jesus. The end game was the proclamation of Jesus.

[19] Isa. 50:7.

[20] Isa. 53:10.

[21] J. E. Goldingay, *The Message of Isaiah 40–55: A Literary-Theological Commentary* (London: T&T Clark International, 2005), pp. 473–477.

[22] G. K. Beale, *The Temple and the Church's Mission: A Biblical Theology of the Dwelling Place of God*, NSBT 17 (Downers Grove: Apollos, 2004), pp. 317–318.

[23] John 2:13–22. See M. L. Coloe, *God Dwells with Us: Temple Symbolism in the Fourth Gospel* (Collegeville: Liturgical Press, 2001), pp. 65–84.

[24] The ongoing expression of this is through the body of Christ, the church, but that is a topic for another occasion. In passing, however, it is worth noting that it anticipates the subject of our next chapter which is the place of the community of faith in the reception of Scripture.

[25] B. J. Koet, 'Isaiah in Luke-Acts', in S. Moyise and M. J. J. Menken (eds.), *Isaiah in the New Testament* (London: T&T Clark International, 2005), pp. 98–100.

[26] For example Luke 24:27. See T. M. Rosica, 'The Road to Emmaus and the Road to Gaza: Luke 24:13–35 and Acts 8:26–40', *Worship* 68 (1994), p. 119.

[27] F. F. Bruce, *The Book of the Acts*, rev. ed., NICNT (Grand Rapids: Eerdmans, 1988), p. 177.

We see once again how God's voice in the written word of Scripture is inseparable from the word of God in Christ. And that word becomes a word to the people who encounter it in later generations. In this instance, the words of the Isaiah scroll speak some five hundred years later to a man whose circumstances could not have been more different than those of the first hearers of the words of Isaiah 53:7–8. Yet through the activity of the Holy Spirit in the heart of the reader, and in the heart of one who became the reader's guide or interpreter, God continued to speak by means of those ancient words. In terms of the issue raised by the aphorism that Francis of Assisi did not utter, with which we began this chapter, an important component of God's speaking is the obedient proclamation of the message of Scripture. Indeed, as we saw in locating this quote, there should be no dichotomy between acting and speaking the word of God; proclamation is never optional.

5. God still speaks

And two millennia later, God continues thus to speak to those who seek him. Part of the vision of Isaiah was an expansion of the notion of the people of God. This pervades the entire Isaiah scroll and especially Isaiah 40 – 55. See for example the expectation that the servant of the Lord would be 'a light for the Gentiles'.[28] The famous tent image of Isaiah 54:2–3 anticipates this expansion, and the everlasting covenant in fulfilment of the hopes invested in David promises to incorporate the 'nations'.[29] If these references remain a little allusive, there is no mistaking the words of Isaiah 56:3–7. Therein the poet/prophet sees a day in which those who now are excluded from the community will take their place in the centre of God's people. This includes 'foreigners', who will 'hold fast to [God's] covenant', but it also includes 'eunuchs'. In a wonderful symmetry this searching Ethiopian official not only finds Jesus but also discovers that his response is part of an ancient vision in which old boundaries are broken and God welcomes all those who respond to his name.[30]

I wonder if the eunuch's interest had been particularly piqued by that reference to eunuchs, or if it was something that Philip was able to point him towards. Sometimes readers of Scripture find obvious

[28] Isa. 42:6.
[29] Isa. 55:3–5.
[30] On the link between the promise in Isaiah and the eunuch of Acts 8 in the mission of God to the nations see C. J. H. Wright, *The Mission of God: Unlocking the Bible's Grand Narrative* (Leicester: IVP, 2006), pp. 493–495.

and particular points of identification which quicken the word of God. At other times, the stories of God in their very particularity and difference carry the voice of God into different circumstances and times. To illustrate this from my own Christian experience, I once was a young man named Timothy, somewhat timid in nature as I embarked on Christian ministry.[31] The encouraging words of the aging apostle Paul to another young man named Timothy[32] were so directly felt by me that the intervening centuries seemed to melt away. On the other hand, the life and circumstances of Jacob as he wrestled with God, as it were, at the ford of the Jabbok and agonized over his coming meeting with his estranged brother Esau could hardly be more different than my own.[33] Yet Jacob's struggle, in its very difference and quickened by the Spirit, speaks just as powerfully to me of vocation and obedience and frailty as do the words of the apostle Paul.

6. Intertextuality: A Postscript

The particular dynamic that we have seen in the encounter between Philip and the Ethiopian eunuch highlights an important technical issue in the reading of Scripture, one of increasing interest to biblical commentators: the phenomenon of intertextuality. Broadly speaking, intertextuality is the notion that one text can affect the meaning or reception of another text when they are put in touch with each other. In one sense, this is nothing new; it is obvious that later texts often make use of earlier texts in order to make a connection or a particular point. But theories of intertextuality work with a range of more subtle ideas.[34]

Two such concern us. The first is that the incorporation of one text into another, whether with a direct quote or by allusion, opens up what could be called a 'surplus of meaning' in the main text.[35] This is nicely illustrated by the passage under discussion. As we have seen, by having the Gentile eunuch reading about the servant

---

[31] I am still a man and still named Timothy and still inclined to timidity, but alas no longer young!

[32] 2 Tim. 1:6–14.

[33] Gen. 32:22–32.

[34] An influential proposal concerning the nature and use of intertextuality in biblical study is that by R. B. Hays, *Echoes of Scripture in the Letters of Paul* (New Haven: Yale University Press, 1989), pp. 14–33. See also P. Tull, 'Intertextuality and the Hebrew Scriptures', *CR:BS* 8 (2000), pp. 88–119.

[35] A phrase used of metaphor in the title of his book by P. Ricoeur, *Interpretation Theory: Discourse and the Surplus of Meaning* (Fort Worth: Texas Christian University Press, 1976), but also applicable to the effects of intertextuality.

in Isaiah 53, the writer of Acts triggers in the reader's mind a host of associations with the book of Isaiah, such as: the so-called servant songs of Isaiah;[36] the theme of the servant in Isaiah; the inclusion of other nations into the people of God; Isaiah's comments about the inclusion of foreigners and eunuchs. All of this is introduced into the story by the two-verse quote from Isaiah 53:7–8 and would not have been available had the writer merely recounted that Philip met an Ethiopian reading the Bible and introduced him to Jesus.

A second effect of intertextuality is that the influence of one text upon another does not only work chronologically; it is more than just a case of earlier texts influencing later ones. The juxtaposition of a later text with an earlier one can impact meaning in both texts. This too can be illustrated from the Acts passage that we have been looking at. The inclusion of the books of Acts and Isaiah in the same canonical collection of writings means that each influences the other, despite the fact that one is at least 500 years older than the other. Philip's application of the humiliated servant of Isaiah 53 to Jesus enhances our understanding of the significance of Isaiah's message as well as our appreciation of the work of Jesus. The servant Israel in the book of Isaiah is now read in the light of Jesus, and the life and work of Jesus is read in the light of the servant in Isaiah.

For our present purposes it is important to note the way that the encounter of one text with another serves to bring the older and/or more distant text into contact with the circumstances of the reader. This happens in Acts 8. The ancient words of Isaiah acquire meaning for the present experience of the eunuch, and presumably also for Philip as a result of this encounter. This dynamic may be extrapolated out into the whole of Scripture, such that the meaning of each part is impacted by the fact of its having been gathered into the canonical collection of Scripture and vice versa. Whenever we read one part of the Bible we bring the other parts with us to its reading.

But there is more to say. Some theoreticians define 'texts' as everything about ourselves that we bring to any reading. While this notion is problematic, it does at least highlight that when we read something we are changed by our reading and by the way that we understand other things that we have read. This also happens in the reading of Scripture in that we are changed by what we read, and our understanding of everything else that we know is changed. With the involvement of the Holy Spirit, this change becomes a change encounter with the God who speaks in Scripture. We have no idea what happened to the Ethiopian eunuch once his *rejoicing* (39) faded and he settled into the 'long obedience in the same direction'

[36] Isa. 42:1–4; 49:1–6; 50:4–9; 52:13 – 53:12.

of faith.[37] But I am pretty sure he was never the same again. And neither are we as we encounter God's word in God's text and in the proclamation and interpretation of that text.

[37] A phrase coined by Friedrich Nietzsche in *Beyond Good and Evil* and appropriated by E. Peterson, *A Long Obedience in the Same Direction: Discipleship in an Instant Society* (Downers Grove: IVP, 1980).

Nehemiah 8
17. Scripture read in community

In the communion service set out in the *New Zealand Anglican Prayer Book* (1989), the person who reads the chosen portion of Scripture concludes by saying, 'Hear what the Spirit is saying to the church,' to which the congregation responds: 'Thanks be to God.' Now, sometimes with particular passages, and the sermon not yet having been preached, it is not at all clear to me, nor I suspect to others around me, what the Spirit might be saying to the church. Yet we parrot our thanks anyway. The part of me that has always wanted to pull the emergency handle in the train to see what happens also wants one day to stand up in church, read 'By night I went out through the Valley Gate toward the Jackal Well and the Dung Gate',[1] and then say 'hear what the Spirit is saying to the church.' I imagine the response would be the same as it always is.

But perhaps I am being unkind to my fellow worshippers. Perhaps their response does not arise from the fact that they have stopped listening properly, like a monosyllabic husband behind his newspaper. Perhaps, rather, the response reflects a deep-seated commitment to the presence of the Spirit in the words of Scripture, no matter how mundane or puzzling they might be, and in the public act of their performance. If it is not always obvious how that may be so with particular passages, that does not deny the importance of the public reading of Scripture as one means by which the word of God is received and acted upon. At the same time, the regular response of my fellow worshippers to the reading of Scripture is not only an affirmation of the effective work of the Spirit in bringing about understanding of particular sections of the Bible as they are read; it is also an affirmation that the Spirit is somehow present as a result of the very act of reading. The regular habit of Bible reading is

---

[1] Neh. 2:13a.

inherently an activity by means of which the reader encounters the words and acts of God.

I make this latter point with some care. I am not saying that the Bible is a talisman that produces God like a genie when its bottle is rubbed. There is nothing innately helpful about having a family Bible on the shelf, or even open on the lectern, other than the possibility that it may be read one day.[2] Nor am I saying that the contents of the Bible are a set of incantations which may be read without understanding in order to bring about a particular effect on behalf of the reader. Sadly, Scripture is all too often treated both as talisman and as incantation, even by those who profess great respect for it. Nevertheless, the practice of public reading of the Bible does open a door onto God's work.

I believe that this occurs at two levels. First, at the level of public theology and civic discourse, regular respect for the Bible as a public document does translate into a wider impact by the message of Scripture interpreted into the life of a society. This of course does not mean that a Bible reading at the opening of Parliament or some other civic occasion necessarily brings about or expresses personal faith in those who hear it read or automatically banishes sin in society; but it does mean that an environment is more likely to emerge in which faith may flourish and the voice of God be heard both personally and at the level of public policy. Secondly, in the matter of personal and intentional listening for the voice of God, the habit of opening the Scriptures helps to effect an environment in which God is encountered. Sometimes my Bible reading is more an obligation than the conduct of a relationship, but the very fact that that reading occurs has both a subliminal effect on me and maintains an environment in which the voice of God in Scripture can speak in a more direct way to my own life and circumstances. In both the public and personal spheres, the Spirit is active in the background when Scripture is read and acknowledged, quite apart from any particular message that may emerge.[3]

In the previous chapter, we saw how the Ethiopian eunuch heard God speak in Christ directly into his situation and his own need of salvation as he read the scroll of Isaiah. Now we turn to Nehemiah 8 for another encounter with God through the reading of the holy text. This time the process is less personal and much more public but

---

[2] Or, as is often the case, as a family record of births, deaths and marriages, but that has nothing to do with its status as Scripture.

[3] M. Habets, 'Reading Scripture and Doing Theology with the Holy Spirit', in M. Habets (ed.), *The Spirit of Truth: Reading Scripture and Constructing Theology with the Holy Spirit* (Eugene: Pickwick, 2010), pp. 89–104.

the same God is encountered. There is both a personal impact on the hearers and an effect on the society of the hearers. The dynamics that emerge from this incident about hearing Scripture, and about its interpretation, give further insight into the manner in which the Bible becomes and is the word of God to those who read it today. Indeed, the account contained in Nehemiah 8 provides a cameo on the human dynamics within which the word of God comes to a group of people when the text is opened and read.

1. The setting

In order to grasp what is going on in this chapter, it is necessary to be reminded of the literary and historical context in which Nehemiah 8 occurs. Historically, as we know from the book of Haggai and the early chapters of Ezra, a number of Jewish exiles returned from Babylon to what had now become the small and sparsely populated Persian province of Yehud, with Jerusalem at its centre.[4] Permission to do so came from the Persian king Cyrus who took over the Babylonian empire in 539 BC, but it seems little progress was made prior to his death in 530 BC. Later, in the time of King Darius, there was a more significant burst of energy under the leadership of Haggai (prophet), Zerubbabel (governor) and Joshua (high priest) around 521 BC. This seems to have resulted in the completion of the renewed temple in about 516 BC.[5]

In the records available to us there is then a long silence of sixty or seventy years until the time of Ezra and Nehemiah. There is debate over how these two men related chronologically to each other: were they working at the same time? Did one come before the other? If so, which one? A likely scenario is that Ezra began his work from around 458 BC and Nehemiah from about 445 BC.[6] At some point their leadership overlapped, as is clear from Nehemiah 8:9. While all of this is subject to debate, the broad outlines of what happened are still clearly visible.

Quite apart from the history recorded in Nehemiah 8, there is also an issue around the text of Nehemiah 8 itself. Most of the book of

[4] For more on the physical details, see O. Lipschits, 'Demographic Changes in Judah between the Seventh and the Fifth Centuries B.C.E.', in O. Lipschits and J. Blenkinsopp (eds.), *Judah and the Judeans in the Neo-Babylonian Period* (Winona Lake: Eisenbrauns, 2003), pp. 323–376; *NIDB* 1, p. 443.

[5] P. A. Verhoef, *The Books of Haggai and Malachi*, NICOT (Grand Rapids: Eerdmans, 1987), pp. 25–32.

[6] F. C. Fensham, *The Books of Ezra and Nehemiah*, NICOT (Grand Rapids: Eerdmans, 1982), pp. 6–8.

Nehemiah is in the first person, in material sometimes described as the Nehemiah Memoir. Yet chapters 8 – 10 constitute a third person account that mostly concerns Ezra. The events of Nehemiah 8 – 10, particularly the reading of the law in chapter 8, seem to belong with the account in Ezra 7 – 10 of the families coming to Jerusalem and the assembly around the question of mixed marriages. Yet the placement of Nehemiah 8 – 10 in the middle of the Nehemiah Memoir implies a time some thirteen years later than events of Ezra 7– 10. It seems strange that Ezra has this public reading of the law (in Neh. 8) so long after those earlier watershed events.[7] This leads some to argue, on the grounds of content and of the sequence of dates, that Nehemiah 8 belongs with Ezra 7 – 10 (specifically, between chs. 8 and 9) and has become misplaced, but to say so denies the evident literary unity of Nehemiah 8 – 10.[8]

There is no tidy answer to this. In any case, the comprehensive reading of the law takes place during the ministries of both Ezra and Nehemiah in the context of epoch-making events in the renaissance of a formal Jewish community on the land to which their ancient memory looked. The exact chronology of these events is probably now lost to us, but the proximity of the reading of the law to them is what concerns us here. In terms of the wider historical context also, it takes place at a time when the community has been back on the land for at least two generations; some progress has been made, but it remains a struggle. There is opposition and discouragement and occasionally also unfaithfulness to contend with. In the midst of all of that Ezra gathers the people to hear *the Book of the Law of Moses* (1).

They meet in a large plaza near one of the gates in the city walls. The lines of the rebuilt wall are now lost to us, as is an exact awareness of the locations of various gates.[9] The Water Gate was on the eastern side of the city,[10] therefore probably overlooking the Kidron Valley and up towards the Mount of Olives. The meeting place would not have been far from the rebuilt temple, perhaps even within sight of it. And so it went on for eight days (18).

[7] D. C. Kraemer, 'On the Relationship of the Books of Ezra and Nehemiah', *JSOT* 59 (1993), pp. 73–92.

[8] F. C. Holmgren, *Israel Alive Again: A Commentary on the Books of Ezra and Nehemiah*, ITC (Grand Rapids: Eerdmans, 1987), p. 122.

[9] On the archaeological difficulties see J. R. Bartlett, 'Editorial: Nehemiah's Wall', *PEQ* 140 (2008), pp. 77–79.

[10] Neh. 3:26.

2. Leadership and opening the book

Ezra was a key figure in this public reading, although his status remains something of a puzzle. He is nowhere described as governor, although some argue that effectively he was that, such was the level of 'secular' influence that he exercised.[11] Those who represent that point of view also argue that his status as 'scribe' (*sōpēr*[12]) could also describe a bureaucratic function within the Persian imperial administration.[13] However, there is a term for governor, the Aramaic term *tiršātā'* (e.g., 9), which is never applied to Ezra although it is to Nehemiah. And generally the descriptions of Ezra as *sōpēr* (scribe/teacher of the law) include an extra rider attaching Ezra's role specifically to the concerns of Israel: 'well versed in the Law of Moses';[14] 'a man learned in matters concerning the commands and decrees of the LORD for Israel'.[15] Even from the mouth of the Persian King Artaxerxes he is a 'teacher of the law of the God of heaven'.[16] This is in contrast to Shimshai, the 'secretary' (*sōpēr*) of the court.[17] It emerges quite strongly that Ezra is primarily concerned with the written law of God, although his resultant leadership role puts him in touch with a wider range of concerns relating to community life.

In that capacity he *opened the book* (5). But he was not alone. *The Levites* (7) were also involved in the reading and interpretation that flowed from the opening of the book. Then *Nehemiah the governor* (9) also got involved in that he seems to have orchestrated the festive response of the people to the reading. We consider below what is entailed in the process of interpretation. For now, it is sufficient to note that leadership is a critical element in the public process of hearing the word of God in Scripture. For the message of God to take root it took Ezra to open the book, a range of Levites to focus on the interpretation, and somebody like Nehemiah to implement it in the society of the day.

[11] The term 'secular' is anachronistic to this context, since the mindset of the age would have regarded even the exercise of civil authority as in some sense sacred, but it makes a useful distinction for our discussion. And it may reflect a distinction in perspective between Ezra and Nehemiah. See Kraemer, 'On the Relationship of the Books of Ezra and Nehemiah', pp. 73–92.

[12] Consistently translated by TNIV as 'teacher of the law': Ezra 7:6, 11; Neh. 8:4, 9.

[13] J. L. Berquist, *Judaism in Persia's Shadow: A Social and Historical Approach* (Minneapolis: Fortress, 1995), p. 110.

[14] Ezra 7:6.

[15] Ezra 7:11.

[16] Ezra 7:12, 21.

[17] Ezra 4:8.

Still today, we need all of these elements. We need people like Ezra and the Levites who have a particular expertise in Scripture, and ability to make it comprehensible to others who do not have the time or opportunity or calling to develop the same expert knowledge. This entails a range of things. At one level it means knowing the languages and cultures and historical and literary backgrounds which have formed the text. At another it involves cultivating the personal life of faith so that a sensitivity and openness to the voice of God develops in the leader. No amount of technical expertise can 'open the book' unless the one opening it does so under the direction of the Holy Spirit.[18] And thirdly, it entails people like Ezra, who stood out from his Levitical associates. The Levites fulfilled their task faithfully, it seemed, but Ezra somehow emerged by virtue of his commitment to the text and of his particular gifting and calling into leadership that impacted the whole of society. Still today, there are those whose public impact is such as to bring the word of God into the public arena and also to encourage others in the practice of reading and interpreting the text. Some such people bring a level of insight that impacts the wider church, and others find themselves in positions where their gifts impel them into leadership within wider society.

Such people are rare, however. More common are those who find themselves in positions like that of Nehemiah *the governor* (9), and whose leadership we also need. As the 'cupbearer' to King Artaxerxes,[19] he was much more than a butler; he was in a key advisory position within the Persian court.[20] As a faithful Jew he obtained the blessing of Artaxerxes to go to Judah and help to address ongoing problems there, and in due course became the governor, probably a Persian imperial appointment. As far as we are aware, Nehemiah had no specialist religious knowledge beyond what any observant Jew in the diaspora would have obtained.[21] He was a leader in Jewish society, not for his particular acquaintance with the law as was the case with Ezra, but because of his courtly and management expertise. In the light of the exposition of the word of God by Ezra and the Levites, Nehemiah was able to organize a communal response to the word in the observance of the Festival of Booths (of which more below). Similarly, the public reception of the words of Scripture as the words and acts of God in our own

[18] See ch. 5 on 2 Pet. 1:19–21.
[19] Neh. 1:11.
[20] *NIDB* 1, p. 810.
[21] Remember that this is now some eighty years since Cyrus permitted the re-formation of the province of Yehud. Many Jewish people have remained in diaspora during that period.

day is in no small part due to leaders in society leveraging what they have been taught and come to understand of the word of God in Scripture. This is as much the work of the Spirit as the ministry of Bible interpretation.

3. Reading the word

The physical description of the reading event is striking in a collection of narratives that are normally sparing of so much detail. The reader can almost see a crowd of men, women and children standing around in the plaza for an entire morning as Ezra and others read and taught. Were there vendors around the sides providing refreshment? Did the women have to nip home to prepare meals or see to a fractious infant? How distracting were the children? Hopefully the weather was better than for Ezra's assembly about mixed marriages.[22] We do not know the answers to these questions, but that they *listened attentively* (3) suggests an unusual degree of receptivity.

This receptivity may have been partly due to the signals that this was a portentous event. All the elements are there: a temporary stage in the form of a *high wooden platform built for the occasion* (4); some pageantry in the gathering of dignitaries flanking Ezra on the stage (4); and the solemn opening of the book (5). When the text mentions that Ezra *opened the book* it is not employing a twenty-first-century evangelical metaphor for thinking about and talking about the contents of the Bible; it refers to the visible physical action of Ezra up on a temporary wooden platform in front of thousands of eyes gathered near the Water Gate. The entire material context vibrates with expectation around this opened book.

It is intriguing that the reading takes place in the plaza by the Water Gate, and not, as was the case for the assembly on mixed marriages in Ezra 10, in 'the square before the house of God'.[23] That it occurs external to the temple, the expected place for such a reading, reflects the dynamic around the leadership considered in the previous section. The impact of Scripture was wrought both by attention to the law led by Ezra and his Levites and by its implementation under the leadership of the governor Nehemiah. The setting of the Water Gate similarly indicates that the importance of 'opening the book' is not confined to the explicitly 'holy places'. It relates to the public life of a people also.

---

[22] Ezra 10:9.
[23] Ezra 10:9. I am grateful to Laidlaw-Carey Graduate School student Joy Hooker for this insight.

Still today various church traditions express the importance of the Bible. Some retain a ceremonial placing of the open Bible at a central point in the meeting place at the start of a service of worship; others observe some kind of liturgical procession, often relating particularly to the reading of the Gospel. Some traditions also maintain a discipline of reading substantial portions of Scripture prescribed by a lectionary. There is a range of ways in which the importance of reading the Bible receives physical and symbolic expression. Of course, none are ultimately effective unless the book is interpreted and implemented, but the effect of maintaining a discipline of doing so and affirming the importance of doing so should not be underestimated. And the commitment of a leadership to that task is also crucial. We might well ask how significant a place church life gives to the opening of the Scriptures by its leadership, and what application it sees of the reading of Scripture to life beyond church.

4. Instructing and giving meaning

For all the importance of what could be called the infrastructure surrounding the reception of the word of God in the reading of the law, the ultimate significance is in the words and acts of God that result. Any focus that is less than that leaves the reader of the text prone to a form of idolatry in which the book and the rituals that surround it become the objects of worship. When Ezra *opened the book* (5) he *praised the Lord* (6) and in response the people *bowed down and worshipped the Lord* (6). Inseparable from their reading was their worship, not of the book but of the Lord of the book.[24]

It was also expected that understanding accompanied the reading. The crowd that gathered consisted of *men and women and all who were able to understand* (2). The Hebrew of this phrase is a little elliptical, but the *and* should probably be read as explanatory, giving the sense: 'men and women, that is, everyone who could understand.' The people in the square were there to understand (8), and it was an understanding not confined to experts. They *understood* (8) because they were *instructed* (7). This instruction entailed three activities on the part of the Levites who assisted Ezra: they *read*, they *[made] it clear* and they *[gave] the meaning*. When this full-orbed reading and interpretation takes place then misplaced and

---

[24] R. Brown, *The Message of Nehemiah: God's Servant in a Time of Change*, BST (Leicester: IVP, 1998), p. 130.

idolatrous veneration of the physical form of Scripture is less likely to occur.[25]

The first component of instruction, the reading act, has been considered above. Suffice to stress again that the word of God must be opened and the actual words must be heard; lip service to the idea of reading is not enough. The Hebrew verb, *qārā'*, translated in verse 8 as *read* is noteworthy. Its primary sense relates to the audible utterance of particular words. It can mean 'to call out' or 'to proclaim', and is less commonly translated simply as 'read'. This implies that even the act of reading in itself is a kind of proclamation. For us who are more likely to make a distinction between reading and proclamation, the breadth of meaning in *qārā'* is an instructive reminder not to despise the reading of the word for its own sake.

But this is normally not entirely sufficient. The readings were also *[made] clear*. The word as used here is closely linked grammatically to the act of reading or proclaiming. The term used is derived from the verb *pāraš*, and it has the sense of separating out or dividing or distinguishing or clarifying. In Aramaic the same word means 'translate',[26] which has led the NRSV and some other translations to read the word in Nehemiah 8:8 as an Aramaism and hence to read 'translate' there also. Some have seen in this verse the precursor to the Targums, highly interpretative Aramaic translations of the Hebrew Scriptures. It is possible that the verse has served as a warrant for the targumic enterprise, but Targums themselves are mostly likely to have been somewhat later. The Hebrew sense of the word is the more likely here. The type of thinking entailed is not too far from the modern Western tradition of critical exegetical thought: careful analysis of something in the attempt to draw out its probable meaning. As Ezra and the Levites read they also apparently wrestled with the technicalities of the text encountered. From a distance of well over 2,000 years, we tend to telescope the timeframes of the Old Testament, and so forget that Ezra and his assistants were handling material that was as far from their own times as we are from the age of Shakespeare. And the events that were being recounted were even more distant. So there were things to explain.

As well as making the text clear, Ezra and the Levites *[gave] the meaning* (8). The phrase thus translated is *śôm śekel*. The verb *śûm* ranges quite widely in meaning around the general idea of establishing or placing something. In this context it probably carries the idea of establishing a case for something as an outcome of a particular

[25] H. G. M. Williamson, *Ezra, Nehemiah*, WBC 16 (Waco: Word, 1985), pp. 298–299.

[26] See Ezra 4:18.

line of thought. And the case that they establish is *meaning*. In Hebrew this noun is unambiguously a wisdom term and refers to insight, skill and discretion, as well as good sense as opposed to foolishness.[27] One of the outcomes of the reading of the law and its interpretation is that it fosters the ability and attitudes to live life wisely in the sight of God. If the *making . . . clear* is similar to what we would call exegesis, then the process of *giving the meaning* is akin to what we might call exposition, the process of applying the word of God into the everyday and devotional lives of the people. As a result of hearing Ezra and the Levites, the people are not only more knowledgeable; they are better equipped to live life wisely.

5. The word of the law of Moses

The reason for this is found in the text that has been read to them. It is described variously as *the Book of the Law of Moses, which the Lord had commanded for Israel* (1), *the Law, which the Lord had commanded through Moses* (14), and *the Book of the Law of God* (18). It is not possible to know which exact body of material was entailed, but it is likely to have been some form or portion of what we now describe as the Pentateuch. 'The Law' in each case translates the word *torah*, but by this stage in Israel's history the term could also in some contexts express the broader agency of God's word. This may be seen in verses such as Isaiah 1:10 and 2:3 where in each instance the *torah* is in parallel with 'the word of the Lord'.

Thus when the people heard the law being read it is likely that they recognized in the words of the text of the *torah* the word of God active in their own times. This reflects the dynamic we have explored in Exodus 19 and Deuteronomy 4,[28] whereby the word of God is encapsulated in the text, then passed on and experienced as the word of God still active in the lives of later hearers and readers. Thus, when the people moved out from the square to share what they had discovered, it was in fact the voice (*qôl*) of God (15)[29] that they took *throughout their towns and in Jerusalem* (15). This is a significant usage as it is another indication that what they had heard was not merely the law read but also the voice of God present. Those ancient words received by Moses from the hand of God now

[27] See for example the use of *śekel* and its related noun *maśkîl* in 1 Sam. 25:3; 1 Chr. 22:12; Jer. 9:23; 1 Chr. 28:19; Dan. 9:22.

[28] See chs. 6 and 7.

[29] The TNIV represents this by *word* (15).

became the very voice of God to a struggling group of the faithful many centuries later. And so they still become today for those who open and read the book.

6. The outcome of understanding

The outcome of this encounter with the word of God given through Moses is that the people *understood* what was being read (8). But understanding must be reflected in response, and I am reminded at this point of a comment from a colleague of mine after preaching in a particular church. As we bemoaned together the widespread neglect of close engagement with the Bible in our churches, he remarked that the response to his exposition of the text had been like pouring water on thirsty ground; his hearers could not get enough. So it seems to have been for Ezra's hearers at the Water Gate. As implied by the narrative, they were powerfully affected, *weeping as they listened to the words of the Lord* (9). This in itself is graphic illustration of the impact of the words of God as the Spirit enlivened the words of the text, and worked through the very event of Scripture itself.

But that on its own was not enough. There needs to be some evident transformation as a result of the reading. In this case it was a transformation from grief to joy (10–12). The joy was expressed in extravagant communal celebration of a festival mandated in the very book of the law from which Ezra and the Levites had been reading (14). What made them want to celebrate was explicitly that *they now understood the words that had been made known to them* (12). They had heard the voice of God in the words of Scripture. When cheap Bibles are readily available in a range of translations representing sectional interests within the Western church, we forget the wonder of the gift that God speaks in the text. For other Christians, where a copy of the Bible in one's own language is a rarity, wonder and joy is a much more instinctive response to that experience.

The people who gathered at the Water Gate celebrated the feast of booths or tabernacles, also known as *Sukkoth* for the name of the *temporary shelters* (14) that the people built for eight days of the celebration. In one sense, it could have been any feast. It was something they discovered in the book of the law, and it reflected their euphoria at the time of their rediscovery of the voice of God.

But the particular festival has some interesting associations. *Sukkoth* was, and still is, one of the main festivals of the Jewish year. It was associated with the end of harvest in the agricultural cycle.

The Levitical material links it with the memory of the people's wandering in the wilderness.[30] The emphasis is a little different in Deuteronomy, where it is conceived as a pilgrimage feast, thus placing the emphasis on the Davidic covenant and the corresponding importance of Jerusalem as the focus of faithful observance.[31] The Deuteronomic tradition also links this feast with reading the *torah*.[32] Still today the observation of *Sukkoth* by Jewish people culminates in the *simḥâ tôrâ* celebrations that mark the end of the annual cycle of readings from the *torah*, or Pentateuch. For the people of Ezra's time, the renewal of *Sukkoth* observance was appropriate for its emphasis on the reading of Scripture. It was also a reminder from Leviticus that the wilderness years of the Babylonian exile were now behind them, and from Deuteronomy that the covenant with David was still operational and Jerusalem and its temple remained a focal point in this relationship. The ancient words of God came afresh into this new context.

This on its own changed everything. But celebrating a feast, while important, leads on to other things. Before the end of the month in which all these events took place, the Israelites were back again, this time 'wearing sackcloth and putting dust on their heads'.[33] They found that knowing the law of God also entailed implementing the law of God into lifestyle. That begins with confession of sins, both individual and communal: 'their sins and the sins of their ancestors.'[34] So the transformation of rediscovering the voice of God entails the transformation of obeying the voice of God, and for the people led by Ezra and Nehemiah this seems to have included a rediscovery of their identity as distinct from their Gentile neighbours. Whatever the technicalities might be concerning the text-historical relationship of Nehemiah 8 to Ezra 8 – 10, it is clear that the reading of the law, the celebratory response to hearing the voice of God in so doing, and the subsequent turn to confession, were all part of the environment that led to the solemn assembly called by Ezra (Ezra 9 - 10) to address the tricky question of those leaders in the renewed community who were married to foreign women. Celebration and hard choice both result from God's speaking.

---

[30] Lev. 23:39–43.
[31] Deut. 16:16–17.
[32] Deut. 31:9–13.
[33] Neh. 9:1.
[34] Neh. 9:2.

7. A cautionary note

Nehemiah 8 paints a wonderful picture of a communal process whereby the Scriptures are transposed from their ancient settings into contemporary circumstances and come alive as the living and transforming voice of God to the hearers. Yet, in the context of seeking to understand the nature of Scripture and its interpretation, as understood by the biblical texts, there are the seeds of at least two dangers in this process that should be noted.

First, the necessity of interpretation that has been highlighted and the accompanying necessity for leaders who are able to interpret skilfully, is an ever-present weak spot, for it is in constant tension with the Reformation principle that each believer is entitled to be his or her own interpreter. The danger is that elites can form whose interpretations are in their own interests or in the service of perverse understandings of Scripture. Sadly, Christian history is replete with examples of powerful misinterpretations of Scripture that have served to mute rather than release the *qôl*, the voice, of God. Of course, no Christian tradition can avoid at some stage taking stances on disputed issues, usually claiming biblical warrant when they do so. But it is important that leaders act with appropriate humility, consciousness that no human interpretation is ever the last word, a confident dependence on the Spirit to guide the interpreter and the community, and a willingness to follow the guidance of the Spirit even into new interpretive paradigms and assumptions. Leadership is important in this whole process, but only insofar as it enables the voice of God to be heard by the entire community of faith.

A corresponding danger has already been alluded to above, namely, the danger of idolatry when it comes to handling the text of Scripture. This is more likely to happen when leaders are abusing their position as interpreters. It can express itself in two different but related ways. The first is that the physical act of opening the Bible, or revering it in some way, can gradually become an end in itself, to the point that those who open or revere it are more interested in the fact that they do so than in what the words of the open book might actually be saying to them. The book remains effectively a silent idol. This is an ever-present danger in any tradition.

A second possibility is even more dangerous, in that it has the potential, not to silence the text, but to make the text speak with a false voice. This is when a community develops a particular paradigm of interpretation imposed by the interpreting elite. The Bible is then only read in the light of that paradigm or set of assumptions, which become more important to the hearers than what the text may actually be trying to say. When that happens the tradition of interpretation of that particular community has become the idol which replaces the God encountered in the text.

Of course, anybody who reads and interprets Scripture brings a set of assumptions and priorities to his or her reading, whether they are consciously articulated or not.[35] And it is important that we do so. Even if we could read in a vacuum devoid of prior commitments, which we cannot, the result would be undesirable as it would distract us from our calling to read in our own contexts. But it is important that we do so mindful of the short step from there to idolatry. To avoid taking that step, every aspect of our interpreting tradition must regularly be submitted to a close reading of the Bible itself and reworked in the light of what is found there. As with the challenge for leaders to remain faithful in interpretation, so interpreting communities must also do their work under the guidance of the Spirit.

To the extent that we do so, the reading of the Bible brings forth the expectant response in us: 'Hear what the Spirit is saying to the church.'

[35] This raises the even larger question of the role and responsibility of readers in the achievement of meaning. This is considered in ch. 19 in the context of an exposition of John 14:15–26.

2 Timothy 3:10–17
18. All Scripture is God-breathed and useful

Gospel truth is and always has been contested. The contest occurs both within and beyond the church. It cannot be otherwise, because the community of the faithful are always called to understand themselves as in some way reflective of God and therefore 'holy'.[1] This was intrinsic to the Holiness Code of Leviticus[2] and was later picked up by the apostle Peter in the context of the early church.[3] In Leviticus holiness has to do with purity and hence with the separation of the pure from the impure. In Peter's application of it, the separation is more along ethical lines; those who follow Jesus live and worship differently from those who do not. This separation and difference regularly engender hostility and opposition. The apostle Paul reminds us that 'to know Christ' means both 'to know the power of his resurrection' and 'participation in his sufferings'.[4] Indeed, Paul goes so far as to suggest to Timothy that *everyone who wants to live a godly life in Christ Jesus will be persecuted* (12).[5] After all, did not Jesus say, 'I did not come to bring peace, but a sword'?[6] This does not mean that Christians should attract trouble simply for the sake of being different; after all, we are also required

---

[1] See the discussion of this in the context of ch. 13 on Matt. 5:17–48.

[2] Lev. 11:44–45.

[3] 1 Pet. 1:15.

[4] Phil. 3:10. On this point see K. J. Vanhoozer, *The Drama of Doctrine: A Canonical-Linguistic Approach to Christian Theology* (Louisville: Westminster John Knox, 2005), p. 81.

[5] I am conscious that the Pauline authorship of this epistle is contested, but I am reading the epistle in its own terms as from 'Paul, an apostle of Christ Jesus' (2 Tim. 1:1). Note P. Trebilco and S. Rae, *1 Timothy*, ABC (Singapore: Asia Theological Association, 2006), pp. 2–4.

[6] Matt. 10:34.

to 'live in peace with everyone'.[7] But it does mean that if we are faithful we will at some point encounter conflict.

Sadly, conflict and even persecution are sometimes experienced within and at the hands of the church. The reading and application of Scripture has been an area of contest from earliest times. The book of Daniel bears traces of contesting parties within Israel.[8] The Qumran material speaks of a community who regarded themselves as the faithful within an apostate nation.[9] In Jesus' day there were divisive and bitter theological debates that spilled into the political sphere around control of the priesthood.[10] Early in the life of the church the Jerusalem council was called to negotiate fractures within the church.[11] And opposition and argument are clearly part of the background to 2 Timothy.[12] This set a pattern that has continued through the life of the church. The sight of three cages in the tower of St Lamberti church in the German town of Münster, in which once hung the bodies of Anabaptist leaders tortured by the bishops whom the Anabaptists had earlier expelled from the town, is a stark reminder of such things. Unfortunately such evidence of inter-church persecution is not difficult to find.[13]

Opposition also comes from those who simply find the claims of Christ unpalatable. This too is nothing new. The Psalmist spoke eloquently of the ravages of the surrounding nations on Israel.[14] Paul's descriptions of his adversity tend not to distinguish between his opponents within the church and those who oppose him from pagan or Jewish standpoints.[15] However we date it, the book of Revelation speaks to those who are persecuted by the pagan empire.[16] In the Western church, with its generally comfortable accommodation to the 'empire', this is not such a familiar scenario. But millions of our Christian brothers and sisters around the world know well that Paul is right when he says: *everyone who wants to live a godly life in Christ Jesus will be persecuted* (12).

---

[7] Heb. 12:14.

[8] Dan. 11:32–35.

[9] See *CD* I.

[10] Mark 12:18. *DJG*, p. 403.

[11] Acts 15.

[12] P. H. Towner, *The Letters to Timothy and Titus*, NICNT (Grand Rapids: Eerdmans, 2006), pp. 569–570, 577.

[13] The evangelical section of the church has not been immune from the tendency to persecute. See D. W. Bebbington, *Evangelicalism in Modern Britain: A History from the 1730s to the 1980s* (London: Unwin Hyman, 1989), pp. 181–228.

[14] Ps. 79:1.

[15] For example 2 Cor. 11:16–28.

[16] G. R. Osborne, *Revelation*, BECNT (Grand Rapids: Baker Academic, 2002), pp. 6–12.

Such an environment of conflict is reflected in the second letter to Timothy. The description of the situation in 2 Timothy 3:1–9 is ambivalent as to whether Paul is writing primarily of dissent within the church or of the church being subjected to attack from those outside their number. The first five verses seem to be describing what might be called the 'spirit of the age', before turning attention to 'teachers [who] oppose the truth'.[17] The reference to Jannes and Jambres sustains the ambiguity. These are the names ascribed by tradition to the magicians of Pharoah's court,[18] so in that respect they represent opposition to the gospel from outside. However, the *Damascus Document* from Qumran refers to them as 'Israelite opponents of Moses and leaders of apostate Israel in Egypt'.[19] Paul is quite possibly also picking up this line of tradition in his letter. The example therefore can work for both contexts: persecution from non-believers and persecution or difficulty from false believers. In any case, the distinction is a blurry one. Much that is false or inadequate within the church is fuelled by our submission to the spirit of the age that surrounds us. Our obsessions with programming and money and the marketing of perception which at their worst end up distorting the truth of the gospel are all behaviours learned from the surrounding culture.

Paul reminds Timothy that one important weapon – arguably an indispensible weapon – in the contest for truth is *the Holy Scriptures* (15), with which Timothy has had a long acquaintance. This is because, according to the writer of this epistle, Scripture *is God-breathed and is useful* (16). That brief iconic phrase, buttressed as it is by a number of other concepts, tells us much of the nature and purpose of Scripture as a means by which God speaks today.

1. All Scripture

Before considering the significance of that, though, several technical issues around the interpretation of 2 Timothy 3:10–17 must be addressed. The first concerns what the writer may have had in mind in referring to *the Holy Scriptures* (15) and *all Scripture* (16). The Greek phrase represented by 'Holy Scriptures' in verse 15 is unique in the New Testament, but it is widely agreed from the evidence of other usages in Hellenistic Judaism that it refers to the

[17] 2 Tim. 3:8.
[18] Exod. 7:11–12.
[19] CD V/17b–19. See *NIDB* 3, p. 198.

Old Testament, probably in the Greek form (the Septuagint).[20] I am also following Howard Marshall's lead in assuming that the phrase is synonymous with the word translated as *Scripture* (16), and that verse 16 is therefore a specification of Scripture at work *[making] ... wise for salvation* (15).[21] Although the reference is almost certainly to what we now call the Old Testament, in the light of the formation of the New Testament these verses may also be taken to apply to all of Christian Scripture.[22]

There is also a question of emphasis, in that the singular *graphē* (16) is not normally used to refer to Scripture as a whole, but rather to a particular passage of Scripture. That being the case, the weight of the opening clause in verse 16, *all Scripture*, is that any given individual section of Scripture is useful, not merely the body of Scripture as a whole.[23] It is a debatable point how substantial this distinction is; at the very least, it is an unqualified endorsement of this particular body of writing. But the singular indefinite noun does stand as a challenge to the notion of a 'canon within a canon' with which all interpreters cannot help but work. We all privilege certain voices within Scripture and all find some parts of it more helpful than other parts; that is the nature of the case given the importance of context in interpretation. But that does not mean that any part is less 'God-breathed' than any other, nor therefore inherently less useful to the life of faith than any other. Not every reading context will inevitably find Leviticus as 'useful' as Romans or James as useful as 2 Chronicles, but the possibility is that some will, and this should be allowed for.

A second technical point relates to the grammatical use of the adjective 'God-breathed'. The Greek form allows for either of two translations: 'all God-breathed Scripture' or 'all Scripture is God-breathed'. The question is an important one, in light of the point above, because the former reading allows the possibility that there is some Scripture of which it could be said that it is perhaps not God-breathed or less God-breathed, and that the Scriptures that are 'useful' for the purposes outlined by Paul are the God-breathed ones. This is clearly a problematic perspective. Although the argument is finely balanced, I side with those who read it as saying 'All Scripture is God-breathed', the reading represented by TNIV and in

[20] R. F. Collins, *I & II Timothy and Titus: A Commentary*, NTL (Louisville: Westminster John Knox, 2002), p. 261.

[21] I. H. Marshall, *The Pastoral Epistles*, ICC (Edinburgh: T&T Clark, 1999), pp. 788–790.

[22] See my argument in ch. 5 for why this is a legitimate interpretive move.

[23] W. H. Gloer, *1 & 2 Timothy-Titus*, SHBC (Macon: Smyth & Helwys, 2010), p. 289: 'each and every part'.

fact by most English versions.[24] This is more than a general theoretical statement about the corpus of texts in the Bible; it is an affirmation that any individual part of that corpus is both *God-breathed* and *useful* (16).

2. God-breathed

But what of this word *God-breathed* (16), *theopneustos*? What exactly does it mean? It is translated by the NRSV, following the trend of a number of English translations, as 'inspired', but this is deeply problematic. The idea of 'inspiration' is a wide-ranging one. If I read the Bible because it is inspired, then I should equally listen to Handel's great oratorio *Messiah*. And perhaps I should read also work by Aristotle or Shakespeare or Milton or Dickens or Joyce, or any other piece of literature that has stood the test of time to be labelled a classic. They are inspired and often inspiring, and they are so because of the incredible capacity of human beings made in the image of God to reflect the creativity of God. So to speak of Scripture merely as 'inspired' does not say anything meaningful about the distinctive nature of the Bible as against any other written text. Even to add the adjective and speak of 'divine inspiration' is problematic, as all human creativity may be said to be an expression of the imaging of God in humanity. The best of art and literature in any culture is as it is because of the participation of men and women in the creativity of God.[25]

That is possibly why Paul uses the word that is well translated by TNIV as *God-breathed*. Its occurrence here, as far as we are able to determine, is the first in the body of Greek literature that is available from antiquity. It is almost as if Paul has created a new word to convey the concept, and perhaps he has.[26] Because this word has no other application in Scripture, it is reasonable to suppose that it was deployed to express some quality that is uniquely true of Scripture, and hence of something that is not true in the same way of other texts. John Goldingay has helpfully characterized the difference between something that is God-breathed and something that is

---

[24] G. W. Knight, *The Pastoral Epistles*, NIGTC (Grand Rapids: Eerdmans, 1992), pp. 445–447.
[25] See N. Wolterstorff, *Art in Action: Toward a Christian Aesthetic* (Grand Rapids: Eerdmans, 1980), especially pp. 192–199. In speaking of the 'best' of art and literature I am referring to matters such as artistic excellence, motivation and impact.
[26] Marshall, *Pastoral Epistles*, p. 794.

'inspired'.[27] Something that is inspired has been, literally, 'breathed into', and by implication in the case of Scripture, breathed into by God. On the other hand, that which is God-breathed, *theopneustos*, has been breathed out by God. It is 'the product of God's creative breath'.[28]

Given that we are probably dealing with a newly-coined word, it would be unwise to pin too much weight on a detailed definition of it. Rather than attempting a technical description of the nature of Scripture with respect to the fact that it is *theopneustos*, 'God-breathed', I take it to be an expression of the uniqueness of Scripture, such as has been unfolding in the passages treated in this volume.[29] What we have seen is the encapsulation in a particular set of texts of the words and actions of God with respect to God's people and cosmos. Somehow, those texts continue to bear the voice of God and the activity of God into subsequent generations as they are read and appropriated. This entire process is soaked in the activity of the Holy Spirit. In that respect it is 'God-breathed' in a way that no other corpus or its reading is.[30]

These verses then should be taken primarily as a statement on the uniqueness and usefulness of Scripture rather than as the basis for a discussion on the 'inspiration' of Scripture, a term that is inherently problematic when it is used to make a qualitative distinction between Scripture and other texts.[31]

3. Useful

Allied to the God-breathed nature of this unique set of texts that we call the Bible is the fact that they are *useful* (16). The Greek adjective that is so translated (*ōphelimos*) is a remarkably pragmatic one. It is relatively rare in the New Testament, as are its close cousins. It appears twice elsewhere in the pastoral epistles.[32] In 1 Timothy the writer is contrasting the usefulness or benefit of physical exercise with 'godliness'. It is a term that focuses on outcomes rather than

---

[27] J. E. Goldingay, *Models for Scripture* (Grand Rapids: Eerdmans, 1994), p. 216.

[28] Ibid.

[29] Of course, there are many more passages that could also have been treated but we are limited by space and time.

[30] A. T. B. McGowan, *The Divine Spiration of Scripture: Challenging Evangelical Perspectives* (Nottingham: Apollos, 2007), pp. 40–43, expresses this with the term 'spiration'.

[31] E. W. Goodrick, 'Let's Put 2 Timothy 3:16 Back in the Bible', *JETS* 25 (1982), pp. 479–487.

[32] 1 Tim. 4:8 and Titus 3:8.

on theoretical notions as to the nature of that which is under discussion. That a different form of the word from the same root is used in 2 Maccabees 8:20, with the sense of booty won in war, is a nice illustration of the pragmatic nature of the field of meaning occupied by the word. This should warn us against setting too high a store by these verses as a resource in technical doctrinal definitions of the nature of Scripture. It is unique in that it is soaked in the breath of God, as we have seen, and is accordingly *useful* in the conduct of the Christian life. The value of these verses is that they convey something of the usefulness of this God-breathed body of material, not that they provide a doctrinal definition of Scripture or its method of inspiration.

This usefulness is considered against the backdrop of all that has so far been noted about the nature of Scripture as the words and acts of God in history and the cosmos and in the ongoing life of creation and of humanity and within the church.

4. In order that . . .

In the wider context of the battle for truth and against error, the usefulness of Scripture as expressed in verse 16 is framed by two statements. The first is the affirmation that the Scriptures *are able to make you wise for salvation* (15). The second expresses the view that the outcome of the usefulness of Scripture is that *all God's people may be thoroughly equipped for every good work* (17). Several important points arise out of this framing of the usefulness of Scripture.

However, before turning to them I note one phrase in verse 15 which I did not include in the quote in the previous paragraph, that is, that the wisdom of salvation is *through faith in Jesus Christ*. This is an important reminder of something that we have already explored, that the Bible is not an end in itself. It is a witness to and is ultimately interpreted by the Word, Christ Jesus.[33] The Scriptures cannot be considered apart from the Word to whom they bear witness.

To turn to the effect of Scripture, first it is the formation of wisdom, *to make you wise* (15). It is important not to mystify the verb *sophizō*; it has to do with the process of teaching or instruction in things pertaining to salvation rather than induction into inaccessible mysteries. The outcome of that acquisition of wisdom is that *all God's people* are *thoroughly equipped for every good work* (17). This phrase is an

[33] See chs. 11–15 in this volume.

emphatic one which is almost impossible to translate literally but which the TNIV expresses with the adverb *thoroughly*. It could be translated literally thus: 'so that the man of God might become *completely proficient, being thoroughly equipped* for every good work.' The two words represented by my italicized phrases share a common root in the Greek that has the sense of completeness, sufficiency, fulfilment, maturity. The wisdom of salvation that is drawn forth from Scripture is enough; there is nothing more necessary.

The adequacy and availability of Scripture is further emphasized by the phrase rendered by TNIV as *all God's people* (17). As indicated above, a more literal rendering would be 'the man (*anthrōpos*) of God'. The term has implications of leadership, but the indefiniteness of the expression in the Greek suggests that any who seek to follow Jesus may be so equipped. Scripture belongs to everybody; it was never meant to be enslaved by experts.

Before concluding this section, a brief disclaimer is in order. It is a point that I have made elsewhere but it is important enough to make again. An assertion as to the sufficiency of Scripture for *all God's people* does not mean that the body of knowledge contained in the Bible is all that anybody, and especially any Christian, needs to know. Knowledge of nuclear physics, brain surgery, Far Eastern languages, art history, earthquake building codes, plumbing, or any other of the almost limitless fields of endeavour is not contained in Scripture, but all of these things are part of God's world and all are potentially part of the call to Christian vocation. What is being asserted is the sufficiency of Scripture for the formation of wisdom and faith in Christ so that the world that God has made may be wisely and faithfully encountered. Any religious tradition that takes the Bible as sufficient for an all-round education is a travesty of the intent of these verses.

5. The process of nurture

Verse 17 opens with *so that*, in the Greek a word that indicates a causal relationship with what precedes it. As a result the equipping of God's people arises out of the process of the application of Scripture, to which we now turn. There are four key terms used to describe that process: *teaching, rebuking, correcting and training in righteousness* (16).[34] In one sense each is inseparable from the others,

---

[34] I am taking the final short phrase *in righteousness* as particularly related to *training in* and not as the culmination of all four verbs. See Towner, *Timothy and Titus*, p. 591.

and cumulatively they express a key part of the process within the community of faith by which the Scriptures are appropriated and heard as the word of God for today. This could be called the process of nurture. At the same time, each element repays some thought on its own terms. The text itself encourages this by attaching the preposition *pros* ('for') to each element in the list, indicating that each has its own contribution to the 'usefulness' of Scripture.

The first is *teaching* (*didaskalia*). This can also be translated as 'instruction'. It conveys the transmission of a body of knowledge from one who teaches to the one who is taught. Sometimes it concerns the body of knowledge itself.[35] Although the distinction between head and heart is in one sense a false one, this is a term that relates more to the acquisition of head knowledge. It is interesting to note that one classical usage of the related noun for teacher, *didaskalos*, was as one who taught actors their lines. In this context, it speaks of a familiarity with God's story as told in Scripture. We might also say, from a distance of twenty centuries of theological and historical reflection on the great events recorded therein, that it entails familiarity with what Christians have discovered to be the significance of that story. The apostle Paul carried within himself a strong sense of responsibility for handing on the teachings or traditions that he had received. In 2 Thessalonians 2:15, in the phrase 'teachings we passed on', the word for 'passed on' is the related verb, *didaskō*. Scripture is 'useful' in this process of passing on the details of the story as well as their supposed significance.

But it is also useful for *rebuking*. Remembering the conflicted context to which these words were written, this is the flip side of the possession of a particular body of knowledge, namely, that there are some traditions or teachings or beliefs that fall outside the story of God's words and actions, or stand as a challenge to them. Scripture is useful in the formation of a sense of that which falls outside the story of God's words and actions in engaging with humanity. There are times when these things are to be named and 'rebuked' or refuted. How and when to do so in a way that commends the gospel is a discussion for another time, but there is a hint about this word that the rebuking should only occur on sound evidence.[36] Where Christians use the Bible oppositionally this should be done carefully and wisely and perhaps even reluctantly when the evidence forces us to it.

Teaching and rebuking have had to do with doctrine. Now come two actions that relate more to personal formation. Scripture is also

---

[35] For example Matt. 5:19; 2 Tim. 4:3.
[36] *BDAG*, p. 315.

useful for *correcting* (*epanorthōsis*). This term appears only here in the New Testament so it is a little difficult to fix its meaning. In 1 Maccabees 14:13 it has the sense of restoration, and in classical Greek it seems to carry a sense of rebuilding or restoring. This is also the case for the closely related noun *anorthōsis*. In that respect it has to do with building or rebuilding character.[37] Once a basis of commonly held truth is laid, and the distinction between truth and falsehood is discerned, the base is formed on which can be set the formation of Christian character. But this may also entail the establishment of Christian identity, the endowment on the reader of Scripture of a place to belong. Scripture is useful thus in drawing its readers into God's story and making it a part of their own story.

And finally there is *training in righteousness*. Training (*paideia*) is not far in meaning from *teaching* (*didaskalia*) although there is also an aspect of training rather than mere teaching about the term. Furthermore, etymologically it implies an analogy with the training of a child, so there is a strong formational aspect to the noun. In that respect it has to do with the development of character as much as knowledge.[38] If there is any doubt about that from the term *paideia* on its own, that this training is *in righteousness* makes quite clear that it relates to being as much as knowing, the heart as much as the head. Something of the content of 'righteousness' (*dikaiosynē*) in the mind of the writer may be seen by comparing 1 Timothy 6:11 and 2 Timothy 2:22, where the same word is included in lists of Christian virtues: 'godliness, faith, love, endurance and gentleness' in 1 Timothy 6:11; and 'faith, love and peace' along with 'a pure heart' in 2 Timothy 2:22. It is not necessary to detail a definition of each term, or of 'righteousness' itself to see that this training concerns the life of faith. That the resultant equipping entails *every good work* (17) also reinforces that the conduct of the life of faith is also in mind.[39]

By means of this fourfold list of action nouns, Scripture is conceived as providing the raw materials for the formation of Christians and of Christian communities, and also provides the knowledge base by means of which the story of Christians and their communities is incorporated into the story of God's encounter with humanity. This is possible because the Scriptures which contain that story are soaked in the Spirit of God, are 'God-breathed', in a way that

[37] Collins, *I & II Timothy and Titus*, p. 264.

[38] R. Saarinen, *The Pastoral Epistles with Philemon & Jude*, BTCB (Grand Rapids: Brazos, 2008), pp. 155–156.

[39] J. I. Packer, *Beyond the Battle for the Bible* (Westchester: Cornerstone, 1980), p. 29.

no other text is. Scripture continues to be the means by which God speaks and acts today.

Given the context of persecution and conflict, the nature of Scripture's usefulness is an important guide to the conduct of the contest for truth with which we began this chapter. Essentially the response proposed here to error and opposition is to establish oneself in the Scriptures and the one to whom they bear witness, to know their contents as well as possible, and to allow one's life to be shaped by the story they contain and by the one who has breathed them out. Of the four actions, 'rebuking' may be seen as a direct engagement with error; the other three are primarily positive actions aimed at nurturing truth. While there is a place for a negative apologetic in Christian encounter with opponents, this must be part of the lifelong project of a positive formation of a soundly-based faith and of Christian character. That, as much as argumentation, is what finally wins the day.

John 14:15–26
19. The Spirit of love and truth

One of the struggles of the New Zealand church, the context from which I write, is the image of the church held by wider society. In a world where increasingly few people have any notion of the biblical story, society's perception of the nature of Christianity is largely derived from its observation of the church. And its observation of the church is likely to be mediated by what gets into the news. And what gets into the news are such things as: the church's opposition to behaviours that society no longer regards as immoral – cohabitation, gay partnerships, contraceptive education for school children and so forth; espousal of causes to the right of the political spectrum; and sexual or other moral failures on the part of church leaders. It is too often not a pretty picture. Sometimes what is reported in the way of moral failure within the church is indefensible; sometimes what is reported is a projection of what the reporter would like the church to be like, the better to ignore or caricature its message. As a result, the church in my country, as in the West generally, lives in a context that illustrates the truth of the first sentence of the previous chapter: 'gospel truth is and always has been contested.'[1] This is the case both within the church and in the interaction of church and society.[2] And it was from within a context of conflict that Paul advised Timothy on the nature and usefulness of Scripture considered in the previous chapter.

It is easy to respond to the situation I describe above in an

[1] There are other parts of the world where opposition is much more flagrant and brutal than that experienced by the Western church.

[2] Ironically, though, it is noticeable that society in New Zealand, one of the most secular of countries, still turns to the church for help in the processing of public grief. This was markedly the case in the recent death of twenty-nine coal miners in the Pike River mine on New Zealand's West Coast, an event that attained national significance.

adversarial manner; indeed, not to do so is counter-intuitive. But that truth is achieved in conflicted contexts does not mean that the reception of truth is inherently a combative process. Unfortunately, to look at parts of the church you would not know that to be the case. Too often we become well known for what we oppose, not because the media distort our message but because that is the voice that we present to the world. When that happens the church has been drawn into the adversarial context in which it finds itself.

But there is an important distinction to be drawn between the context in which the reader of Scripture does his or her work and the manner in which that work is done. The counterpoint to a contested environment for the gospel, such as that conveyed in Paul's second letter to Timothy, is a response characterized by positive presentation of gospel truth. This entails the responsibility to become known for what we are in favour of more than for what we are against. That does not mean that Christians are required to be nice people who never disagree with anybody and simply roll over to the spirit of the age. The positive presentation of truth always has the potential to unearth enemies of truth, for 'people loved darkness instead of light because their deeds were evil'.[3] But enmity must come about as response to the winsome living out of the gospel rather than as an outcome of adversarial behaviour. This may be summarized in the call to love and truth. It is in the dynamic of love activated by the Holy Spirit of truth that the word of God becomes most audible. And it is to that dynamic that we now turn in an examination of part of Jesus' final discourse with his disciples in John 14:15–26.

1. Love

Jesus' promise of the Spirit is interlaced by the theme of love. The opening sentence calls for the disciples to love Jesus (15). They in turn are *loved by my Father* and by Jesus (21). Somehow we sense also as we read verses 23–24 that this love into which the disciples are caught up is the very love enjoyed within the Godhead between the Father and the Son. This becomes more explicit at John 15:10: 'If you keep my commandments, you will remain in my love, just as I have kept my Father's commands and remain in his love.' A little further on in the discourse it also becomes evident that this Godhead love into which the disciples are incorporated emanates out to characterize relationships between the disciples themselves:

[3] John 3:19.

'This is my command: Love each other.'[4] To repeat a point made above, this dynamic of love is not always a guarantee of peace. Jesus was clear on that a little later in his discourse when he warns the disciples that this very love is capable of attracting hatred and opposition.[5]

This volume has been concerned to demonstrate that God speaks in Christ and in the text and therefore still today. On the evidence of Jesus' final discourse as recorded in the Gospel of John, an important aspect of the ongoing communication between God and humanity is that it is soaked in love. The words of Scripture are a central part of that communication, and so therefore is their interpretation. That means that the process of reading and interpretation is also imbued with love. If, as has been suggested, 'exegesis is prayer',[6] we might also say that exegesis is love.[7] What that might entail gradually emerges in an examination of these words.

2. The Paraclete

It is not possible to derive an accurate technical description of the Godhead from these verses, if in fact it is possible or desirable to do so at all, but it is clear that this process of love is fuelled by the work of the *advocate* (16; *paraklētos* in Greek). This is a term whose meaning is subject to much debate.[8] Etymologically, the sense of the word is of one who is called to be alongside another one. The English translation 'advocate' is in that respect a good one, as it contains the idea of somebody who takes the part of another and is present with him or her. In another respect, however, the translation is problematic in that 'advocate' in English has also acquired connotations of a protagonist in a formal courtroom setting, one perhaps more interested in the advancement of an argument than the care of a person.[9] The Greek word being translated is more inclusive of the notion of 'compassion' within its meaning. The Spirit, as one who is called alongside to take the part of another, also

[4] John 15:17. For a theological exposition of this principle, see M. Volf, *After Our Likeness: The Church as the Image of the Trinity* (Grand Rapids: Eerdmans, 1998), pp. 192–198.
[5] John 15:18–25.
[6] C. C. Black, 'Exegesis as Prayer', *Princeton Seminary Bulletin* 23NS (2002), pp. 131–145.
[7] On this possibility, see N. T. Wright, *The New Testament and the People of God*, COQG 1 (Minneapolis: Fortress, 1992), pp. 63–64.
[8] A. J. Köstenberger, *John*, BECNT (Grand Rapids: Baker Academic, 2004), p. 435.
[9] *DJG*, p. 349.

cares deeply and compassionately about the one for whom the Spirit advocates.

Note that in verse 16 the promise from Jesus is that *another* advocate will be given to the disciples, one with no expiry date who will extend beyond the timeframe of the earthly life of Jesus. This implies that the love between Jesus and his followers will be sustained *for ever* by the agency of the advocate, also known as *the Spirit of truth* (17).

The significance of the relationship and its continuity with Jesus is emphasized by the vocabulary employed in verse 17b. This Spirit is one who will *live with* and *be in* the disciples. The Greek phrase translated as *live with*, *menō para*, foreshadows Jesus' comments on the vine in that the verb *menō*, translated by TNIV as 'remain' and referring to the relationship of Jesus himself with his disciples,[10] is the same as the one used here of the paraclete. As for the paraclete, the outworking of Jesus 'remaining in' the disciples is love.[11] There is a difference, however, in that the preposition governing the indirect object of the verb is *para* ('with') in chapter 14 rather than *en* ('in') as it is later in the discourse. Prepositions are notoriously unstable in most languages, including New Testament Greek, so care must be taken in drawing too well-defined a distinction of meaning based on their occurrence. Nevertheless, it does seem that the choice of *para* here is a deliberate play on words with the term *para*clete, and implies a relationship between two beings. As one who draws alongside, the paraclete draws alongside the disciple. This is slightly different from the idea of incorporation into Christ implied by the vine imagery of chapter 15. However, that image and the idea of incorporation is then implied in the final phrase of verse 17 regarding the paraclete, who, as well as drawing alongside, *will be in* the disciples. By means of this portmanteau foreshadowing of chapter 15 – living with and being in – the writer indicates that the 'Spirit of truth', the paraclete, both incorporates the believer and is in relationship with the believer. The two ideas remain in creative tension with each other.

Given that the reading and interpretation of Scripture flow from and reflect the love of God, as I will argue below, this tension between relationship and incorporation is also a feature of reading and interpreting Scripture. On the one hand, we encounter the Scriptures as autonomous responsible beings meeting an entity other than and different from ourselves. We bring all that we are to the task: our context, abilities, learning and experience. We initiate a conversation with the text such that the potential meaning of

[10] John 15:4–10.
[11] John 15:12–14.

the text is drawn out by the particular reader/interpreter in a way that would not be possible for any other reader/interpreter. This does not mean that the text can be made to say anything the reader wants it to say, but it does mean that the reader has a responsibility to 'make' meaning as he or she reads, to hear the voice of the text in all its particularity and relevance. On the other hand, the reader/interpreter is in some way incorporated into God and reads as one indwelt by the Spirit.[12] This means that the words of Scripture are able to be perceived as God's words with all the possibilities that flow from that.

This tension is relevant to how a Spirit-dwelt exegesis of love relates to postmodern understandings of reader responses to the text. The respect for the personality of the reader implicit in Jesus' promise does seem to place a responsibility on the reader to bring him or herself into the reading. To that extent, a careful listening to people like Jacques Derrida,[13] with his emphasis on deconstruction, and Elizabeth Schussler Fiorenza with her hermeneutic of suspicion, is important.[14] For they challenge us to know well what we bring to the conversation with Scripture, and to acknowledge that we do not read in a vacuum but out of a context and a set of assumptions. A hermeneutic of suspicion, for example, teaches us at the very least to deconstruct and suspect the assumptions and distortions that beset our own readings, but also to understand that our own experience and context may enrich our readings.

At the same time incorporation into the love of God leads to a reading that identifies closely with the text itself, because in the Spirit we dwell in the God whose story is told by the text. This engenders in the Christian reader an ethic of reading that takes seriously the intentions of the text, as far as they may be discerned.[15] To this extent, a reading that is tuned by the indwelling presence of the Spirit allows the text to speak with its own voice. Somehow both

---

[12] W. Olhausen, 'A "Polite" Response to Anthony Thiselton', in C. Bartholomew, C. Greene and K. Möller (eds.), *After Pentecost: Language and Biblical Interpretation*, Scripture and Hermeneutics 2 (Carlisle: Paternoster, 2001), pp. 127–128.

[13] The issues raised by the work of Jacques Derrida are neatly summarized by J. Barton, 'Beliebigkeit', in Y. Sherwood (ed.), *Derrida's Bible (Reading a Page of Scripture with a Little Help from Derrida)* (New York: Palgrave MacMillan, 2004), pp. 301–303.

[14] E. Schüssler Fiorenza, *In Memory of Her: A Feminist Theological Reconstruction of Christian Origins* (New York: Crossroads, 1983), especially her introductory material (pp. 1–96).

[15] Note the reference to the 'morality' of reading in the sub-title to the influential volume by K. J. Vanhoozer, *Is There a Meaning in this Text? The Bible, the Reader and the Morality of Literary Knowledge* (Leicester: Apollos, 1998).

an appreciation of the independence of the reader from the text and an indwelling respect for the text itself must feature in an exegesis of love.

3. The Spirit of truth

This paraclete, who draws alongside the follower of Jesus, is also *the Spirit of truth* (17). This implies that the dynamic of love of which Jesus speaks has also to do with knowing and understanding. The first hint in that direction is that the people of God have not been *[left] . . . as orphans* (18). The coming of the paraclete as the Spirit of truth encapsulates God's commitment in Christ to maintaining a conversation with humanity. The quest for truth is not one that we undertake alone; it is one that takes place within the context of knowing God. It is something that has been made possible by the incarnation of God in Christ and remains possible through the ongoing work of the Spirit who draws alongside.[16]

This has implications for Christian knowing, not least that any quest for truth is undertaken in conversation with the great story of God's involvement with humankind that is contained in the pages of Scripture. As previously discussed, this does not mean that all that needs to be known resides within the pages of the Bible. I do not open the Bible to learn quantum physics or Japanese, yet both branches of knowledge are part of the good earth that God has made and asked us to explore, and I may be taught from both branches of knowledge by those whom the writer of John's Gospel might categorize as in 'the world'. It does mean, however, that all knowledge is best received and understood against the backdrop of God's ongoing involvement in his creation and his redemption of the world that he has made and its inhabitants.

John somewhat complicates this by his insistence that there are those who do not have this relationship with the truth that comes through knowing God. He is at his most blunt at verse 19: *the world will not see me anymore, but you will see me.* This is reinforced in verse 24: *Anyone who does not love me will not obey my teaching.* Does this mean that only Christians can achieve competence in various skills and knowledge? This appears to be at odds with the notion indicated above that God's truth is not confined to the religious dimension of life, and it is certainly at odds with experience. Part of the resolution to this lies in an appreciation of the use in

---

[16] In that respect this exegesis and epistemology of love is a thoroughly Trinitarian enterprise.

John's Gospel of the word *kosmos* or 'world'.[17] This word sometimes simply refers to the created order, all of which is loved by the
creator; at other times it refers to that part of the created order that
chooses not to acknowledge the creator. It is the latter understanding
that is in play here. So the Gospel writer is not saying that compre-
hension and even a measure of enlightenment in its broadest sense is
only available to Christians. He is saying that understanding in the
light of God's story in Christ and through the Holy Spirit gives a
unique – and we can say even a particularly true – appreciation of
the way the world works and is.[18] Christians ought then to bring a
value-added contribution to the task of exegesis and to the wider
enterprise of epistemology – of the very nature of our knowing –
because of our participation in the love of the Godhead. That is one
of the consequences of the promise of Jesus here recorded.

But a word of warning: this does not eliminate the need for humility on the part of Christian readers and interpreters of Scripture. For
creation also springs from the love of God, and creation, flawed and
broken as it may be, still in some measure reflects that love. There
is plenty of truth in the world that God has made that may come in
surprising ways and from surprising sources.

4. The teaching

There are several points at which the love of the Father, Jesus
and the paraclete are explicitly linked with the word of God. Our
passage opens with Jesus' own directive, *if you love me, keep my
commands* (15). This is repeated in verse 21. The same point is made
using slightly different vocabulary in verse 23: *Anyone who loves me
will obey my teaching*.

Jesus then draws the same continuity link between himself and
the paraclete with respect to his commands or teaching that we
have already noted with respect to love. The baton of teaching represented by *all this [Jesus has] spoken while still with* the disciples
(25) will be grasped by the paraclete, who will *remind [the disciples]
of everything [Jesus has] said to [them]* . The Spirit will also *teach
[them] all things* (26). There are two categories of instruction here
– everything which Jesus has conveyed to his disciples and 'everything' *per se* – with just the hint that the instruction of Jesus is a
subset of a wider field of knowledge that the Holy Spirit will convey

---

[17] *DJG*, pp. 889–890.
[18] N. Wolterstorff, *Art in Action: Toward a Christian Aesthetic* (Carlisle:
Solway, 1980), pp. 67–78.

to believers. The teaching of Jesus does not end with his death, resurrection and ascension; it continues, and perhaps is even enhanced, through the agency of the Sprit drawing alongside and indwelling followers of Jesus. We might even suppose that the Spirit provides the dynamic behind the process of memory described in John 2:22.[19]

The first important question to consider is what Jesus may have meant in referring to his *commands* and to his *teaching*. In particular, was he referring only to the content of his spoken communications with the disciples or was there something wider in mind? The evidence of the Gospel itself is mixed. More often than not, reference to Jesus' 'words' or 'word' refer to his particular utterances. However there are hints that these are gradually forming into something that transcends the immediate context. A technical word for that is the *kērygma*, the proclamation of the gospel witnessed to by the earliest believers and now encapsulated in Scripture.[20] John 12:47–49 suggests that possibility, as does John 17:6. In the latter context, Jesus is commending his disciples into the future without him and a recurrent theme therein is that they will take his 'word' with them into that future. For the first generation, that may well have been the orally shared memory of Jesus' words, but we know that that 'word' was subsequently formed into a text bearing witness to the 'word' and the Word.

Correspondingly, 'commands' in this context should not be thought of merely as a prescriptive list of instructions.[21] The Greek *entolē* is overwhelmingly the term of choice by the Septuagint to translate *miṣwâ*, commandment. In the Old Testament usage, most evident in Psalm 119, this is virtually synonymous with *torah*, a term that implies a body of teaching. So it is that reference to Jesus' 'commands' may also be understood as a reference to a body of teaching rather than merely to particular utterances in the imperative mood.

There is a tantalizing glimpse of the interaction between the word as *kērygma* and the Word, Jesus, in John 2:22.[22] The context is Jesus' cleansing of the temple which culminates in Jesus' cryptic identification of himself with the temple building. Only at the end of his earthly life were the disciples able to figure out what he was talking about. They did so by reflection on 'the scripture and the words that Jesus had spoken'.[23] We have seen elsewhere that the

---

[19] See ch. 9.
[20] *EDT*, pp. 653–654.
[21] D. A. Carson, *The Gospel According to John* (Leicester: IVP, 1991), p. 498.
[22] See the treatment of this verse in ch. 9.
[23] John 2:22.

notion of Scripture, while having its most obvious referent to the Old Testament, also gradually came to include certain writings from the apostolic age.[24] Together these writings – the Old Testament and the apostolic – along with the spoken words of Jesus bring understanding to the disciples. By the end of the book of Revelation, the author of that book expects that the text created by the spoken word contains the words of God.[25]

With respect to the context of John 14, it is unlikely that the disciples understood the paraclete as one who would deliver texts to them. If they understood at all at that pre-resurrection point, they would probably have assumed some kind of continuation of the oral interaction with their existing Scriptures and traditions that were the hallmark of Jesus' teaching with them. The wider *kērygma*, however, shows the gradual formation of a written testimony to the things bequeathed to the disciples by Jesus. Furthermore, the work of the Spirit of truth was seen to be a crucial element in the formation of the textual witness.[26] By the time of the formation of the Gospel of John, one or two generations after the discourse recorded in John 14,[27] it would have been clear to the followers of Jesus that part of the role of the advocate was the scriptural preservation of Jesus' words. These themselves become part of the spreading circle of witness envisaged by John's Gospel.[28]

From this distance we may then see that one of the outcomes of the formation and preservation of Scripture is a continuation of the dynamic of love and truth with which Jesus is concerned in his final discourse. The truth encapsulated in the Scriptures springs from the loving heart of the Godhead, and is discerned by the disciples who themselves are caught up into this love and truth and bear witness to it in the formation of the Scriptures. The Scriptures themselves, breathed as they are by the Spirit, continue to bear the love and truth of God's word. They become the very means by which the words of God, the truth and the acts of God who is love, continue to speak and act in the lives and communities of those who preserve and interpret them.

[24] See on 2 Pet. 1:19–21 in ch. 5.

[25] Rev. 22:7.

[26] 1 Pet. 2:1–19. See also Rev. 22:7. The work of prophecy was assumed to be the work of the Spirit, so the binding of the words of prophecy into a scroll implies the preservation in text of the witness of the Spirit.

[27] On the dating of the Gospel of John, see B. Milne, *The Message of John: Here is Your King*, BST (Leicester: IVP, 1993), p. 25.

[28] For example John 15:26–27.

5. 'Keeping' the w/Word

By focusing on knowing with respect to love in my consideration of John 14, I have thus far omitted to acknowledge an important aspect of this experience, namely, the requirement to 'keep' the teaching and commands of Jesus. This aspect peppers the final discourse of Jesus. Verses 15 and 21 speak of 'keeping' the commands; and verses 23 and 24 draw a line between those who *obey* and those who do not. In fact, the same Greek word, *tēreō*, is translated by TNIV as both 'keep' (15 and 21) and 'obey' (23 and 24). While *tēreō* may in certain contexts include the idea of obedience, it primarily entails guarding or preserving or protecting something. It contains the idea of taking responsibility for the well-being of something. And that something, as we have seen, is the teaching and commands of Jesus.

Since there is a Greek verb available to the writer which more explicitly means 'to obey', presumably the more allusive term has been used here for a reason. We have been gradually uncovering a dynamic of love and reception of truth which reflects the word of God made visible in Christ and sustained through the Spirit. Participation in this dynamic is made possible by the text of Scripture which has come to embody the words and commands of God. Therefore, the attitude which is adopted towards this text is critical. That is why Jesus calls for his disciples to 'keep' his commands and words. This may include obedience to the text but it entails much more than that. It also asks the follower of Jesus to take on a responsibility for the Scriptures: to care for them; to foster them; to guard them; to preserve them; and to read and interpret them. In so doing we express our love for God and our participation in God's love for us.

6. Christ shows himself

The outcome of the process uncovered above is that Jesus may be made known to his disciples. The train of thought goes like this. On the day that the earthly presence of Jesus is no longer available, anyone who loves Jesus is also loved by the Father and will be loved by Jesus in return. Moreover, to such people, despite his physical absence, Jesus will show himself. One of the disciples, Judas, then asks about this promise of Jesus to show himself with the question, *why do you intend to show yourself . . .* (22)? The phrase translated as *why do you intend* (*ti genonen*) is difficult to capture exactly. The sense is more 'what has happened' or 'how can it be' that you are about to show yourself to us.[29] The expression implies that Jesus has somehow cut across the assumptions of his listeners, as he was often wont to do. Most commentators assume at this point that the problem is that Judas and his colleagues were expecting a more visible and politicized manifestation of the presence of Jesus, hence his use of the phrase *and not to the world* (22).

But it is also possible that Judas' puzzlement arises from the notion that Jesus will continue to reveal himself to those who had not known him in the flesh but somehow do still see him and hence know him. These are certainly the terms in which Jesus responds, whether because he is deliberately adding a new dimension to the question or because that was how he too understood the question. In a sense, for my purposes it does not matter which. What is important is that what follows in the answer is an explanation, albeit still somewhat cryptic, which picks up on the two aspects of the question posed by Judas. The first is clarification as to why this manifestation of himself is *not to the world*. We have discussed something of this above and will not revisit it now. The second is an explanation as to how Jesus will continue to make himself known. In brief, he does so through both the word and the love contained in that word that he has spoken and that will continue to be available through the ministration of *the Advocate, the Holy Spirit* (26). The logic of this train of thought is that the love of the Father and the Son for each other and for the disciples, and which is returned by the disciples, the truth that is generated out of this love, and the teachings and the text that bear witness to this truth and love, all reveal Jesus.

The verb that contains this notion of revelation is *emphanizō*, which Jesus uses to express that he will *show* himself to future disciples (21) and which Judas then echoes in his clarificatory question (22). It occurs only here in John's Gospel and eight other times in the New Testament. There are similarly ten uses in the Greek Old Testament (the LXX including apocryphal books), only four of which are not in the apocryphal material and hence with a Hebrew equivalent available to us. At one level the word simply concerns passing on information, although there is a sense of it being information that could not otherwise have been known by the recipient.[30] It can contain a hint of mystery and otherworldly communication.[31] And on at least one occasion it speaks of the appearing of the heavenly

[29] B. F. Westcott, *The Gospel according to St John* (London: James Clark & Co, 1958 [1880]), p. 207, suggests: 'how is it that?'
[30] For example Acts 23:15, 22; 24:1; 25:2, 15; 2 Macc. 3:7; 11:29.
[31] For example Wis. 17:4; 18:18; Matt. 27:53.

Christ.[32] There is nothing too portentous about the word when it translates from Hebrew except at Exodus 33:13. However, what is interesting is that on two of the three occasions in the Septuagint that it translates the Hebrew, it translates a word which has a similar range of meaning – from fairly everyday to quite revelatory[33] – as that contained within the Greek *emphanizō*.

The consequence of all this is that when Jesus speaks of 'showing' himself to those who love him and obey his teaching he could be understood in more than one way. For those who have ears to hear, there is a hint of revelation about the term. This is all the more the case given the context of the final discourse set by the prologue to the Gospel, which speaks of light and darkness and of the *logos* coming into the world as light.[34] When the light 'shines' in the darkness the word is *phainō*,[35] a verb from the same stem as *emphanizō*. At one level of meaning in John 14, when Jesus talks of showing himself to his followers he is speaking of their enlightenment. This enlightenment emerges from the Trinitarian activity of the Godhead, by which the believer is drawn into the love that characterizes the Godhead, and the truth that emerges thence. An indispensible part of this process is the teaching both of Jesus the Word and the Spirit of truth who continues that teaching. And an essential part of that teaching is its formation, preservation and interpretation in the texts of Scripture.

These verses themselves only hint at the importance of the text itself, but in doing so they reflect other contexts examined in this volume, where the place of Scripture in the encounter with the risen Christ and the Holy Spirit is more explicit. At the same time, they leave no doubt as to the enlightening resource – the text of Scripture – available to those whom Jesus loves and who themselves seek to express that love in a sometimes hostile world.

[32] Heb. 9:24.
[33] Isa. 3:9; Esth. 2:22.
[34] John 1:4, 5, 9.
[35] John 1:5.

2 Thessalonians 2:13–17
20. Holding fast the traditions

A feature of our postmodern world is the paradoxical coexistence of tendencies towards both tribalization and globalization. By this I mean that across the world there is a reassertion of local values and aspirations, while at the same time the forces of globalization continue apace.[1] So, to cite one expression of the paradox, various indigenous peoples continue to seek local expressions of nationhood while also drinking Coca-Cola and Starbucks coffee and wearing clothes made in China. The impulses are at times contradictory and ironic. I have noticed, for example, that the troubles of various countries are routinely placed at the feet of the United States, arguably the nation that most epitomizes the phenomenon of globalization, while at the same time citizens of those countries are flocking to live in the USA and to enjoy the perceived advantages of so doing. I suspect that this is not the only context in which the tension between global aspiration and local commitment can be observed.

One expression of this tension emerges in the debate around tradition and history. Generalizations are always dangerous, but I think it is a commonplace that the impetus to globalization tends to focus on future possibility, change, financial and economic imperative and individual aspiration, while the impetus to tribalization tends to focus on past identity, community values and preservation or retrieval of tradition.[2] This is seen also in the constant tug between conservation and development, and between tradition and new forms of being and knowing. The irony is that both sides of the tug are necessary for growing a healthy society, and it is unfortunate that they are so often set in opposition to each other.

[1] M. Featherstone, *Undoing Culture: Globalization, Postmodernism and Identity* (Thousand Oaks: Sage, 1995), pp. 86–101.
[2] Ibid., pp. 103–125.

The tension is felt in the matter of how to respond to the biblical story also. Is it the task of the church to be open to the new wind of the Spirit bringing freshness and change? Or is the task of the church to preserve a story and hand it on, preferably unchanged? If the answer is thought to be the latter, biblical interpretation will focus on the intention of the text in its original setting. The danger of such an approach when taken too far is that the text becomes a dead letter with little perceived relevance to the contemporary situation, and a corresponding loss of confidence in the contemporary work of the Spirit. If the answer is thought to be the former, interpretation will focus more on the context of the interpreter and the needs of the interpreter's context. The danger of such an approach when taken too far is in a willingness to suspend aspects of the biblical story in the light of the imperatives of contemporary experience, and in so doing to lose the expectation that the text might challenge the contemporary context, or to set the text and the Spirit artificially at odds with each other.[3]

As with much else in this debate, the two aspects ought not to be in opposition to each other; to set them thus is to create a false dichotomy. The Spirit constantly blows both in the life of believers and through their reading of the text, giving fresh insights for new challenges and contexts. At the same time, the preservation of the story of the work of God in Christ, and still through the Spirit from the earliest days of human encounter with God, orients the believing reader to fresh experience of God at work.[4] Throughout this volume we have seen the interaction of the word and action of God, its preservation in the text, and the activity of the Spirit as the text is read in the light of Christ. Together this may be described as the words and actions of God, or a little more technically, the speech-act of God.

In his second letter to the Thessalonian church, Paul evokes the picture of receiving and handing on tradition. In doing so, he focuses on one side of the paradox above and reflects, at the conclusion of this exploration of the message of Scripture, on the importance of respect for what has been received and the responsibility to nurture and hand it on to others. This has clear implications for the handling of Scripture, as we will see. But at the same time Paul

---

[3] Compare M. J. Sawyer, 'The Father, the Son, and the Holy Scriptures?', in M. J. Sawyer and D. B. Wallace (eds.), *Who's Afraid of the Holy Spirit? An Investigation into the Ministry of the Spirit of God Today* (Dallas: Biblical Studies Press, 2005), pp. 253–277, and J. K. A. Smith, 'The Closing of the Book: Pentecostals, Evangelicals, and the Sacred Writings', *JPT* 11 (1997), pp. 49–71.

[4] For an even-handed approach to this matter, see J. Pelikan, *The Vindication of Tradition* (New Haven: Yale University Press, 1984).

makes clear that the encounter with the tradition received (including Scripture) is a deeply transformative experience. It could hardly be further from a meeting with the letter of an inanimate text. In that respect, his thought on this point helps to form a summary of the ground traversed in this volume.

1. Delusion

The context in which Paul writes is a struggle around how to understand 'the day of the Lord'.[5] There has been false teaching claiming to be that of Paul. The apostle firmly identifies the source of this teaching as deceptive and characterized by displays of power and self-exaltation.[6] Sadly, there are people who choose to believe the lie that they have been sold. The outcome is what Paul calls a 'powerful delusion' that is owned by the people who have chosen to believe the lies they are told.[7] The apostle is clear that the responsibility for this state of affairs lies as much with those who believe the false teacher as with 'the man of lawlessness' himself.[8]

All of the above is in stark contrast to what we considered in the previous chapter as present in Jesus' final discourse to his disciples recorded in John 14 – 17. Those chapters were woven from the love and truth to be found in relationship with the trinitarian God. It is remarkable then that the work of the lawless one and those who believe his lies is the exact opposite: a refusal 'to love the truth' (literally 'love of truth')[9] means that love and truth are absent in such discourse. The resulting 'powerful delusion' in its turn further exacerbates the power of the lie.[10]

Verse 13 then opens with the contrastive *but*. What follows is therefore in contrast to the powerful delusion of the lies of the lawless one and as such is thereby a response to the loss of love for truth, which loss ultimately results in collapse into delusion of some sort. For the Thessalonians those delusions took particular forms. In our own day they look somewhat different. In any case, what is

---

[5] 2 Thess. 2:2. See G. K. Beale, *1–2 Thessalonians* (Downers Grove: IVP, 2003), p. 201, on Paul's use of this term.

[6] 2 Thess. 2:4, 9–10.

[7] 2 Thess. 2:11.

[8] 2 Thess. 2:3. Who 'the man of lawlessness' might be is not of immediate interest to us but see E. J. Richard, *First and Second Thessalonians*, SP 11 (Collegeville: Liturgical Press, 1995), p. 327.

[9] 2 Thess. 2:10.

[10] 2 Thess. 2:11.

called for from both the early Thessalonian Christians and from us is the rediscovery of love and/for the truth.

2. In relationship

The first point that Paul makes is that love and truth are found in a relationship. He thanks God for *brothers and sisters loved by the Lord* (13). Most English translations follow the lead of the Authorized Version and emphasize this point with the translation 'beloved'. These believers who are beloved of the Lord are saved through the *sanctifying work* (13) of the Spirit. The noun in question (in Greek *hagiasmos*), suggests the idea of making holy, which has the sense of setting apart for a purpose. By the work of the Spirit this setting apart is occurring in the lives of the Thessalonian *brothers and sisters* (13) to whom Paul writes as an expression of the fact that they are beloved by God.

In the same verse the companion to the work of the Spirit in salvation is *belief in the truth* (13). The word 'belief' is a problematic translation of *pistis*, which is a term that might equally be translated as 'faith'. Whereas the English word 'belief' suggests intellectual assent to a proposition, the Greek is more redolent of relationship. Belief as faith suggests trusting in somebody. Whether Paul intends God or Christ or the Spirit as that somebody is in one sense immaterial; the point here is that truth is attained in the context of a relationship with the divine.

Truth and love, therefore, are expressions of being in relationship with God. In that respect Paul is here reinforcing what Jesus so powerfully conveyed to his disciples in his final discourse, and which the church so carefully nurtured into the Gospel of John. In the context of this volume, this is an important reminder that Scripture is not the end goal; it is both a signpost and a means to the end goal of a relationship between God and humanity from which love and truth may emerge. I make this point carefully, not in any way to disparage the importance of a high view of the significance of Scripture, but as a reminder that it is possible to pay so much attention to the Bible that a kind of idolatry of the book can develop. It should not be forgotten that the destiny of followers of Jesus is that they *might share in [his] glory* (14), not that they might be expert exegetes.

3. Set apart

There is a further aspect to this relationship that should not be lost sight of, and that is that it is purposeful. This is not stated explicitly but is implicit in three phrases or words: *sanctifying work*, *share in the glory* and *firstfruits* (13–14). We have already noted above the connection of *sanctifying work* with the concept of *hagios* or that which is holy. Inherent in that notion is setting aside for sacred use.[11] The mention of *firstfruits* points in the same direction. It is a little hard to pin down exactly what Paul had in mind by this expression, as it is similarly difficult in James 1:18 where there is also use of the term with reference to followers of Jesus. If we take the background concept of the firstfruits as an offering of the first and best of the harvest to God, then Paul's brothers and sisters beloved of God are similarly people who have been set aside as special in that they are being offered to God.[12]

Both of those concepts refer to something that happens to believers at the hands respectively of *God* and *the Spirit* (13). The call to *share in the glory* (14) is more active with respect to believers. The TNIV representation of the Greek term *peripoiēsis* as 'share' does not quite capture the sense; NRSV gets closer with 'obtain'.[13] It is still not perfect, but it is better in that it hints at an active involvement with the glory of God on the part of believers. The concept suggests a subject who takes responsibility for the care of and involvement in something. It conveys much more in this context than a picture of believers hanging around the edges hoping for a brief and occasional bask in the glory of God. Although the terminology is different, it foreshadows a notion more fully developed in the book of Revelation, that Christians are given to share in the cosmic responsibility exercised by Christ himself.[14] This in its turn reflects the vision of one like a son of man in Daniel 7, in which the 'holy people of the Most High' will be endowed with the 'sovereignty, power and greatness of all the kingdoms under heaven'.[15] This is an eschatological vision to some extent not yet realized, but Paul reflects the beginnings of a hope in this direction for those to whom he wrote in the passage under discussion.

[11] *DPL*, p. 400.
[12] B. Witherington, *1 and 2 Thessalonians: A Socio-Rhetorical Commentary* (Grand Rapids: Eerdmans, 2006), p. 233.
[13] G. L. Green, *The Letters to the Thessalonians*, PNTC (Leicester: Apollos, 2002), p. 328.
[14] Rev. 3:21; 5:10.
[15] Dan. 7:27.

4. Stand firm and hold fast

To recap, in their struggle to know how to respond to the day of the Lord some Thessalonian believers have been led astray by a 'lawless one' in an environment that is characterized by the absence of truth and love and love for truth, with a consequent liability to delusion. In response Paul reminds his readers that their very salvation has been birthed in the love of God and the truth that is conceived in relationship with God. This has powerful effects on their status and calling.

What then follows is introduced by the strong causal phrase, *so then* (*ara oun*, 15). Both elements of the phrase can stand on their own to express inference from or consequence on what has just preceded in a line of thought. When they are combined the consequential link is further emphasized. This doubling is beloved of Paul in whose letters are the only occurrences in the New Testament.[16] In moving from thanks for his readers' participation in all that has been expressed in verses 13 and 14, the apostle is connecting the contents of verses 13 and 14 as strongly as he knows how to his urging to *stand firm and hold fast* (15).

The direction of the connectivity is interesting. Generally, 'so then . . .' asks the reader to see what is about to follow as a consequence or logical outcome of what has immediately preceded. The importance of tradition or *teachings* (15), or what I argue below we would call Scripture, is therefore a result of the believers' salvation and sanctification in the Spirit, a result of the love of God and the truth in which they trust, a result of their participation in the glory of Jesus. These things are not won by holding firm to Scripture; they are in fact outworked in the holding firm to Scripture. This is a somewhat different dynamic than that expressed in 2 Timothy 3: 10–16,[17] wherein the indispensability of Scripture in the formation of the believer was more the emphasis. The juxtaposition of the 2 Thessalonians material with the 2 Timothy material indicates that both directions are important. Scripture is indispensible in the formation of faith and apprehension of the word of God in the life of the church and the believer; at the same time, an appreciation of the word of God and the development of relationship with God outworks itself in a focus on Scripture. The two dynamics feed off each other.

Before considering in more detail what is meant by 'teachings', what of this instruction to *stand firm and hold fast* (15)? The 'and'

---

[16] Of the eleven other occurrences, see for example Rom. 8:12 and 1 Thess. 5:6.
[17] Examined in ch. 18.

may be read as explanatory.[18] Therefore *[holding] fast to the teachings* is an expansion on the notion of standing firm: stand firm, that is, hold fast to the teachings. The word translated as *stand firm* was occasionally used by Paul to express the idea of standing firmly in something: for example in the faith, in the Lord, in one spirit.[19] The term translated as *holding fast* has a somewhat broader range of meaning than the English, which implies clinging to something in a crisis, such as a log in a flooded river. That is one aspect of its meaning, but it has the more positive senses of taking control of something or holding something in place or providing support or overcoming obstacles in attaining an object. It speaks of an active appropriation of something, in this case *the teachings* (15).[20] Standing firm by holding to the teachings, or traditions, then, entails much more than clinging to them like a drowning man; it potentially also entails working with them, proclaiming them, studying and wrestling with them, striving for understanding of them. In sum, it is a committed, even an innovative, response on the part of the recipient. For Paul, part of this active response was to *[pass] on* (15) these things.

If we may take these 'teachings' to include Scripture, this is an affirmation that an important aspect of the life of faith is a determined effort to wrest meaning from the texts that are encountered, and in turn to pass on what is discovered there as part of the ongoing witness of the church. While the onus on the recipients themselves to pass on *the teachings* is not part of this passage, it is inherent in the exegetical responsibilities that we discerned in John 14 – 15.[21] We might suppose that this imperative to hand on the message of Jesus became more important to the church as the early Christians became gradually more removed in time from the great events around the life of Jesus.[22] It was also noticeable in the attitude of the book of Deuteronomy towards the texts of the law of God.[23] In participating in this dynamic of receiving and passing on the word of God we hear the voice and meet the action of God in our lives and in the world around us.[24]

---

[18] F. F. Bruce, *1 & 2 Thessalonians*, WBC 45 (Dallas: Word, 1982), p. 193.

[19] 1 Cor. 16:13; Phil. 4:1; 1:27.

[20] *BDAG*, p. 564.

[21] See ch. 19.

[22] E. Best, *The First and Second Epistles to the Thessalonians* (London: Adam & Charles Black, 1972), p. 318.

[23] See ch. 7.

[24] J. E. Goldingay, *Daniel*, WBC 30 (Dallas: Word, 1989), p. ix, reflects helpfully on this ongoing responsibility on the part of Christians.

5. The teachings

So far I have relied on the assumption that these verses may be taken as applicable to Scripture, but that assumption needs to be tested. There are a range of terms in these verses that imply some body of knowledge or truth presupposed by Paul. The first is reference to *our gospel* (14). Then come *the teachings*, which are experienced either by *word of mouth or by letter* (15). Paul's 'gospel' constitutes the declaration of the good news, conveyed through the Greek noun *euangelion*. He uses the same word in his first letter to the same group of people, and the context there suggests the activity and contents of Paul's preaching.[25] The same thing is probably intended here also. 2 Thessalonians 1:8 also makes clear that the good news concerns Jesus Christ, by which we might suppose both the story of his life and the apostle's understanding of the significance of that life.[26] The good news of salvation through Jesus Christ, conveyed by the preaching of the good news by Paul, is apparently in mind.

The *teachings* (15, *paradoseis*) or 'traditions' is a less context-specific and slightly more problematic concept. It is a term variously used in the New Testament. In the synoptic Gospels it occurs most often in a negative comparison of the tradition of the elders with the word of God during disputes with the Pharisees.[27] However, this is not a comment on the value of traditions *per se*; it is a comment on the particular traditions which dulled rather than brought forth the word of God. While alert to the dangers of deadening tradition,[28] Paul also has a lively sense of the value of tradition as the vehicle of keeping and handing on matters essential to salvation.[29] In this particular context it refers most obviously to his own teaching and preaching, *whether by word of mouth or by letter* (15). While centred on Jesus Christ, the wider content of this teaching and tradition might be sensed from a reading of 1 Thessalonians 4.

In the context of the study of Scripture undertaken in this volume, however, the idea can be widened out a little further. The verb that is related to the noun translated as 'teachings' (*paradoseis*) is *paradidōmi*, which has the sense of handing over or handing on something. A tradition is something that has been maintained and passed on. Paul uses the same term in 1 Corinthians 11:23 with respect to the tradition of the Lord's Supper. In Jude 3 the faith that

[25] 1 Thess. 1:5. See Best, *Thessalonians*, p. 74.
[26] See Bruce, *1 & 2 Thessalonians*, p. 14, including details of the background in Isaiah on which the word builds.
[27] See Mark 7:8–13; Matt. 15:6.
[28] See Col. 2:8.
[29] See 1 Cor. 11:2.

has been 'entrusted' is entrusted by 'the Lord'. This seems to be more widely conceived than the particularity of the letter writer's contribution, and hence of Paul's own contribution. As was noted in our study of 2 Peter 1:19–21,[30] which letter bears a number of commonalities with the letter of Jude, the category of Scripture was beginning to include apostolic material while also looking back to the Old Testament Scriptures.[31] Moving now into the Synoptics, Luke uses the same verb in Luke 1:2 to refer to the handing down of 'the things which have been fulfilled among us' by 'eye witnesses and servants'.[32] I argued in that context that 'the things which have been fulfilled' refer not just to the life of Jesus, the main subject of the Gospel, but also to the scriptural tradition which was brought to fruition by the life of Jesus.[33]

When Paul refers the Thessalonians to *the teachings* (15) he was probably in the first instance calling to mind all of the material that he himself had conveyed to them by various means concerning Jesus. However, it is clear from elsewhere in the Pauline corpus that this would also have included his access to the early church's memory of Jesus Christ.[34] And by the time of the Gospel of Luke, perhaps a generation or so later than this letter, reflection on the life and significance of Jesus was based on a body of collected material, which included Old Testament as well as apostolic texts which were beginning to be conceived of as in some way authoritative. In that context it is possible to read the urgings of Paul to believers to *stand firm and hold fast to the teachings* (15) to be a statement that may be applied to the handling of Scripture.

6. In every good deed and word

For Paul, the upshot of all this is the wish that Jesus Christ, and God his Father with him, might establish the Thessalonian believers *in every good deed and word* (17). This is the outcome of the love and truth that results from knowing God. This participation in love and truth leads on naturally to a wrestling with the Scriptures and, on the evidence seen in 2 Timothy and John 14 – 15, also arises out of that same wrestling. In this way, as we have seen repeat-

[30] See ch. 5.
[31] 2 Pet. 3:16. For further on the relationship between 2 Peter and Jude see T. R. Schreiner, *1, 2 Peter, Jude*, TNAC 37 (Nashville: Broadman & Holman, 2003), pp. 415–419.
[32] Luke 1:1.
[33] See ch. 8.
[34] D. E. Garland, *1 Corinthians*, BECNT (Grand Rapids: Baker, 2003), p. 512.

edly throughout this volume, the reader hears and sees the words and acts of God both historically and in the life of the believer and the church, as well as the cosmos inhabited by the believer. As we have seen at various points,[35] the pervasive presence of the Holy Spirit in the formation, reading, interpretation and application of Scripture ensures that the sacred texts need never become the dead letter of tradition. There is no better counter than this to 'powerful delusion'.[36]

Without this collection of texts we call the Bible, 'deed and word' of God would be dimly discerned and barely perceived. With the Bible we may know that God does indeed speak and act, that he does so in the texts of Scripture, that it is in Jesus Christ that these texts speak most clearly to us, and that this remains as true today as when the Scriptures were first formed. But more importantly even than that, the word of God continues to speak the work of God in each of us, and in the church and the world of which we are a part. It is over to us now to respond with our own *deed and word* (17).

Thanks be to God.

---

[35] See especially chs 5 and 19.
[36] 2 Thess. 2:11.

Study guide

HOW TO USE THIS STUDY GUIDE

The aim of this study guide is to help you get to the heart of what Tim has written and challenge you to apply what you learn to your own life. The questions have been designed for use by individuals or by small groups of Christians meeting, perhaps for an hour or two each week, to study, discuss and pray together. When used by a group with limited time, the leader should decide beforehand which questions are most appropriate for the group to discuss during the meeting and which should perhaps be left for group members to work through by themselves or in smaller groups during the week.

PREVIEW. Use the guide and the contents pages as a map to become familiar with what you are about to read, your 'journey' through the book.

READ. Look up the Bible passages as well as the text.

ANSWER. As you read look for the answers to the questions in the guide.

DISCUSS. Even if you are studying on your own try to find another person to share your thoughts with.

REVIEW. Use the guide as a tool to remind you what you have learned. The best way of retaining what you learn is to write it down in a notebook or journal.

APPLY. Translate what you have learned into your attitudes and actions, considering your relationship with God, your personal life, your family life, your working life, your church life, your role as a citizen and your world-view.

Introduction (pp. 23–30)

1. What do you understand by 'the Bible', 'the Scriptures' and 'the word of God'? Is it important to distinguish between them (pp. 23–24)?
2. What are the author's four key propositions and why does he prefer a 'narrative rather than a systematic approach' (pp. 24–25)?
3. What aspects of speech-act theory are helpful in a study of the word of God (pp. 25–27)?
4. What three aspects or effects of God's speaking emerge (pp. 27–28)?
5. How does Psalm 119 illustrate the insights of speech-act theory in relation to the word of God (pp. 28–30)?
6. Why is the word of God described as a 'conversation' (p. 30)?

PART 1. GOD SPEAKS

Psalm 19
1. The glory of God made known (pp. 33–45)

1. Can you think of a similar experience when you sensed that God was speaking to you 'in the silence of his creation' (pp. 33–34)?

'I knew beyond a shadow of a doubt that I rested in the centre of God's perfectly formed love, a love shown in Jesus that no evil can ultimately obscure. How did I know? Because the heavens of God declared it and because the law of the Lord in Scripture interpreted it for me' (p. 34).

---

2. Why do many commentators see Psalm 19 as two distinct psalms and what is the argument for its coherence (pp. 34–36)?
3. What is the paradox in verses 1–4 and what attempts can be made to resolve it (pp. 36–37)?
4. In what ways does Psalm 19 reflect the language and thought of Genesis 1–3 and Isaiah 40–55 (pp. 38–39)?
5. How is the concern about idolatry in Isaiah 40–55 reflected in the language of Psalm 19 and what contemporary parallels can be adduced (pp. 39–41)?
6. Is there a connection between verses 6 and 7 and if so how is it developed (p. 41)?

7. How should we understand the word *torah* (pp. 41–42)?
8. What features are evident in verses 7–9 and what three key points do they convey (pp. 42–43)?
9. Which expression is 'the odd one out' in verses 7–9 and why has it been included (pp. 43–44)?
10. What concept of knowing (epistemology) has dominated Western thought in the modern period and how does an understanding of Psalm 19 challenge it (pp. 44–45)?

Isaiah 55
2. God's word goes forth (pp. 46–60)

1. In what ways does the background of Isaiah 40–55 resonate with our own times (pp. 46–47)?
2. What do linguists mean by the terms *locution, illocution* and *perlocution* (pp. 48–49)?
3. How does Walter Brueggemann describe the logical flow of Isaiah 55 (pp. 49–50)?
4. What earlier passages in Isaiah can be linked with chapter 55 and in what way (pp. 50–51)?
5. In what ways can the metaphor in verse 10 be unwrapped and developed (pp. 51–52)?
6. How is the metaphor of verse 10 applied in verse 11 (pp. 52–55)?
7. What aspects of the covenant-making word of God are evident in verses 1–5 and what are their historical precedents (pp. 55–57)?
8. How does the translation of verse 6 affect our understanding of verses 6–9 (pp. 57–58)?
9. What is the paradox in verses 6–11 and how is it resolved (pp. 58–59)?

'The miracle of the incarnation is that this God enters into the world of humanity and enables the gap to be bridged. One effect of this is that through the activity of God's word it becomes possible for humankind to begin to see the world through God's eyes, and so to begin to form ways of life that more adequately reflect the truth and goodness of God' (p. 58).

---

10. How does the vocabulary of verses 12–13 suggest the scope of the transformation spoken about in these verses (pp. 59–60)?

Proverbs 30:1–9
3. The wisdom of God's word (pp. 61–71)

1. To what extent do you recognize in your own life the mixture of aspiration and frustration described by the author (p. 61)?
2. What two interpretive decisions have to be made about these verses and how do they affect our understanding of them (pp. 62–63)?
3. What significance should be placed on the fact that Agur son of Jakeh is the author of this section and how do the authorship of Proverbs 31 and the terminology of Daniel 1 reinforce it (pp. 63–65)?
4. What is 'the dilemma of the human condition' and how is it expressed in verses 1–4 (pp. 65–66)?
5. What characteristics of the word of God emerge in verses 5–6 (pp. 66–67)?
6. In what sense can we – or should we – speak of God's word as infallible (pp. 67–69)?
7. What should we understand by 'the sufficiency of Scripture' (pp. 69–70)?
8. How does the notion of lying link Agur's prayer with what goes before and what is implied by linking these two forms of falsehood (pp. 70–71)?

Amos 3:1–8
4. The Lord God has spoken (pp. 72–83)

1. What evidence is there that God's word is 'also a word for the everyday' (pp. 72–73)?
2. What aspects of Amos 3:3–8 reflect typical features of wisdom literature (pp. 73–74)?
3. How does the grammar of these verses reinforce andd develop the argument (pp. 74–75)?
4. Which fresh aspect of God's word is revealed in verse 7 and what nuances of translation should reflect it (pp. 75–76)?
5. What three important things about the word of God does this verse tell us (p. 76)?
6. Why is it difficult to define precisely how Amos's contemporaries would understand his role as a prophet (pp. 76–77)?
7. On what grounds can we affirm with Amos that God's counsel is always available to God's people (pp. 77–79)?
8. How does the first of Amos's 'bookends' address the issues of his day (pp. 79–80)?

9. How does the second 'bookend' draw on and develop the earlier material (pp. 80–82)?
10. Does the use of poetic imagination in the understanding of God's word make it less authoritative (pp. 82–83)?

2 Peter 1:19–21
5. Through men and women moved by the Spirit (pp. 84–96)

1. What issues are generated by the humanity of Scripture and what insights can help those who struggle with it (pp. 84–86)?

'It is difficult to discover that the ancient and ever-new set of documents we call the Bible has a long history of compilation and collection, a variegated track record of authorship, a diversity of perspectives, and a corresponding tendency to call forth competing interpretations from the ranks of its readers' (p. 84).

---

2. What assumptions are made in this chapter about the authorship, date and context of 2 Peter (pp. 86–87)?
3. How should we understand the TNIV's 'prophetic message', 'prophecy of Scripture' and 'prophecy' in verses 19–21 (pp. 87–88)?
4. Is it legitimate to apply Peter's 'prophetic message' to the New Testament Scriptures (pp. 88–89)?
5. What interpretation has the comparative adjective in verse 19 led to and do you agree that there is a meaningful ambiguity in the comparison (pp. 89–90)?
6. How is the importance of Peter's statement in verse 20 signalled (pp. 90–91)?
7. What is the relationship between *prophecy* and *interpretation* in verse 20 and is it possible for different understandings of this relationship to coexist (pp. 91–94)?
8. What is not meant by 'carried along by the Holy Spirit' (p. 94)?
9. What are the three dimensions to the Spirit's involvement in the development of the prophetic word (pp. 94–96)?
10. In what ways does the Spirit's activity impact the past, present and future of the believer's life and the life of the church (p. 96)?

PART 2. GOD SPEAKS IN THE WRITTEN WORD

Exodus 19–20
6. The spoken word written (pp. 99–111)

1. In what way are the concepts of *tapu* and *ḥerem* similar and why are they difficult for the Western mind to grasp (pp. 99–100)?
2. What does Richard Hays mean by the 'palpable word' of God and what caution should be exercised in that assessment (pp. 100–101)?
3. What are the 'two important dynamics' in the encounter at Sinai and what conclusions should we draw from them (pp. 101–103)?
4. What limits are placed on the people's meeting with God and why is there an indication that the mountain itself is not intrinsically holy (pp. 103–105)?
5. How does God intervene to facilitate the encounter with his people across the boundaries of holiness (pp. 105–107)?
6. What is the coincidence of vocabulary between Exodus 33:19 and 34:5 and what does it underline (p. 107)?
7. Why is it important that the spoken word of God should become the written word (pp. 108–109)?
8. What questions are raised by the 'paradox of responsibility' in the production of the preserved text (pp. 109–111)?

Deuteronomy 4:1–20
7. The covenant remembered (pp. 112–125)

1. What is your personal response to the issues characterized as *the furnace* and *the inheritance* (pp. 112–114)?
2. In what historical setting was the book of Deuteronomy formed and what lessons can be learned from that context (pp. 114–115)?
3. What is meant by 'this blurring of the distinction between the visual and the verbal' (pp. 115–116)?
4. What is involved in the call to teach God's law (pp. 116–118)?
5. How does translation differ from transposition and do you find these metaphors helpful (pp. 117–118)?
6. What two results of failure to 'remember' are described in verses 9, 10 (pp. 118–119)?
7. What are the effects of remembering in a community soaked in the word of God (pp. 119–120)?

8. What ambiguity do we find in verse 20 and are the different possibilities mutually exclusive (pp. 120–122)?
9. Why is it difficult to read Deuteronomy today (pp. 122–123)?
10. What positive points can be made in response to the difficulty (pp. 153–155)?

Luke 1:1–4
8. The written word as witness (pp. 126–136)

1. What is the 'ugly ditch' between theology and history and what scriptural event highlights it 'most vividly' (pp. 126–127)?
2. What are the possible responses to the problem and how do you evaluate them (pp. 127–128)?
3. How did Old Testament writers of history view themselves and where is that view reflected in the New Testament (pp. 128–129)?
4. In what ways does the grammar of Luke 1:1–2 contribute to the meaning and what further focus is introduced in verses 3 and 4 (p. 129)?
5. What do *pragmata* and *logos/logoi* mean and what is the implication of their use here (pp. 129–130)?
6. How is *hypēretēs* used in the New Testament and what light does that throw on its use here (pp. 130–131)?
7. How is *plēroō* used in the New Testament and what is its significance here (pp. 131–132)?
8. What contrasts does Luke draw in these verses and how is his approach described (pp. 132–134)?

'For Luke there is no 'ugly ditch' between theology and history. His account of the life and significance of Jesus is as thorough and careful and comprehensible as it can be, with a concern to connect what he finds with all that is already known, just as any good modern approach to history should be. At the same time it is earthed in a deep commitment to what he is writing about' (p. 134).

---

9. What is the meaning of *asphaleia* and how is it achieved (pp. 134–136)?

John 2:13–25
9. The Scriptures and the resurrection of the Word (pp. 137–145)

1. How do a mental 'suspense account' and the linguistic category of relevance relate to our understanding of God's word (pp. 137–139)?
2. What four elements induced belief in the disciples and how was 'relevance in communication' achieved (pp. 139–140)?
3. What two pairings are implicit in verse 22 (p. 140)?
4. How does the NRSV differ from the TNIV in its translation of *logos* and why is it significant (pp. 140–141)?
5. In what way do the two pairings in verse 22 take us back in to speech-act territory (pp. 141–142)?
6. What is unusual about the use of *egeirō* in verses 19–20 and is its use in verses 19–22 just a literary play on words (p. 143)?
7. In what ways does John take Luke's understanding of history a step further (p. 144)?
8. In John's Gospel does belief always have the same connotations (p. 145)?

Matthew 12:1–21
10. The Scriptures interpreted and fulfilled by Jesus (pp. 146–154)

1. Are there aspects of institutional Christianity that you find frustrating and what should be the correct response to them (pp. 146–147)?
2. In what ways can the word of God in Scripture be misused (p. 147)?

'God meets us in our humanity and not in some unearthly dimension. Constantly we must hold together commitment to God through allegiance to human expressions of that commitment, with a recognition that the human expressions themselves are conditional and temporary' (p. 147).

---

3. Who were the Pharisees and what motivated them (pp. 147–148)?
4. Why did the Pharisees take issue with Jesus and on what grounds did he respond to them (p. 149)?

5. What was the paradox at the heart of Sabbath observance and where else is this paradox evident (p. 150)?
6. How did Jesus differ from the Pharisees in his reading of Hosea 6:6 (pp. 151–152)?
7. Is the debate between Jesus and the Pharisees merely a hermeneutical one (pp. 152–153)?
8. 'Things can go wrong.' Why is this and how can it be avoided (pp. 153–154)?

PART 3. GOD SPEAKS IN CHRIST

John 1:1–14
11. The Word made flesh (pp. 157–164)

1. Why is language so important (pp. 157–158)?
2. In what way is the opening phrase of Genesis much more than a chronological statement and how does this influence our understanding of John 1:1 (pp. 158–159)?
3. What is significant about the use of *pros* in John's prologue (pp. 159–160)?
4. How does the reference to John the Baptist highlight the uniqueness of Jesus as the Word of God (pp. 160–161)?
5. In what ways does the theme of light echo the creation account in Genesis (pp. 161–162)?
6. Why does the theme of birth into the family of God take us beyond the creation account (pp. 162–163)?
7. What are the links between the theme of glory in verse 14 and passages in the Old Testament (pp. 163–164)?

Hebrews 1:1–4
12. In these last days God has spoken (pp. 165–174)

1. Who was Marcion, what was his teaching and what was his legacy to later generations (pp. 165–166)?
2. In what ways can Christians today still reflect the position taken by Marcion (pp. 166–167)?
3. How does the original Greek form of verses 1 and 2a help us to understand their meaning (pp. 167–169)?
4. What is the connection between the concept of Jesus as *heir of all things* and the one who *made the universe* (pp. 169–171)?
5. Is 'representation' an adequate translation of the Greek

charaktēr and how significant is the description of the Son as
the radiance of God's glory (pp. 171–172)?
6. Why is it not enough to speak about God as creator and how
does Christ's work as redeemer link with Exodus 19 (pp.
172–173)?
7. How would the term 'angel' be understood by the earliest
hearers or readers of this epistle (pp. 173–174)?
8. In what respect was Marcion right and in what respect was he
wrong (p. 174)?

Matthew 5:17–48
13. Christ fulfils the Scriptures (pp. 175–186)

1. What responses have been given to the command in Leviticus,
'Be holy because I am holy' both within Scripture and beyond
it (pp. 175–177)?
2. What is new in the discourse of Matthew 5:21–48 and how does
the original language signal it (pp. 177–178)?
3. Why are verses 17–20 important in the light of what follows (p.
178)?
4. By speaking of 'the Law or the Prophets' was Jesus excluding
the psalms and wisdom literature of the Old Testament (pp.
179–180)?
5. What is different about verses 33–36 and what point does it
make obvious (pp. 180–181)?
6. Is the prohibition of murder restricted to the taking of human
life (p. 181)?
7. What is the 'similar dynamic' at work in verses 27–30 (pp.
181–182)?
8. In what way is the focus on divorce different from that on
murder and adultery and what are its implications (pp. 182–
183)?
9. What was the original purpose of the *lex talionis* and what effect
does Jesus' teaching bring about (pp. 183–184)?
10. What was the Jewish understanding of the covenant and how
did the life and work of Jesus redefine it (pp. 184–185)?
11. How should we understand Jesus' instruction to 'be perfect'
and what should be our response to it (pp. 185–186)?

---

*'Always Jesus as the Word draws the reader to a clearer and deeper
appreciation of the word of God as preserved in Scripture, and
always he calls the reader on to live the word/ Word as well as*

read it. For those who teach, there is a particular responsibility to get this right' (p. 186).

Romans 10:5–13
14. God's word and righteousness (pp. 187–193)

1. How is the sin of the Tower of Babel evident in our contemporary world and what is God's answer to it (pp. 187–188)?
2. What themes are drawn together by Paul's use of Joel 2:32 (p. 189)?
3. Can you think of ways in which you might be guilty of the 'tendency to domesticate Jesus' to your own ends (pp. 189–190)?
4. What does Paul mean by righteousness and what are the two implications he develops from it (pp. 190–191)?
5. What are the three elements that work together in the dynamic of righteousness (pp. 191–192)?
6. Why is a danger still inherent in a true understanding of these three elements (pp. 192–193)?

Revelation 5
15. Worthy to open the scroll (pp. 194–204)

1. In what senses is the Christian experience (a) similar to and (b) different from that of Vladimir and Estragon in 'Waiting for Godot' (pp. 194–196)?
2. How should we understand the word 'forever' in Revelation 5:13 (p. 196)?
3. How does the vision build up to the climax of the opening of the scroll (p. 197)?
4. What different interpretations have been suggested for the scroll and what problems do they present (pp. 197–198)?
5. What does the scroll as 'an evocative symbol' evoke (pp. 198–199)?
6. Does the particular scroll of Revelation 5 have anything to say about the wider canvas of Scripture (p. 199)?
7. What is intended by the sealing of the scroll and in what ways does the description of the Lamb echo the seven seals (pp. 200–201)?
8. In what ways does the representation of Jesus as both the Lion and the Lamb develop the 'boundary-crossing' nature of his work (pp. 201–203)?
9. What is the effect of the unsealing of the scroll (pp. 203–204)?

PART 4. GOD SPEAKS TODAY

Acts 8:26–39
16. Individual encounters with the word of God
(pp. 207–218)

1. What important truth is conveyed by the words attributed to St Francis of Assisi (pp. 207–208)?
2. What do we know about the Ethiopian eunuch and his circumstances (pp. 209–210)?
3. What do the details of the story tell us about the way God speaks (p. 210)?
4. What was the Holy Spirit's role in the encounter between the eunuch and Philip (pp. 210–211)?
5. What is meant by the three-legged stool of authority? What should – and should not – be inferred from this perspective (pp. 211–213)?

'While a guide was essential to the Ethiopian eunuch and to any reader of Scripture, the guide is never as important as Scripture and finally does not have a mandate to define the meaning of Scripture over against the text. The signpost should not be confused with the way itself' (p. 212).

---

6. Trace the background and subsequent development of the servant theme in Isaiah. How is it significant for God's voice in the written word of Scripture (pp. 213–215)?
7. Which detail in Isaiah's scroll may have resonated with the Ethiopian official and can you think of any such resonances in your own experience (pp. 215–216)?
8. What is 'intertextuality' and how is it demonstrated in Acts 8 and Isaiah 53 (pp. 216–218)?

Nehemiah 8
17. Scripture read in community (pp. 219–232)

1. How should we respond to parts of the Bible that do not seem immediately understandable or helpful (pp. 219–220)?
2. Is the mere presence or reading of the Bible necessarily a good thing (pp. 220–221)?
3. What is the literary and historical context of Nehemiah 8 (pp. 221–222)?

4. What evidence is there that leadership is a critical element in the public process of hearing the word of God in Scripture (p. 223)?
5. What elements of leadership evident in Nehemiah 8 ought to be reflected in our own time (pp. 224–225)?
6. How does the description of the event underline its significance and are there any lessons for us to apply today (pp. 225–226)?
7. How should we understand the three activities on the part of the Levites who assisted Ezra (pp. 226–228)?
8. Why is the occurrence of *qôl* in verse 15 significant (pp. 228–229)?
9. What were the emotional responses to the word of God and what occasioned them (p. 229)?
10. What is the background of *Sukkoth* and how did that shape the people's response (pp. 229–230)?
11. What two dangers are inherent in the pursuit of understanding and interpreting the text of Scripture (pp. 231–232)?

2 Timothy 3:10–17
18. All Scripture is God-breathed and useful (pp. 233–243)

1. Where do we find evidence of hostility and conflict in the history of God's people (pp. 233–234)?
2. Why is the reference to Jannes and Jambres ambiguous and does the ambiguity present a problem (p. 235)?
3. What technical issues around the interpretation of 2 Timothy 3:10–17 must be addressed (pp. 235–237)?
4. Why is 'God-breathed' a better translation of *theopneustos* than 'inspired' (pp. 237–238)?
5. What meaning is conveyed by the Greek word *ōphelimos* (pp. 238–239)?
6. What important reminder is contained in the phrase *through faith in Jesus Christ* (p. 239)?
7. How do the two statements which frame verse 16 add to our understanding of the usefulness of Scripture (pp. 239–240)?
8. What approach to Scripture would constitute 'a travesty of the intent of these verses' (p. 240)?
9. What four elements combine to form 'the process of nurture' and what is the distinctive contribution of each (pp. 240–243)?

John 14:15–26
19. The Spirit of love and truth (pp. 244–255)

1. What is your response to the picture of the Western church presented here (pp. 244–245)?
2. How is the theme of love developed in this part of John's Gospel (pp. 245–246)?

'The counterpoint to a contested environment for the gospel, such as that conveyed in Paul's second letter to Timothy, is a response characterized by positive presentation of gospel truth. This entails the responsibility to become known for what we are in favour of more than for what we are against' (p. 245).

---

3. What is the meaning of the Greek word *paraklētos* and what does it reveal about the role of the Holy Spirit (pp. 246–247)?
4. Is it legitimate to see a significance in the use of *para* rather than *en* in this chapter (p. 247)?
5. What can we learn from the tension between relationship and incorporation (pp. 247–249)?
6. What difference does being a Christian make (and not make) to the quest for truth (pp. 249–250)?
7. What did Jesus mean by his *commands* in this context (pp. 250–251)?
8. How does John 2:22 illustrate the role of the Spirit with respect to the teaching of Jesus (pp. 251–252)?
9. What is the sense of the word *tēreō*, and which translation fits better, in this context (p. 253)?
10. What is it that puzzled Judas (not Iscariot) and how did Jesus answer (pp. 253–254)?
11. Why is *emphanizō* an interesting word to describe the self-revealing of Jesus (pp. 254–255)?

2 Thessalonians 2:13–17
20. Holding fast the traditions (pp. 256–265)

1. What is meant by 'the paradoxical coexistence of tendencies towards both tribalization and globalization' and how is it reflected in the contemporary church (pp. 256–258)?
2. What were the nature and the result of the 'powerful delusion' threatening the Thessalonian church (pp. 258–259)?

3. What are the evidences of a genuine relationship with God (p. 259)?
4. What truths are implicit in *sanctifying work, share in the glory* and *firstfruits* and how does the second of these terms differ from the other two (p. 260)?
5. What are the two dynamics in 2 Thessalonians 2:13–17 and 2 Timothy 3:10–16 and how do they feed off each other (p. 261)?
6. What is the relationship between 'standing firm' and 'holding fast' and what are the implications for our handling of Scripture (p. 262)?
7. What are the component parts of the body of truth presupposed by Paul (pp. 263–264)?
8. On what grounds is it legitimate to include New Testament Scriptural material in Paul's injunction to 'hold fast to the teachings' (pp. 263–264)?
9. What is the ultimate aim of Paul's instructions for his original readers – and for us (pp. 264–265)?

The Bible Speaks Today: Old Testament series

The Message of Genesis 1 – 11
The dawn of creation
David Atkinson

The Message of Genesis 12 – 50
From Abraham to Joseph
Joyce G. Baldwin

The Message of Exodus
The days of our pilgrimage
Alec Motyer

The Message of Leviticus
Free to be holy
Derek Tidball

The Message of Numbers
Journey to the promised land
Raymond Brown

The Message of Deuteronomy
Not by bread alone
Raymond Brown

The Message of Judges
Grace abounding
Michael Wilcock

The Message of Ruth
The wings of refuge
David Atkinson

The Message of Samuel
Personalities, potential, politics and power
Mary Evans

The Message of Chronicles
One church, one faith, one Lord
Michael Wilcock

The Message of Ezra and Haggai
Building for God
Robert Fyall

The Message of Nehemiah
God's servant in a time of change
Raymond Brown

The Message of Esther
God present but unseen
David G. Firth

The Message of Job
Suffering and grace
David Atkinson

The Message of Psalms
1 – 72
Songs for the people of God
Michael Wilcock

The Message of Psalms
73 – 150
Songs for the people of God
Michael Wilcock

The Message of Proverbs
Wisdom for life
David Atkinson

The Message of Ecclesiastes
A time to mourn, and a time to dance
Derek Kidner

The Message of the Song of Songs
The lyrics of love
Tom Gledhill

The Message of Isaiah
On eagles' wings
Barry Webb

The Message of Jeremiah
Against wind and tide
Derek Kidner

The Message of Ezekiel
A new heart and a new spirit
Christopher J. H. Wright

The Message of Daniel
The Lord is King
Ronald S. Wallace

The Message of Hosea
Love to the loveless
Derek Kidner

The Message of Joel, Micah and Habakkuk
Listening to the voice of God
David Prior

The Message of Amos
The day of the lion
Alec Motyer

The Message of Obadiah, Nahum and Zephaniah
The kindness and severity of God
Gordon Bridger

The Message of Jonah
Presence in the storm
Rosemary Nixon

The Message of Zechariah
Your kingdom come
Barry Webb

The Bible Speaks Today: New Testament series

The Message of the Sermon on the Mount (Matthew 5 – 7)
Christian counter-culture
John Stott

The Message of Matthew
The kingdom of heaven
Michael Green

The Message of Mark
The mystery of faith
Donald English

The Message of Luke
The Saviour of the world
Michael Wilcock

The Message of John
Here is your King!
Bruce Milne

The Message of Acts
To the ends of the earth
John Stott

The Message of Romans
God's good news for the world
John Stott

The Message of 1 Corinthians
Life in the local church
David Prior

The Message of 2 Corinthians
Power in weakness
Paul Barnett

The Message of Galatians
Only one way
John Stott

The Message of Ephesians
God's new society
John Stott

The Message of Philippians
Jesus our Joy
Alec Motyer

The Message of Colossians and Philemon
Fullness and freedom
Dick Lucas

The Message of Thessalonians
Preparing for the coming King
John Stott

The Message of 1 Timothy and Titus
The life of the local church
John Stott

The Message of 2 Timothy
Guard the gospel
John Stott

The Message of Hebrews
Christ above all
Raymond Brown

The Message of James
The tests of faith
Alec Motyer

The Message of 1 Peter
The way of the cross
Edmund Clowney

The Message of 2 Peter and Jude
The promise of his coming
Dick Lucas and Christopher Green

The Message of John's Letters
Living in the love of God
David Jackman

The Message of Revelation
I saw heaven opened
Michael Wilcock